LEARNING
MATHEMATICS

Archie E. Lapointe   Nancy A. Mead   Janice M. Askew

Prepared for the National Center of Education Statistics,
U.S. Department of Education and the National Science Foundation

February 1992   Report No. 22-CAEP-01

The International Assessment
of Educational Progress   ETS   *IAEP*

EDUCATIONAL TESTING SERVICE

Educational Testing Service, (ETS) is a private, not for profit corporation devoted to measurement and research, primarily in the field of education. It was founded in 1947 by the American Council on Education, the Carnegie Foundation for the Advancement of Teaching, and the College Entrance Examination Board.

The Center for the Assessment of Educational Progress (CAEP) is a division of ETS devoted to innovative approaches to the measurement and evaluation of educational progress. The present core activity of CAEP is the administration of the National Assessment of Educational Progress (NAEP), under contract from the U.S. Department of Education. CAEP also carries out related activities, including the International Assessment of Educational Progress (IAEP), state assessments, and special studies such as the National Science Foundation-supported Pilot Study of Higher-Order Thinking Skills Assessment Techniques in Science and Mathematics.

The work upon which this publication is based was performed pursuant to Grant No. SDE-8955070 of the National Science Foundation, and additional funding was provided by the U.S. Department of Education through Interagency Agreement No. IAD-91-0222. Supplementary funds were provided by the Carnegie Corporation of New York.

This report, No. 22-CAEP-01, can be ordered from the Center for the Assessment of Educational Progress at Educational Testing Service, Rosedale Road, Princeton, New Jersey 08541-0001.

Library of Congress Card Number: 91-078082

ISBN: 0-88685-120-3

Introduction

Ah, la belle chose,
que de savoir quelque chose.

Ah, what a lovely thing it is,
to know something.   Molière

Each of the countries that participated in the second International
Assessment of Educational Progress (IAEP) did so for its own reasons.
Some wanted to compare their results with those of neighbors or
competitors. Others wanted to learn about the educational policies and
practices of countries whose students seem to regularly achieve success in
mathematics and science. Still others wanted to establish a baseline of data
within their own countries against which they can measure progress in the
future.

All participants, however, shared a common interest in identifying
what is *possible* for today's 9- and 13-year-old children to know and to be
able to do in mathematics and science. While critics warn of the dangers of
promoting an educational olympiad, the benefits of periodically gathering
comparative data must be considered. Knowledge of what is *possible*
produces new enthusiasm, raises sights, establishes new challenges, and
ultimately can help improve personal and societal performance.

Some might say that a study that compares the United States with
Slovenia or England with São Paulo, Brazil is inappropriate or irrelevant.
Education is, in fact, imbedded in each society and culture, and
performance should not be studied or described without considering the
important differences from country to country. The life of a 13-year-old in
a rural Chinese community is very different from that of his or her peer
growing up in a middle-class Paris apartment. And yet, these two young
citizens may well meet in the global marketplace 20 years from now. And if
they do, chances are they will rely on the mathematics and science they
learned in this decade to succeed in the complex business and technological
environment of 2012.

While recognizing the fundamental differences from country to
country, the participants in the second IAEP project assembled tests that
focus on the common elements of their curriculums, and in order to form
the contexts for interpreting the student achievement data, they added sets

of questions about students' home background and classroom experiences and the characteristics of the schools they attend.

This report, then, is organized according to those contexts that surround and affect student performance: the curriculum, classroom practices, home environments, and the characteristics of countries and their education systems. While survey research projects like IAEP cannot establish cause-and-effect relationships, these studies can provide clues that may help explain high and low performance.

Occasionally, the findings are counter-intuitive. For example, in some countries, less well-trained teachers with large classes and poor-quality instructional materials sometimes produce students who achieve truly exceptional results. In other countries, students of better paid, better trained teachers, who work in schools that are more generously supported perform less well on the IAEP tests. The results presented in this report will highlight some of these paradoxes.

One possible reaction to this report would be for a country to examine the results and attempt to find out how to become *Number 1* in the world. A more thoughtful course of action would be for each country to use this information to set reasonable goals that are in harmony with its own values and culture.

The achievement results reported here can help identify what is *possible* for 9- and 13-year-olds to achieve and the descriptive information can suggest practices and curriculums that others are using successfully. It seems reasonable to expect that each country may find elements worth emulating in the practices of its neighbors and competitors.

ABOUT THE PROJECT   In 1990-91, a total of 20 countries surveyed the mathematics and science performance of 13-year-old students and 14 also assessed 9-year-olds in the same subjects. An optional short probe of the geography achievement of 13-year-olds and an experimental performance-based assessment of 13-year-olds' ability to use equipment and materials to solve mathematics and science problems were also conducted by some participants and their results will be presented in forthcoming reports.

Some countries drew samples from virtually all children in the appropriate age group; others confined their assessments to specific geographic areas, language groups, or grade levels. The definition of populations often followed the structure of school systems, political divisions, and cultural distinctions. For example, the sample in Israel focused on students in Hebrew-speaking schools, which share a common curriculum, language, and tradition. The assessment in Slovenia reflected the needs and aspirations of this recently separated republic of Yugoslavia. The restriction to certain grades in the Portuguese assessment was necessitated by a very dispersed student population resulting from a unique education system that allows students to repeat any grade up to three times. All countries limited their assessment to students who were in school, which for some participants meant excluding significant numbers of age-eligible children. In a few cases, a sizable proportion of the selected schools or students did not participate in the assessment, and therefore results are subject to possible nonresponse bias.[1]

A list of the participants is provided below with a description of limitations of the populations assessed. Unless noted, 90 percent or more of the age-eligible children in a population are in school. For countries where more than 10 percent of the age-eligible children are out of school a notation of *in-school population* appears after the country's name. In Brazil, two separate samples were drawn, one each from the cities of São Paulo and Fortaleza. In Canada, nine out of the 10 provinces drew separate samples of 13-year-olds and five of these drew separate samples of English-speaking and French-speaking schools, for a total of 14 separate samples. Four Canadian provinces, six separate samples, participated in the assessment of 9-year-olds.[2] These distinct Canadian samples coincide with the separate provincial education systems in Canada and reflect their concern for the two language groups they serve.

PARTICIPANTS

BRAZIL	Cities of São Paulo and Fortaleza, restricted grades, in-school population
CANADA	Four provinces at age 9 and nine out of 10 provinces at age 13
CHINA	20 out of 29 provinces and independent cities, restricted grades, in-school population
ENGLAND	All students, low participation at ages 9 and 13
FRANCE	All students
HUNGARY	All students
IRELAND	All students
ISRAEL	Hebrew-speaking schools
ITALY	Province of Emilia-Romagna, low participation at age 9
JORDAN	All students
KOREA	All students
MOZAMBIQUE	Cities of Maputo and Beira, in-school population, low participation
PORTUGAL	Restricted grades, in-school population at age 13
SCOTLAND	All students, low participation at age 9
SLOVENIA	All students
SOVIET UNION	14 out of 15 republics, Russian-speaking schools
SPAIN	All regions except Cataluña, Spanish-speaking schools
SWITZERLAND	15 out of 26 cantons
TAIWAN	All students
UNITED STATES	All students

---

[1] Percentages of age-eligible children excluded from samples and percentages of sampled schools and students that participated are provided in the Procedural Appendix, pp. 131-132 and 134-135.

[2] Taken together, the Canadian samples represent 94 percent of the 13-year-olds and 74 percent of the 9-year-olds in Canada. An appropriately weighted subsample of responses was drawn from these samples for the calculation of the statistics for Canada.

Typically, a representative sample of 3,300 students from 110 different schools was selected from each population at each age level and half were assessed in mathematics and half in science.[3] A total of about 175,000 9- and 13-year-olds (those born in calendar years 1981 and 1977, respectively) were tested in 13 different languages in March 1991.[4]

Steps to ensure the uniformity and quality of the surveys were taken at all stages of the project. While procedures could not always be followed in exactly the same way in each of the separate assessment centers, overall compliance was very high, as shown in the quality control procedures provided in the figure on the next page.[5] Translations and adaptations of assessment materials were carefully checked for accuracy. All questions were pilot-tested in participating countries before they were used in the final assessment. Comparable sampling designs were used by all participants and the quality of their implementation was carefully checked and documented. Participants were provided with training and computer software to facilitate their tasks and to ensure uniformity and quality. Test administrators were trained to administer the tests to students using the same set of instructions and time limits. The standardization of administration procedures was carefully checked within each country and across countries by an international monitoring team. While the reports of the quality control observers were for the most part completed check lists, some impressionistic observations of international monitoring team members are interspersed throughout this report to give a more personal view of the test administrations in several countries. The accuracy of the database was validated through independent checks of a random selection of completed student test booklets and school questionnaires; the accuracy of the data analysis was validated by comparing the results obtained using different statistical programs and computer equipment.

---

[3]The numbers of schools and students in each sample are provided in the Procedural Appendix, pp. 134-135.

[4]Because their school years begin in March instead of September, Brazil, Korea, and Mozambique assessed six months earlier in September 1990, and to compensate for the earlier assessment in Brazil and Korea, they sampled students who were six months older (born between July 1, 1976 through June 30, 1977). Mozambique assessed students born in 1977 in mathematics only.

[5]Additional documentation of data collection is provided in the Procedural Appendix, pp. 139-141 and in Adam Chu, et al, *IAEP Technical Report*, Princeton, NJ, Educational Testing Service, 1992.

TRANSLATIONS OF ASSESSMENT MATERIALS INDEPENDENTLY VERIFIED Achievement and background questions and student directions were adapted and translated within each country and then checked independently by language experts in the United States. All countries used the same artwork and physical page layouts for their tests.

PILOT TEST OF ASSESSMENT QUESTIONS Achievement and background questions were pilot-tested with groups of students from each participating country (except Slovenia, which joined the project late) to determine which questions would work best in the final assessment.

SAMPLES INDEPENDENTLY VERIFIED Samples for each population were drawn using agreed-upon procedures and were independently checked in the United States to ensure that procedures were followed accurately and that sampling weights were appropriately calculated.

PROCEDURAL MANUALS AND TRAINING PROVIDED Procedural manuals were developed for coordinating the project, drawing samples, administering the assessments, conducting a quality control program, and entering results into a database. Regional training sessions were held at which the individuals from each assessment center who actually performed the tasks were provided detailed instructions and hands-on experiences.

COMPUTER SOFTWARE PROVIDED Specially developed computer software was provided to the participants to facilitate sampling and data entry and to ensure uniformity and quality.

STANDARDIZED TEST ADMINISTRATION Test booklets were administered to students using the same instructions and the same time limits in each participating country. To ensure procedures were understood, test administrators, usually school personnel, were trained in 20 out of 29 assessment centers.

ON-SITE OBSERVATION OF ASSESSMENTS Unannounced observations of 10 to 20 percent of the test administrations were conducted by 22 out of 29 assessment centers.

INDEPENDENT QUALITY CONTROL In all countries except Brazil and Mozambique, an independent, trained observer interviewed the country project manager about all aspects of the project and visited one or more test administration sites. In most cases, the observer was fluent in the language of the assessment.

DATA FILES AND DATA ANALYSIS VALIDATED The scoring of open-ended mathematics questions was checked in 10 percent of the booklets by 27 out of 29 assessment centers and in all cases, accuracy of scoring was 98 percent or higher. Each country validated its own data files, using software provided by the project, to ascertain their quality and accuracy. Data files were also independently validated by comparing the responses of a random set of 10 student booklets and 10 school questionnaires of each type to the data entered into the databases. If data files contained 1 percent errors or greater, participants were asked to rekey all the responses. This happened in one case. Data analysis procedures were checked by calculating statistics using different programs and computer equipment and comparing the results.

ASSESSMENT QUESTIONS CHECKED FOR CURRICULAR OR CULTURAL BIAS Assessment results were checked to verify that responses to individual questions could be summarized without misrepresenting curricular or cultural differences within particular countries. Cluster analyses and analyses of differential item functioning (DIF) resulted in the removal of one mathematics question at each age level, two science questions at age 9, and eight at age 13 before final analyses were conducted.

A major challenge of international studies is to provide fair comparisons of student achievement. Some of the problems faced by these studies are similar to those of any survey research project. For example, samples must be adequately drawn, test administration procedures must be scrupulously adhered to, care must be taken to produce accurate data files. These concerns are not trivial. However, international studies must also address a number of unique issues that stem from the differences in language, culture, and education systems of the participating countries.[6]

Three areas of concern warrant special attention: the representativeness of the target population, the appropriateness of the measures, and educational and cultural differences. As indicated earlier, some participants confined assessments to particular geographic areas, language groups, or grade levels and in some cases, significant numbers of age-eligible children were not attending school and in other cases, participation rates of schools or students were low. These limitations are described in more detail in the figure on the following page. There is simply no way to measure the bias introduced when certain groups of children are excluded from a sample or when response rates are low; their participation could have raised performance scores, lowered them, or not affected them at all.

To address concerns of representativeness, all populations have been named on all of the figures and in the text in ways that highlight the major limitations of their assessment. For example, Italy is listed in the figures and in the text as "Emilia-Romagna," the actual province that was assessed, and China is listed in the figures as "China — in-school population, restricted grades, 20 provinces and cities," and in the text as "China (in-school population)," its major limitation.

Countries also differ with respect to the appropriateness of the curricular areas the IAEP assessment sought to measure. All countries participated in the development of the mathematics and science frameworks that guided the design of the instruments; curricular experts in each country reviewed all potential questions for their appropriateness for their own students.[7] While acceptable to all, the resulting tests do not match all countries' curricula equally well. Differences in curriculum emphasis are documented alongside the performance of each country in various curricular areas in Chapter Two.

---

[6]A thoughtful treatment of the issues involved in international studies is discussed in Norman M. Bradburn and Dorothy M. Gilford, Eds., *A Framework and Principles for International Comparative Studies in Education*, Washington, D.C., National Academy Press, 1990.

[7]A full discussion of the development of frameworks and selection of questions is provided in Center for the Assessment of Educational Progress, *The 1991 IAEP Assessment, Objectives for Mathematics, Science, and Geography*, Princeton, NJ, Educational Testing Service, 1991.

Descriptions of Limited Populations**

	Included		Excluded	
Brazil, Age 13	3%	13-year-olds in grades 5 through 8 in cities of São Paulo and Fortaleza.	97%	13-year-olds in grades other than 5 through 8 in São Paulo (20% of those in school) and in Fortaleza (34% of those in school). 13-year-olds not in school (8% of those in São Paulo and 15% of those in Fortaleza). 13-year-olds in schools in other cities and rural areas.
Canada, Age 9	74%	9-year-olds in English-speaking schools in British Columbia and New Brunswick. 9-year-olds in English- and French-speaking schools in Ontario and Quebec.	26%	9-year-olds in French-speaking schools in New Brunswick. 9-year-olds in six other provinces and territories.
China, Age 13	38%	13-year-olds in 17 provinces and independent cities of Beijing, Tienjing, and Shanghai in middle schools (grades 7 through 9).	62%	13-year-olds below grade 7 in 20 provinces and cities (10% of those in school). 13-year-olds not in school (about 49% of 13-year-olds). 13-year-olds in schools in 9 provinces and autonomous regions with predominantly non-Chinese populations.
Israel, Age 9	71%	9-year-olds in public Hebrew-speaking schools.	29%	9-year-olds in non-public Hebrew-speaking schools (about 7%). 9-year-olds in Arabic schools (about 20% of 9-year-olds).
Israel, Age 13	71%	13-year-olds in public Hebrew-speaking schools.	29%	13-year-olds in non-public Hebrew-speaking schools (about 10%). 13-year-olds in Arabic schools (about 20% of 13-year-olds).
Italy, Age 9	4%	9-year-olds in schools of Emilia-Romagna province.	96%	9-year-olds in 19 other provinces.
Italy, Age 13	6%	13-year-olds in schools in Emilia-Romagna province.	94%	13-year-olds in 19 other Italian provinces.
Mozambique, Age 13	1%	13-year-olds in schools of cities of Maputo and Beira.	99%	13-year-olds not in school (about 75% of 13-year-olds). 13-year-olds in other cities and rural areas.
Portugal, Age 9	81%	9-year-olds in grades 3 and 4.	19%	9-year-olds in grades other than 3 and 4 (about 16%).
Portugal, Age 13	68%	13-year-olds in grades 5 through 9.	32%	13-year-olds in grades other than 5 through 9 (about 18% of those in school). 13-year-olds not in school (about 16%).
Soviet Union, Age 9	63%	9-year-olds in Russian-speaking schools in 14 republics.	37%	9-year-olds in non-Russian-speaking schools in 14 republics. 9-year-olds in schools in Uzbeckistan republic.
Soviet Union, Age 13	60%	13-year-olds in Russian-speaking schools in 14 republics.	40%	13-year-olds in non-Russian-speaking schools in 14 republics. 13-year-olds in schools in Uzbeckistan republic.
Spain, Age 9	80%	9-year-olds in all Spanish-speaking schools except those in schools except those in the Catalan autonomous community.	20%	9-year-olds in all schools in the Catalan autonomous community. 9-year-olds in exclusively Valencian- and Basque-speaking schools.
Spain, Age 13	80%	13-year-olds in all Spanish-speaking schools except those in the Catalan autonomous community.	20%	13-year-olds in all schools in the Catalan autonomous community. 13-year-olds in exclusively Valencian- and Basque-speaking schools.
Switzerland, Age 13	76%	13-year-olds in German-, French- and Italian-speaking public schools in 15 cantons.	24%	13-year-olds in private and Romansch schools in 15 cantons. 13-year-olds in the remaining 11 cantons.

**Unless noted above, all other populations included 90 percent or more of their age-eligible children.

Furthermore, the testing format — multiple-choice and short-answer questions — is not equally familiar to students from all countries. To address this issue, participants were given the option of administering a practice test to sampled students prior to the assessment. Finally, since countries differ in the age at which students start school and policies for promotion, students at ages 9 and 13 are further along in their schooling in some countries than in others.[8] While all results presented in this report represent performance of all students in each age group, participants were also provided with results broken down by the two most common grade levels for students in each age group.

International results must ultimately be interpreted in light of the educational and cultural context of each country. The countries participating in IAEP are large and small, rich and poor, and have varied ethnic, religious, language, and cultural traditions. Likewise, educational goals, expectations, and even the meaning of achievement vary from nation to nation. As a reminder of these differences among countries, results are presented along with relevant contextual information that is designed to help the reader interpret their significance.

---

[8]See the Procedural Appendix, pp. 137-138 for the distribution of students by grade level.

Highlights

• Factors that impact academic performance interact in complex ways and operate differently in various cultural and educational systems. There is no single formula for success.

• The IAEP results demonstrate what is *possible* for 9- and 13-year-olds to achieve in mathematics. This information can be instructive to policy makers as they attempt to set goals and standards for their own young citizens.

• In almost all 13-year-old populations, at least 10 percent of the students performed very well (20 points or more above the IAEP average) and at least 10 percent performed poorly (20 points or more below the IAEP average). In China (in-school population), however, even students in the 10th percentile performed close to the IAEP average.

• In about one-third of the populations, 13-year-old boys performed significantly better than girls that age. Nevertheless, in almost all populations, three quarters or more of the students felt "mathematics is for boys and girls about equally."

• Most countries include whole-number operations in their instructional programs for age 13. Students in many countries that emphasize geometry or algebra performed well in those topics as well as in mathematics overall. Taiwan, a high-performing population, is an exception: their schools do not emphasize geometry at this age level. Although Spain (except Cataluña), Portugal (restricted grades), São Paulo (restricted grades), and Fortaleza (restricted grades) all emphasize algebra at age 13, students in those places were lower performers.

• Teaching practices, types of instructional materials, teacher background, and classroom organization vary from country to country for children at age 13; moreover, these factors do not distinguish between high-performing and low-performing populations.

- Within individual populations, greater frequency of teacher presentation and independent work are associated with higher performance for the majority of IAEP participants, suggesting either the importance of intensity of instruction in general or of these practices in particular.

- Thirteen-year-old students in most participating countries do not spend a great deal of time doing mathematics homework. The most common response is one hour or less *each week* in all populations except Korea and Israel, where the norm is two to three hours weekly and China, where the most common response is four hours or more weekly.

- Thirteen-year-olds are much more likely to spend their spare time watching television than studying. The norm is two to four hours of television viewing *each day* in all but two IAEP populations. In China (in-school population), 65 percent of the students reported watching little or no television on a daily basis. Slightly more than one-half of the students in France reported watching one hour or less of television each day.

- While socioeconomic factors seem to be associated with mathematics performance at age 13 in many IAEP populations, so are students' out-of-school activities. Amount of leisure reading and time spent on all homework is positively related to mathematics achievement, while amount of time spent watching television is negatively related in about one-half participating countries.

- The range of average performance across the 14 populations participating in the IAEP assessment at age 9 was 20 points, and in almost all populations, at least 10 percent of the students performed very well (20 points or more above the IAEP average) and at least 10 percent performed poorly (20 points or more below the IAEP average).

- The difference in performance between 9- and 13-year-olds in each of the 14 populations ranged from a 22- to 32-point increase.

Mathematics Performance of 13-Year-Olds

CHAPTER ONE

Quel che si impara in gioventú,
Non si dimentica mai piú.

What is learned in youth,
Will never be forgotten.

Italian Proverb

The results presented in this chapter reflect some of what 13-year-olds know and can do in mathematics in the 20 countries. The percentages displayed in the tables and graphs reflect the percentages of questions that groups of students from the various populations answered correctly. In addition to group averages, the figures display how the best students (90th to 99th percentiles) and the least successful (1st to 10th percentiles) from each population performed on the assessment. Next to each printed statistic, in parentheses, is an estimate of sampling error.[9] It is especially important to consider the imprecision in the estimates when comparing two populations with similar results.

Results are presented separately for two groups: **comprehensive populations** and **populations with exclusions or low participation.** Comprehensive populations are those that included in the assessment

---

[9]The estimate of sampling error provided is a jackknifed standard error. It can be said with 95 percent certainty that for each population of interest, the value for the whole population is within ± 2 standard errors of the estimate for the sample.

virtually all age-eligible children within a defined group, even if the group was limited to a specific geographic area or a certain language group. Populations with exclusions or low participation are those that excluded from the assessment a significant proportion (more than 10 percent) of 13-year-olds from within the defined group, typically because not all grade levels were assessed or because some children were not in school, or those where participation of sampled schools and students was low (less than 70 percent).

In the figures that follow, two kinds of data are displayed: the comparative achievement results as well as indicators of cultural and educational differences. These cultural and educational characteristics are drawn from international databases, country questionnaires completed by project directors, school questionnaires completed by school administrators, and student questionnaires completed by the assessed students. The source of each piece of descriptive data is indicated by a footnote.

The descriptive data permit easier and more thoughtful interpretation of the significance of achievement results. Key characteristics of participants, their education systems, classrooms, homes, and students are presented, along with a graphic representation of achievement in the attached fold-out CHART. The average percents correct and distribution of scores are repeated in FIGURE 1.1. After the introduction of overall achievement results in this chapter, they are discussed in more depth, along with contextual information, in the chapters that follow.

ᴱIAEP

| t of
ts Who
ositive
es
s Math[8, 9]	**COMPREHENSIVE POPULATIONS**
71	**Korea**
79	**Taiwan**
85	**Switzerland** 15 Cantons
76	**Soviet Union** Russian-speaking Schools in 14 Republics
85	**Hungary**
81	**France**
86	**Emilia-Romagna, Italy**†
90	**Israel** Hebrew-speaking Schools
94	**Canada**
91	**Scotland**†
88	**Ireland**
83	**Slovenia**
89	**Spain** Spanish-speaking Schools except in Cataluña
90	**United States**†
77	**Jordan**
	POPULATIONS WITH EXCLUSIONS OR LOW PARTICIPATION
79	**China** In-school Population, Restricted Grades, 20 Provinces & Cities
91	**England** Low Participation‡
84	**Portugal** In-school Population, Restricted Grades†
83	**São Paulo, Brazil** In-school Population, Restricted Grades
86	**Fortaleza, Brazil** In-school Population, Restricted Grades
88	**Maputo and Beira, Mozambique** In-school Population, Low Participation‡

re based on responses of four attitude questions.

ᴱDUCATIONAL TESTING SERVICE

92823-07217 • S21M25 • 251822 • Printed in U.S.A.

The results are presented in Figure 1.1. The green bars indicate the average percent correct for each population and take into account the imprecision of these estimates due to sampling. When the bars overlap, as they do in many cases, it indicates that the performances of those populations do not differ significantly.

The average score across the comprehensive populations and populations with exclusions or low participation, represented by a vertical dashed line, is 58 percent.[10] Students in Scotland, Ireland, Slovenia, and England (low participation) performed at about the IAEP average.

The highest performing students were those assessed in China (in-school population), with an average of 80 percent correct. The other populations performing above the average, from highest to lowest, were Korea, Taiwan, Switzerland (15 cantons), Soviet Union (Russian-speaking schools), Hungary, France, Emilia-Romagna, Israel (Hebrew), and Canada. As the overlapping bars on the figure indicate, performance levels were essentially the same for many of these populations.

Students from Spain (except Cataluña) and the United States scored just below the IAEP average and those from Portugal (restricted grades) somewhat lower. Lower still was the performance of students from Jordan and São Paulo (restricted grades) and the two lowest performing groups were the students assessed in Fortaleza (restricted grades) and those from Maputo-Beira (in-school population).

The performance of the individual Canadian populations which contribute to the overall Canada score ranged from 53 to 69 percent correct. However, as the overlapping bars in the figures indicate, the scores often are not significantly different from one population to another. Nova Scotia, Newfoundland, Ontario (English), Manitoba (English), and New Brunswick (English) all performed about at the IAEP average.

Those scoring above the average, from highest to lowest, were Quebec (French), Saskatchewan (French), British Columbia, Quebec (English), Alberta, Manitoba (French), Saskatchewan (English), and New Brunswick (French). Ontario (French) is the only Canadian population that scored below the IAEP average.

---

[10] The IAEP average is the unweighted average of the scores of the comprehensive populations and populations with exclusions or low participation. An unweighted average has been chosen to describe the midpoint because it is not influenced by the differential weights of very large and very small populations.

Mathematics, Age 13
Distribution of Percent Correct Scores by Population*
Part 1

FIGURE 1.1

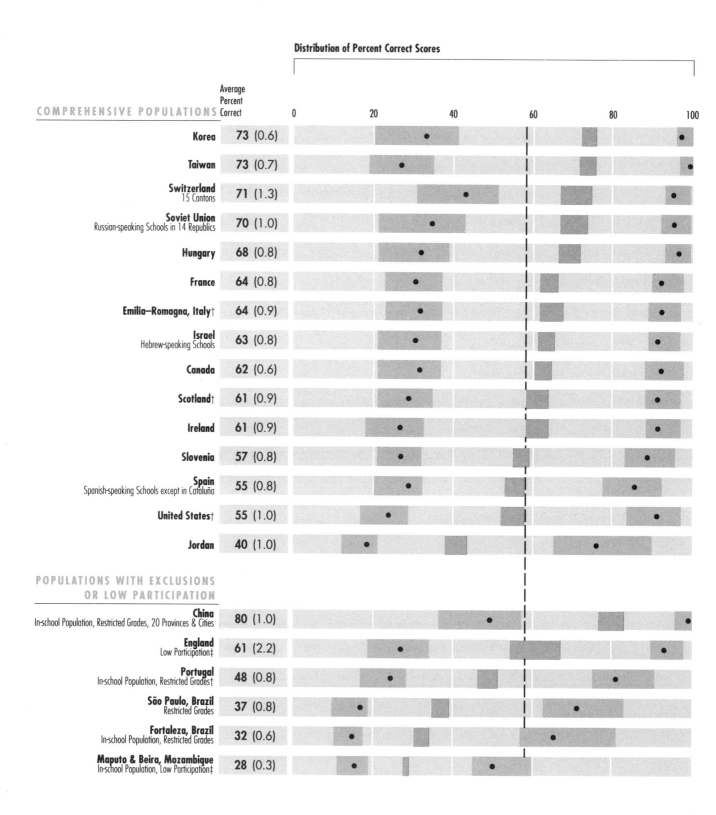

Distribution of Percent Correct Scores

COMPREHENSIVE POPULATIONS	Average Percent Correct				
Korea	73 (0.6)				
Taiwan	73 (0.7)				
Switzerland 15 Cantons	71 (1.3)				
Soviet Union Russian-speaking Schools in 14 Republics	70 (1.0)				
Hungary	68 (0.8)				
France	64 (0.8)				
Emilia–Romagna, Italy†	64 (0.9)				
Israel Hebrew-speaking Schools	63 (0.8)				
Canada	62 (0.6)				
Scotland†	61 (0.9)				
Ireland	61 (0.9)				
Slovenia	57 (0.8)				
Spain Spanish-speaking Schools except in Cataluña	55 (0.8)				
United States†	55 (1.0)				
Jordan	40 (1.0)				

POPULATIONS WITH EXCLUSIONS OR LOW PARTICIPATION

China In-school Population, Restricted Grades, 20 Provinces & Cities	80 (1.0)				
England Low Participation‡	61 (2.2)				
Portugal In-school Population, Restricted Grades†	48 (0.8)				
São Paulo, Brazil Restricted Grades	37 (0.8)				
Fortaleza, Brazil In-school Population, Restricted Grades	32 (0.6)				
Maputo & Beira, Mozambique In-school Population, Low Participation‡	28 (0.3)				

▨ Average percent correct with simultaneous confidence interval controlling for all possible comparisons among comprehensive populations, populations with exclusions or low participation, and Canadian populations based on the Bonferroni procedure (the average ±2.79 standard errors).

● Bullet is 5th and 95th percentile. ▨ are 1st to 10th percentiles and 90th to 99th percentiles.

┊ IAEP Average

* Jackknifed standard errors are presented in parentheses.

† Combined school and student participation rate is below .80 but at least .70; interpret results with caution because of possible nonresponse bias.

‡ Combined school and student participation rate is below .70; interpret results with extreme caution because of possible nonresponse bias.

FIGURE 1.1

Mathematics, Age 13
Distribution of Percent Correct Scores by Population*
Part 2

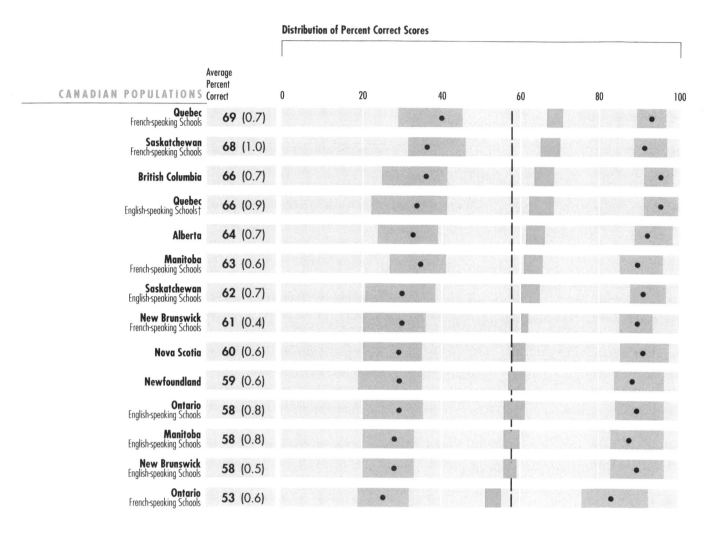

Distribution of Percent Correct Scores

CANADIAN POPULATIONS	Average Percent Correct	
Quebec French-speaking Schools	69 (0.7)	
Saskatchewan French-speaking Schools	68 (1.0)	
British Columbia	66 (0.7)	
Quebec English-speaking Schools†	66 (0.9)	
Alberta	64 (0.7)	
Manitoba French-speaking Schools	63 (0.6)	
Saskatchewan English-speaking Schools	62 (0.7)	
New Brunswick French-speaking Schools	61 (0.4)	
Nova Scotia	60 (0.6)	
Newfoundland	59 (0.6)	
Ontario English-speaking Schools	58 (0.8)	
Manitoba English-speaking Schools	58 (0.8)	
New Brunswick English-speaking Schools	58 (0.5)	
Ontario French-speaking Schools	53 (0.6)	

▨ Average percent correct with simultaneous confidence interval controlling for all possible comparisons among comprehensive populations with exclusions or low participation and Canadian populations based on the Bonferroni procedure (the average ±2.79 standard errors).
● Bullet is 5th and 95th percentile. ▨ are 1st to 10th percentiles and 90th to 99th percentiles.
┊ IAEP Average

* Jackknifed standard errors are presented in parentheses.
† Combined school and student participation rate is below .80 but at least .70; interpret results with caution because of possible nonresponse bias.

Achievement reflects the percent correct on 75 questions. Responses to one question included in the assessment were removed from the results after a series of data analysis steps explored the consistency of performance across countries, topics, and individual items. These procedures were designed to identify questions that were not functioning in the same way across all populations.[11] Such items are not considered to be *bad items*; they simply did not seem to measure the same content or skill in all of the populations, probably because of curricular differences or because of cultural or linguistic idiosyncrasies.

[11] See the Procedural Appendix, p. 142-143, and the *IAEP Technical Report* for a detailed discussion of cluster and differential item functioning analyses.

Averages provide a useful picture of group performance among participants. However, the technological leaders of the 21st century will probably come from the highest-performing students in schools today. Figure 1.1 also shows the range of correct responses for the top-performing students from each population (the 90th through the 99th percentiles). These data reflect the achievement levels of the best students. Of equal concern is what can be done to improve the results of each population's poorest performers. Also displayed are the ranges of results for the lowest performing students in each population assessed (the 1st through the 10th percentiles). The average percents correct for students at the 5th and 95th percentiles are indicated by a bullet inside the shaded bar.[12]

Percentiles represent locations in the distribution of scores. If the average percent correct for the 5th percentile is 30 percent, it means that the 5 percent of the population who are the lowest scorers answered 30 percent or fewer of the questions correctly. If the average percent correct for the 95th percentile is 90, the 5 percent of the population who are the highest scorers answered 90 percent or more of the questions correctly.

The pattern of results for high and low achievers tend to mirror the averages, but they also demonstrate that in almost all populations there are some very good students (scoring at least 20 points above the IAEP average) and some poor students (scoring at least 20 points below the IAEP average). Some extremes can be noted. Students in the 10th percentile from China (in-school population) performed close to the IAEP average and those in the 10th percentile from Switzerland (15 cantons) answered over one-half of the questions correctly. Only the very best students assessed in Maputo-Beira (in-school population) attained scores at the IAEP average.

---

[12] Performance of students at the very bottom of the distribution (the lowest 1 percent) and at the very top (the highest 1 percent) are not represented on the figure because very few students fall into these categories and their performance cannot be estimated with precision.

FIGURE 1.2 reports the average mathematics performance for males and females at age 13 and the degree to which students agreed that mathematics is equally appropriate for both groups. In nearly every population, almost all students assessed agreed with the statement "mathematics is for boys and girls about equally." Performance of females and males did not differ significantly in most (all but eight) of the comprehensive populations and populations with exclusions or low participation. The performance of boys was significantly higher than that of girls in Switzerland (15 cantons), France, Emilia-Romagna, Canada, Ireland, Spain (except Cataluña), China (in-school population), and Fortaleza (restricted grades). These finding in some cases confirm and in other cases contradict those of other national and international studies.[13] Inconsistencies in results may be due to differences in the content coverage of assessments, since in many countries, girls typically perform better in some topics and boys in others, or to differences in sample designs.

For most Canadian populations, boys outscored girls about as much as they did for Canada as a whole. However, because sampling errors are greater for the individual Canadian populations, these differences are not statistically significant. Newfoundland is a notable exception. Here the performance of girls was significantly higher than that of boys.

Interestingly, the three countries that were more likely to view mathematics as gender-linked — Korea, Taiwan, and Jordan — did not exhibit significant differences in performance by gender. In Korea, 27 percent of the students felt that mathematics is more for boys and 17 percent that it is more for girls; in Taiwan, 15 percent felt that mathematics is more for boys and 8 percent felt that it is more for girls; and in Jordan, 15 percent of the students felt that mathematics is more for boys and 9 percent that it is more for girls.

---

[13] For example, results for England replicated those of the first IAEP study but contradict findings from national monitoring studies and the Second International Mathematics Study.

Mathematics, Age 13

Percentages of Students Reporting Math Is Equally for Boys and Girls and Average Percents Correct*

FIGURE 1.2

Part 1

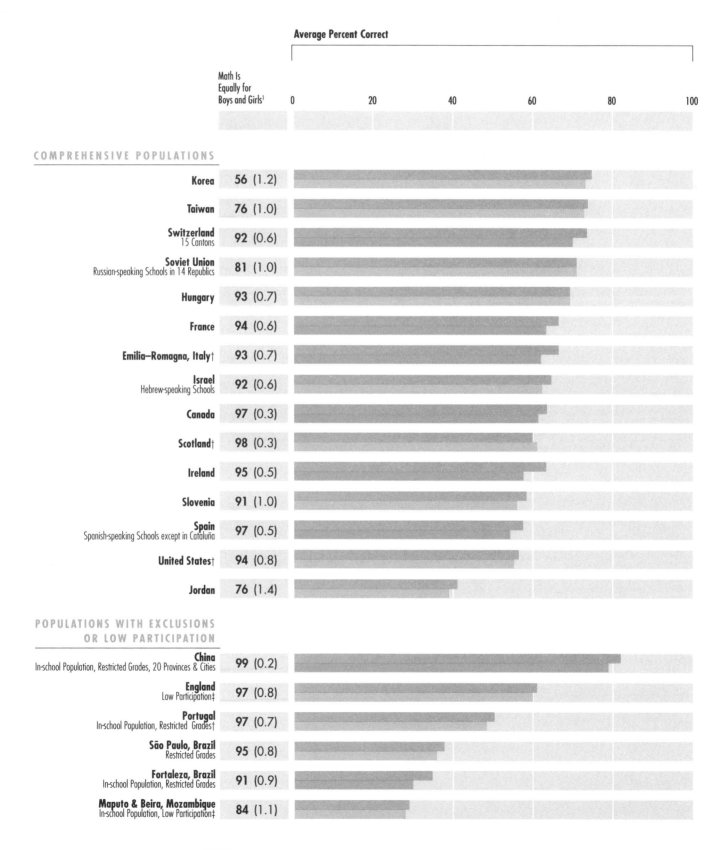

	Math Is Equally for Boys and Girls[1]	Average Percent Correct
COMPREHENSIVE POPULATIONS		
Korea	56 (1.2)	
Taiwan	76 (1.0)	
Switzerland 15 Cantons	92 (0.6)	
Soviet Union Russian-speaking Schools in 14 Republics	81 (1.0)	
Hungary	93 (0.7)	
France	94 (0.6)	
Emilia–Romagna, Italy†	93 (0.7)	
Israel Hebrew-speaking Schools	92 (0.6)	
Canada	97 (0.3)	
Scotland†	98 (0.3)	
Ireland	95 (0.5)	
Slovenia	91 (1.0)	
Spain Spanish-speaking Schools except in Cataluña	97 (0.5)	
United States†	94 (0.8)	
Jordan	76 (1.4)	
POPULATIONS WITH EXCLUSIONS OR LOW PARTICIPATION		
China In-school Population, Restricted Grades, 20 Provinces & Cities	99 (0.2)	
England Low Participation‡	97 (0.8)	
Portugal In-school Population, Restricted Grades†	97 (0.7)	
São Paulo, Brazil Restricted Grades	95 (0.8)	
Fortaleza, Brazil In-school Population, Restricted Grades	91 (0.9)	
Maputo & Beira, Mozambique In-school Population, Low Participation‡	84 (1.1)	

Males
Females
Statistically significant differences between groups at the .05 level.
* Jackknifed standard errors are presented in parentheses.
† Combined school and student participation rate is below .80 but at least .70; interpret results with caution because of possible nonresponse bias.
‡ Combined school and student participation rate is below .70; interpret results with extreme caution because of possible nonresponse bias.
[1] IAEP Student Questionnaire, Age 13.

 IAEP

Mathematics, Age 13

FIGURE 1.2

Percentages of Students Reporting Math is Equally for Boys and Girls and Average Percents Correct*
Part 2

Average Percent Correct

	Math Is Equally for Boys and Girls[1]	0	20	40	60	80	100

CANADIAN POPULATIONS

Quebec French-speaking Schools	95 (1.2)
Saskatchewan French-speaking Schools	97 (1.2)
British Columbia	95 (0.7)
Quebec English-speaking Schools†	97 (0.3)
Alberta	96 (0.6)
Manitoba French-speaking Schools	95 (0.9)
Saskatchewan English-speaking Schools	96 (0.5)
New Brunswick French-speaking Schools	95 (0.5)
Nova Scotia	97 (0.5)
Newfoundland	96 (0.6)
Ontario English-speaking Schools	97 (0.5)
Manitoba English-speaking Schools	95 (0.6)
New Brunswick English-speaking Schools	96 (0.5)
Ontario French-speaking Schools	94 (0.7)

■ Males
▨ Females
▨ Statistically significant differences between groups at the .05 level.
* Jackknifed standard errors are presented in parentheses.
† Combined school and student participation rate is below .80 but at least .70; interpret results with caution because of possible nonresponse bias.
[1] IAEP Student Questionnaire, Age 13.

IAEP

While the mathematics achievement ranged from 28 to 80 average percents correct, there is evidence of the potential of each population, as demonstrated in the performance of the top 10 percent of the students in each country. The data from the bottom 10 percent remind us that even the most successful countries have students who need further help and encouragement.

Most students in most participating countries believe that mathematics is equally important for boys and girls. Still, in more than one-third of the comprehensive populations and populations with exclusions or low participation, behavior does not match attitude and 13-year-old boys perform significantly better than girls at that age.

While it is tempting to look only at which country is *Number 1*, the IAEP results can only be useful if they inform educators, policy makers, and the public about characteristics of high and low performers. To that end, the achievement results are examined in relation to school, home, and societal factors in the chapters that follow.

TAIWAN March 15, 1991

The motto of the modern, suburban, junior high school was "Perserverance, Determination, Justice, and Honesty: Be Free from Laziness, Awkwardness, Partiality, and Falsehood." The serious challenges of this admonition did not seem to inhibit the enthusiasm of about 20 pom-pom girls clad in cheerful yellow and white costumes rehearsing their routines in the warm, humid sunshine.

"This junior high has only been coeducational for a couple of years," I was informed as soon as I entered the door. And indeed I noticed almost as many boys as girls in their crisp blue uniforms hurrying up and down the four flights of stairs to their classes in the 107 classrooms. As we drank tea and ate shaobing and youtiao in the contemporary lounge outside the main office, the dean told me that the change had caused the faculty to re-evaluate the content of the home economics courses.

The sampled students filed quietly into the large, modern, sloped auditorium. They quickly seated themselves at the desks facing a stage, whose walls were covered with paintings of distinguished figures and several scrolls of calligraphy written by school officials urging students to apply themselves. One of them warned ominously, "When you go to use your knowledge, you will regret that you haven't learned more."

The pleasant, enthusiastic, 13-year-old faces remained that way throughout the exercise. The student's natural and unselfconscious courtesy expressed itself in bows and "she'she's" (thank-you's), as they left the room.

ETS Quality Control Observer

Curriculum

CHAPTER TWO

O homem é o autor de si mesmo.
Man is his own author.

Delfim Santos

While politicians and the public may be most interested in the overall performance of children, these findings have only limited utility for educators charged with developing student competence. Knowledge and skills are taught in segments that are usually organized around topics featured in the curriculum and in textbooks. Results showing that students perform poorly can only sound a general alarm. Teachers and administrators must know which are the specific areas of students' strength and weakness before they can target their limited time and resources.

While initial analyses of the data confirm that questions across all of the topic areas can be summarized without masking important differences between populations, results by topic presented in this chapter do show some variation.[14] This is understandable because countries differ in their

---

[14] A country-by-topic interaction analysis using Hartigan and Wong's K-Means cluster analysis technique indicated that the differences in performance from topic to topic do not confound the main effects of overall performance. This means that the relative performance of countries would remain essentially the same if a group of items from a particular topic or topics were removed from the overall summary measure. More details of this analysis are provided in the Procedural Appendix, p. 142, and in the *IAEP Technical Report*.

approaches to teaching mathematics to 13-year-olds. While the IAEP assessment was based on a consensus description of the topics and cognitive processes that all participants agreed were both taught in their schools and appropriate for this age group, the assessment is not aligned with any specific country's curriculum. The materials included in the assessment are neither given equal emphasis nor taught on the same time schedule in all participating countries. Furthermore, the importance ascribed to what is *not* covered by the IAEP assessment varies from country to country.

The results for students of age 13 are presented in this chapter for five content areas typically taught in mathematics: **Numbers and Operations; Measurement; Geometry; Data Analysis, Statistics and Probability;** and **Algebra and Functions.** The distribution of questions by topic is shown in FIGURE 2.1. Three quarters of the questions used a multiple-choice format and the remaining questions required students to write their answers on lines provided.

FIGURE 2.1

Mathematics, Age 13:
Numbers of Questions by Topic

Numbers and Operations	Measurement	Geometry	Data Analysis, Statistics and Probability	Algebra and Functions	Total
27	13	11	9	15	75

NUMBERS AND OPERATIONS About 35 percent of the assessment of 13-year-olds focused on Numbers and Operations, a total of 27 questions. Samples of a relatively easy and of a relatively hard question from this category and their average difficulty levels are shown in FIGURE 2.2.[15] Short descriptions of all of the questions in this category and their average difficulty levels are provided in the Data Appendix along with the same information for items in the other four content areas. The questions for 13-year-olds assessed students' basic understanding of numerical operations as well as of concepts of number lines, place values, negative numbers, multiples, odd and even, fractions, decimals, percents, and ratios. Questions require students to add, subtract, multiply, and divide using whole numbers (including negative numbers), fractions, and decimals. Many tasks are imbedded in problems that require one or more operations.

---

[15] The difficulty level for sample questions for this and subsequent topics is an unweighted average of the item percents correct across the comprehensive populations and populations with exclusions or low participation.

FIGURE 2.2
Mathematics, Age 13:
Sample Test Questions for Numbers and Operations

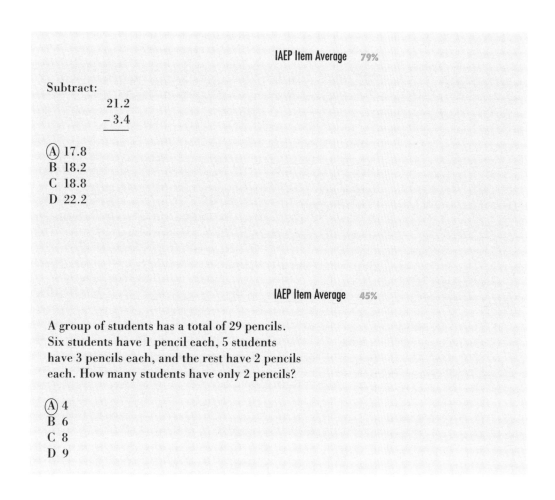

IAEP Item Average   79%

Subtract:

$$\begin{array}{r} 21.2 \\ -\,3.4 \\ \hline \end{array}$$

Ⓐ 17.8
B 18.2
C 18.8
D 22.2

IAEP Item Average   45%

A group of students has a total of 29 pencils.
Six students have 1 pencil each, 5 students
have 3 pencils each, and the rest have 2 pencils
each. How many students have only 2 pencils?

Ⓐ 4
B 6
C 8
D 9

Comprehensive populations and populations with exclusions or low participation are listed in order of performance across all mathematics questions in FIGURE 2.3. The bars display both the IAEP average across all populations in the two groups and the average percents correct for each population for Numbers and Operations. The numeric averages and standard errors for this topic and the other content and process categories are provided in the Data Appendix.

In general, the relative performance of the two population groups on Numbers and Operations mirrors their overall achievement in mathematics. This is shown by the fact that the bars representing the topic averages generally follow the same pattern as the green bars representing overall averages in Figure 1.1 in Chapter One.

The patterns of performance were examined to see if the performance of a population on a particular topic was different from its overall performance and some exceptions were identified. Since the average difficulty level of the questions in the various topics and across all topics differs, performance was examined in relative terms. The difference between a population's topic average and the IAEP topic average was compared with the difference between the population's overall average and the IAEP overall average. If the difference between those deviations was greater than what might be expected due to sampling error, the population's performance on that topic was identified as an exception. In some cases, performance on a topic was identified as higher compared to achievement overall and in some cases it was identified as relatively lower than performance in general.[16]

For example, students in Maputo-Beira (in-school population) were identified as performing at relatively higher levels in Numbers and Operations than they did overall. On this topic, these students scored 27 points below the IAEP Numbers and Operations average of 61 but across all mathematics questions, they scored 30 points below the IAEP overall mathematics average of 58. Students assessed in the Soviet Union (Russian-speaking schools) performed less well in Numbers and Operations relative to their performance overall because they scored 8 points above the IAEP topic average but scored 12 points above the IAEP overall average. In both cases, these differences, in absolute terms, are greater than would be expected due to sampling error. Scotland is the only other population that was identified as performing differently in Numbers and Operations as compared with its overall performance. Like the Soviet Union (Russian-speaking schools), its performance was lower in this topic relative to its overall mathematics achievement.

[16] For these analyses of achievement by topics, populations are cited as deviating from their normal pattern if the difference between their deviation from the mean for the topic and their deviation from the overall mean is twice the standard error of difference between these deviations, or greater. Further details of these analyses are provided in the Procedural Appendix, p. 143, and the *IAEP Technical Report*.

Mathematics, Age 13

Percentages of Schools that Emphasize Five Numbers and Operations Subtopics and Average Percents Correct for Numbers and Operations*

FIGURE 2.3

	Percent of Schools Emphasizing A Lot [1]					Average Percent Correct					
	Whole Numbers Operations	Common Fractions	Decimal Fractions	Ratio and Proportions	Percents	0	20	40	60	80	100
COMPREHENSIVE POPULATIONS											
IAEP Topic Average											
Korea	47 (6.5)	19 (4.1)	30 (7.1)	10 (3.0)	3 (1.5)						
Taiwan	33 (6.4)	24 (4.6)	15 (5.6)	52 (7.1)	7 (2.4)						
Switzerland 15 Cantons	75 (5.2)§	72 (6.5)§	81 (5.8)§	43 (8.2)§	41 (4.2)§						
Soviet Union Russian-speaking Schools in 14 Republics	46 (4.2)	54 (4.5)	60 (5.1)	27 (3.9)	17 (3.8)						
Hungary	72 (5.7)	90 (2.7)	89 (3.3)	15 (***)	60 (7.7)						
France	43 (6.3)	81 (4.0)	57 (6.2)	51 (6.5)	23 (8.7)						
Emilia-Romagna, Italy†	49 (5.0)	46 (5.9)	50 (5.4)	63 (5.4)	49 (6.5)						
Israel Hebrew-speaking Schools	71 (9.2)	63 (7.8)	53 (6.6)	18 (4.9)	55 (7.5)						
Canada	72 (2.4)	52 (2.3)	63 (2.1)	48 (2.6)	57 (2.3)						
Scotland†	69 (9.5)	23 (5.8)	70 (9.1)	34 (5.5)	51 (8.8)						
Ireland	77 (4.3)	76 (5.2)	57 (6.0)	44 (6.2)	62 (5.7)						
Slovenia	77 (6.5)	61 (***)	40 (5.8)	14 (8.5)	26 (7.9)						
Spain Spanish-speaking Schools except in Cataluña	93 (2.5)	92 (2.6)	56 (5.9)	50 (7.2)	50 (7.5)						
United States†	49 (9.9)	54 (***)	52 (***)	38 (***)	42 (***)						
Jordan	61 (9.4)	21 (5.4)	25 (7.8)	75 (7.7)	61 (8.9)						
POPULATIONS WITH EXCLUSIONS OR LOW PARTICIPATION											
China In-school Population, Restricted Grades, 20 Provinces & Cities	23 (5.1)	24 (5.2)	21 (5.7)	20 (5.5)	22 (6.4)						
England Low Participation‡	49 (***)	10 (4.9)	44 (***)	43 (***)	50 (***)						
Portugal In-school Population, Restricted Grades†	62 (8.1)	66 (7.9)	42 (6.9)	19 (5.5)	6 (3.6)						
São Paulo, Brazil Restricted Grades	61 (7.2)	44 (8.3)	28 (5.3)	33 (8.8)	22 (5.6)						
Fortaleza, Brazil In-school Population, Restricted Grades	78 (4.7)	48 (7.1)	38 (7.4)	46 (6.7)	34 (7.0)						
Maputo & Beira, Mozambique In-school Population, Low Participation‡	70 (0.0)	40 (0.0)	45 (0.0)	20 (0.0)	11 (0.0)						

* Jackknifed standard errors are presented in parentheses.
*** Jackknifed standard errors are greater than 9.9
† Combined school and student participation rate is below .80 but at least .70; interpret results with caution because of possible nonresponse bias.
‡ Combined school and student participation rate is below .70; interpret results with extreme caution because of possible nonresponse bias.
§ Results represent percent of classrooms in schools.
[1] IAEP School Questionnaire, Age 13.

Figure 2.3 also shows the percentage of schools from each population that reported they emphasized various numbers and operations subtopics *a lot* in the modal grade for 13-year-olds in their country (typically grade 7 or 8).[17] Patterns of instruction vary from country to country. Most countries still provide instruction on whole number operations at this level but emphasis on the more complex operations differs, with some countries focusing on common and decimal fractions, others on ratios and proportions, and still others on percent. Several high-performing populations — Korea, Taiwan, and China — do not emphasize the various numbers and operations subtopics as much at this age level as the other populations do.

MEASUREMENT   The 13 Measurement questions focused on understanding basic measurement concepts and applying them in typical classroom problems and real-world situations. Questions required students to work with units of length and to solve problems involving length, width, perimeter, area, volume, and surface area, primarily of squares, rectangles, cubes, and rectangular solids. The ability to read scale drawings was also assessed. Typical measurement questions are presented in FIGURE 2.4.

Questions such as those in the first example were adapted from non-metric to metric units in countries as appropriate, but the actual quantities involved in the measurements were not changed. Some questions expressed in metric units, like those in the second example, were administered in both metric and non-metric countries, but these tasks did not require students to understand nor to be able to use metric units to solve the problem.

---

[17] Several questions in the IAEP age 13 school questionnaire focused on the teachers and educational program for the grade in which most 13-year-olds are enrolled, or the modal grade. Each country tailored its questionnaire to indicate the appropriate title for that grade — e.g., junior high 2 in Korea and Taiwan, 7th class in German Switzerland, 8th year in French and Italian Switzerland, 8th class in the Soviet Union.

FIGURE 2.4

Mathematics, Age 13:
Sample Test Questions for Measurement

IAEP Item Average   60%

The area of a rectangle is 24 square inches
and the measures of its length and width are
whole numbers. Which of the following are
NOT possible dimensions for the rectangle?

A length = 6 inches, width = 4 inches
B length = 8 inches, width = 3 inches
Ⓒ length = 12 inches, width = 12 inches
D length = 24 inches, width = 1 inch

IAEP Item Average   33%

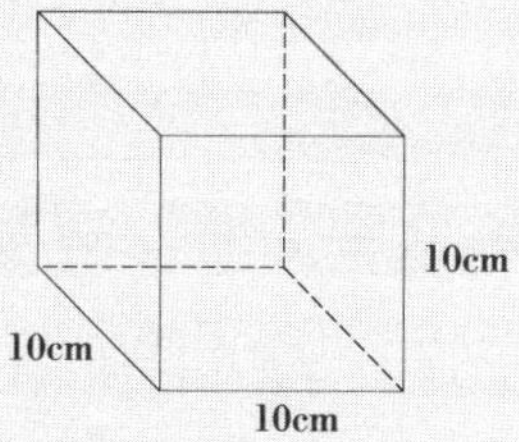

10cm

10cm

10cm

What is the total surface area of the cube shown above?

A   240 square centimeters
B   400 square centimeters
Ⓒ   600 square centimeters
D   1,000 square centimeters

As FIGURE 2.5 shows, Measurement is a topic in which students
from Emilia-Romagna did better compared with their overall mathematics
achievement; its schools reported that they gave this topic heavy emphasis
at this age level. Thirteen-year-olds in Maputo-Beira (in-school population)
also had relatively higher scores on this topic than they did on the
mathematics test as a whole. Israel (Hebrew), Spain (except Cataluña), the
United States, and Portugal (restricted grades) performed less well in this
topic compared to their total mathematics performance. As was seen for
Numbers and Operations, the high-performing populations of Korea,
Taiwan, and China (in-school population) did not emphasize measurement
at this age level.

Mathematics, Age 13

Percentages of Schools that Emphasize Measurement and Average Percents Correct for Measurement*

FIGURE 2.5

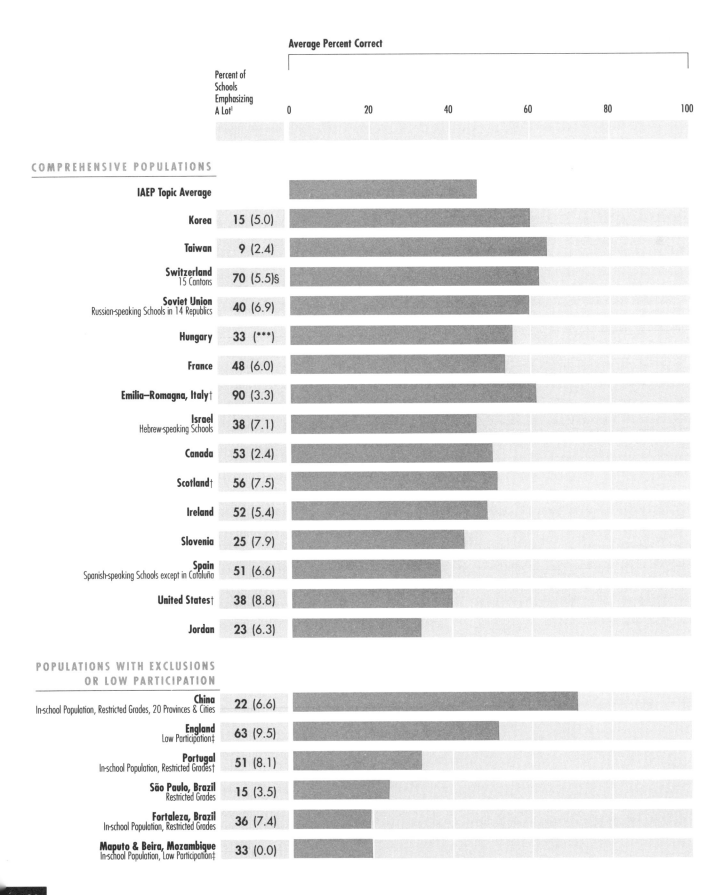

Average Percent Correct

	Percent of Schools Emphasizing A Lot[1]	
COMPREHENSIVE POPULATIONS		
IAEP Topic Average		
Korea	15 (5.0)	
Taiwan	9 (2.4)	
Switzerland 15 Cantons	70 (5.5)§	
Soviet Union Russian-speaking Schools in 14 Republics	40 (6.9)	
Hungary	33 (***)	
France	48 (6.0)	
Emilia–Romagna, Italy†	90 (3.3)	
Israel Hebrew-speaking Schools	38 (7.1)	
Canada	53 (2.4)	
Scotland†	56 (7.5)	
Ireland	52 (5.4)	
Slovenia	25 (7.9)	
Spain Spanish-speaking Schools except in Cataluña	51 (6.6)	
United States†	38 (8.8)	
Jordan	23 (6.3)	
POPULATIONS WITH EXCLUSIONS OR LOW PARTICIPATION		
China In-school Population, Restricted Grades, 20 Provinces & Cities	22 (6.6)	
England Low Participation‡	63 (9.5)	
Portugal In-school Population, Restricted Grades†	51 (8.1)	
São Paulo, Brazil Restricted Grades	15 (3.5)	
Fortaleza, Brazil In-school Population, Restricted Grades	36 (7.4)	
Maputo & Beira, Mozambique In-school Population, Low Participation‡	33 (0.0)	

* Jackknifed standard errors are presented in parentheses.
*** Jackknifed standard errors are greater than 9.9.
† Combined school and student participation rate is below .80 but at least .70; interpret results with caution because of possible nonresponse bias.
‡ Combined school and student participation rate is below .70; interpret results with extreme caution because of possible nonresponse bias.
[1] IAEP School Questionnaire, Age 13.

  IAEP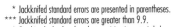

FIGURE 2.6

Mathematics, Age 13:
Sample Test Questions for Geometry

IAEP Item Average 75%

In which of the following figures is the
dotted line a line of symmetry?

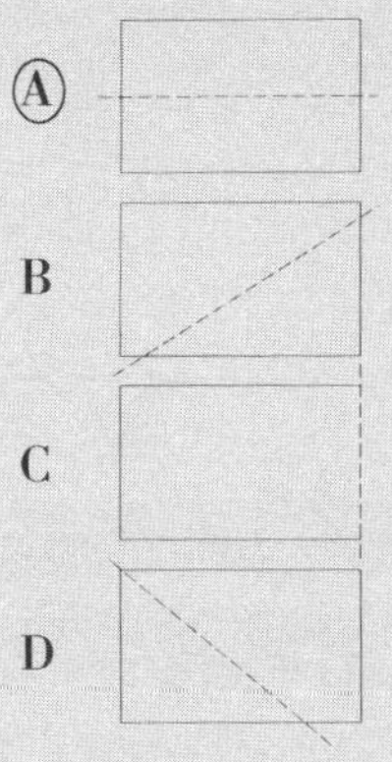

(A)

B

C

D

IAEP Item Average 41%

The measure of one acute angle of a right triangle is 50°.
What is the measure of the other acute angle?

Answer: _____ *40* _____ degrees

GEOMETRY The IAEP Geometry tasks, which represented 15 percent of the
assessment, assessed properties of circles, rectangles, triangles, cubes,
angles, and lines of symmetry. The 11 different questions required students
to visualize geometric figures and to demonstrate knowledge in typical
classroom and practical situations. Two examples are shown in FIGURE 2.6.

The assessment results for Geometry are presented in FIGURE 2.7.
France, Emilia-Romagna, and Scotland all performed better in this topic,
compared with their performance overall. Geometry was a major part of
the curriculum at this age level in all Emilia-Romagna schools. Ireland, the
United States, São Paulo (restricted grades), and Fortaleza (restricted
grades) performed relatively less well in Geometry than they did overall.
Many top-performing populations emphasized geometry at this age level:
Korea, the Soviet Union (Russian-speaking schools), Hungary, Emilia-
Romagna, and China (in-school population). An exception is Taiwan, a
high performer overall, where geometry was not emphasized at age 13.

FIGURE 2.7

Mathematics, Age 13
Percentages of Schools that Emphasize Geometry and Average Percents Correct for Geometry*

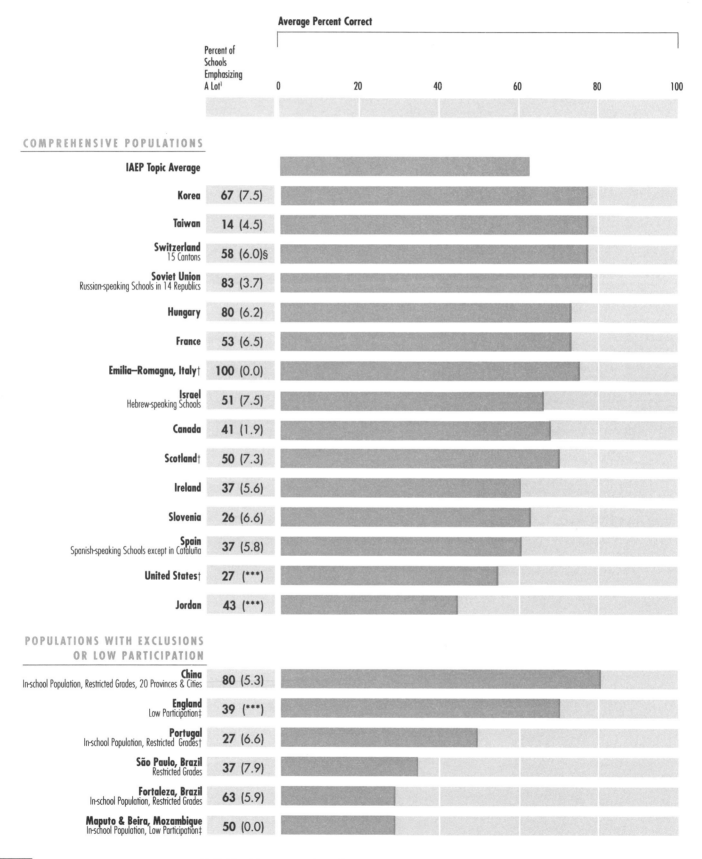

Average Percent Correct

	Percent of Schools Emphasizing A Lot[1]	

COMPREHENSIVE POPULATIONS

IAEP Topic Average		
Korea	67 (7.5)	
Taiwan	14 (4.5)	
Switzerland 15 Cantons	58 (6.0)§	
Soviet Union Russian-speaking Schools in 14 Republics	83 (3.7)	
Hungary	80 (6.2)	
France	53 (6.5)	
Emilia–Romagna, Italy†	100 (0.0)	
Israel Hebrew-speaking Schools	51 (7.5)	
Canada	41 (1.9)	
Scotland†	50 (7.3)	
Ireland	37 (5.6)	
Slovenia	26 (6.6)	
Spain Spanish-speaking Schools except in Cataluña	37 (5.8)	
United States†	27 (***)	
Jordan	43 (***)	

POPULATIONS WITH EXCLUSIONS OR LOW PARTICIPATION

China In-school Population, Restricted Grades, 20 Provinces & Cities	80 (5.3)	
England Low Participation‡	39 (***)	
Portugal In-school Population, Restricted Grades†	27 (6.6)	
São Paulo, Brazil Restricted Grades	37 (7.9)	
Fortaleza, Brazil In-school Population, Restricted Grades	63 (5.9)	
Maputo & Beira, Mozambique In-school Population, Low Participation‡	50 (0.0)	

* Jackknifed standard errors are presented in parentheses.
*** Jackknifed standard errors are greater than 9.9.
† Combined school and student participation rate is below .80 but at least .70; interpret results with caution because of possible nonresponse bias.
‡ Combined school and student participation rate is below .70; interpret results with extreme caution because of possible nonresponse bias.
§ Results represent percent of classrooms in schools.
[1] IAEP School Questionnaire, Age 13.

 IAEP

The nine questions in this category assessed a sample of data analysis (7), statistics (1), and probability (1) tasks. Students were required to read and interpret bar charts, line graphs, circle graphs, and data tables, to compute an arithmetic mean, and to demonstrate an understanding of basic probability concepts. Since this topic area focused on mathematical applications, the tasks were cast in a variety of practical settings. Sample questions from this topic are shown in FIGURE 2.8.

A large number of exceptions to the overall pattern of performance are seen in FIGURE 2.9. Six populations performed better in this topic compared to their overall achievement: France, Canada, Scotland, the United States, England (low participation), and Portugal (restricted grades). The Soviet Union (Russian-speaking schools), Slovenia, Jordan, and Maputo-Beira (in-school population) achieved at relatively lower levels in this topic, and China (in-school population), which did not emphasize this topic at age 13, scored below its usual superior level.

In almost all participating countries, schools indicated that they emphasized charts and graphs more than they did probability and statistics topics; in the assessment, most of the questions fell into the area of charts and graphs. These questions proved to be relatively easy compared with questions in other topics.

FIGURE 2.8

Mathematics, Age 13:
Sample Test Questions for Data Analysis, Probability, and Statistics

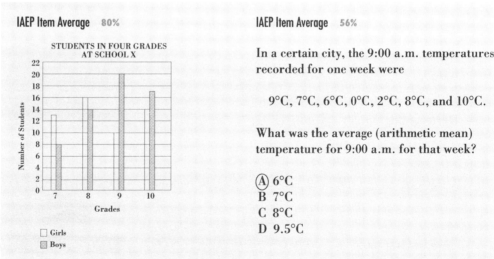

IAEP Item Average 80%

STUDENTS IN FOUR GRADES AT SCHOOL X

☐ Girls
▨ Boys

Which of the following is a true statement about the information shown in the graph above?

A Grade 8 has the least number of students.
Ⓑ Grade 9 has twice as many boys as girls.
C Grade 10 has more girls than boys.
D Grades 8 and 10 have the same number of students.

IAEP Item Average 56%

In a certain city, the 9:00 a.m. temperatures recorded for one week were

9°C, 7°C, 6°C, 0°C, 2°C, 8°C, and 10°C.

What was the average (arithmetic mean) temperature for 9:00 a.m. for that week?

Ⓐ 6°C
B 7°C
C 8°C
D 9.5°C

Mathematics, Age 13

Percentages of Schools that Emphasize Tables and Graphs, Probablility, and Statistics and Average Percents Correct for Data Analysis, Probability, and Statistics*

FIGURE 2.9

	Percent of Schools Emphasizing A Lot[1]			Average Percent Correct					
	Tables and Graphs	Probability	Statistics	0	20	40	60	80	100

COMPREHENSIVE POPULATIONS

	Tables and Graphs	Probability	Statistics	Average Percent Correct
IAEP Topic Average				
Korea	37 (7.1)	53 (6.5)	11 (3.3)	
Taiwan	35 (6.9)	0 (0.0)	15 (8.5)	
Switzerland 15 Cantons	20 (3.7)§	0 (0.0)§	0 (0.0)§	
Soviet Union Russian-speaking Schools in 14 Republics	67 (3.3)	0 (0.0)	3 (1.1)	
Hungary	45 (***)	0 (0.0)	2 (1.6)	
France	39 (7.7)	0 (0.0)	17 (4.4)	
Emilia–Romagna, Italy†	87 (3.9)	41 (6.3)	34 (6.0)	
Israel Hebrew-speaking Schools	28 (7.4)	9 (4.4)	12 (2.3)	
Canada	18 (1.9)	5 (1.1)	8 (1.4)	
Scotland†	56 (8.1)	3 (2.4)	9 (3.2)	
Ireland	47 (5.6)	3 (1.5)	28 (5.0)	
Slovenia	56 (4.9)	1 (1.6)	6 (3.5)	
Spain Spanish-speaking Schools except in Cataluña	28 (5.4)	8 (3.4)	7 (2.6)	
United States†	18 (***)	9 (6.8)	13 (8.7)	
Jordan	6 (3.5)	0 (0.0)	0 (0.0)	

POPULATIONS WITH EXCLUSIONS OR LOW PARTICIPATION

	Tables and Graphs	Probability	Statistics	Average Percent Correct
China In-school Population, Restricted Grades, 20 Provinces & Cities	15 (6.3)	5 (2.5)	9 (4.5)	
England Low Participation‡	53 (***)	11 (5.3)	29 (***)	
Portugal In-school Population, Restricted Grades†	32 (6.7)	12 (9.2)	16 (9.4)	
São Paulo, Brazil Restricted Grades	10 (3.5)	6 (2.9)	5 (2.6)	
Fortaleza, Brazil In-school Population, Restricted Grades	34 (7.1)	10 (8.0)	7 (8.1)	
Maputo & Beira, Mozambique In-school Population, Low Participation‡	33 (0.0)	11 (0.0)	0 (0.0)	

* Jackknifed standard errors are presented in parentheses.
*** Jackknifed standard errors are greater than 9.9.
 † Combined school and student participation rate is below .80 but at least .70; interpret results with caution because of possible nonresponse bias.
 ‡ Combined school and student participation rate is below .70; interpret results with extreme caution because of possible nonresponse bias.
 § Results represent percent of classrooms in schools.
 [1] IAEP School Questionnaire, Age 13.

Twenty percent of the assessment, 15 questions, measured Algebra and Functions. Examples of two of the questions are shown in FIGURE 2.10. Students were asked to demonstrate an understanding of algebraic and functional concepts and use these concepts to solve problems involving formulas, verbal descriptions, diagrams, and tables. Students were required to express relationships in equations, to substitute numbers for variables, and to solve formulas for one variable.

The results for this topic are presented in FIGURE 2.11. The Soviet Union (Russian-speaking schools), Hungary, Israel (Hebrew), China (in-school population), and Fortaleza (restricted grades), scored well in this topic compared with their performance overall, while Emilia-Romagna, Canada, and Maputo-Beira (in-school population) achieved at relatively lower levels than they did in mathematics in general. Except for Switzerland (15 cantons), high-performing populations tend to emphasize Algebra and Functions a lot. However, some lower-performing populations also emphasized this topic: Spain (except Cataluña), Portugal (restricted grades), São Paulo (restricted grades), and Fortaleza (restricted grades).

FIGURE 2.10   Mathematics, Age 13:
Sample Test Questions for Algebra

IAEP Item Average   80%

If $x - 5 = 12$, what does x equal?

Answer: _____ *17* _____

IAEP Item Average   44%

x	2	3	4	5
y	7	10	13	16

The table above shows a relationship between x and y.
Which of the following equations expresses this
relationship?

A $y = x + 5$
B $y = x - 5$
C $y = \frac{1}{3}(x - 1)$
Ⓓ $y = 3x + 1$

Mathematics, Age 13
Percentages of Schools that Emphasize Algebra and Average Percents Correct for Algebra*

FIGURE 2.11

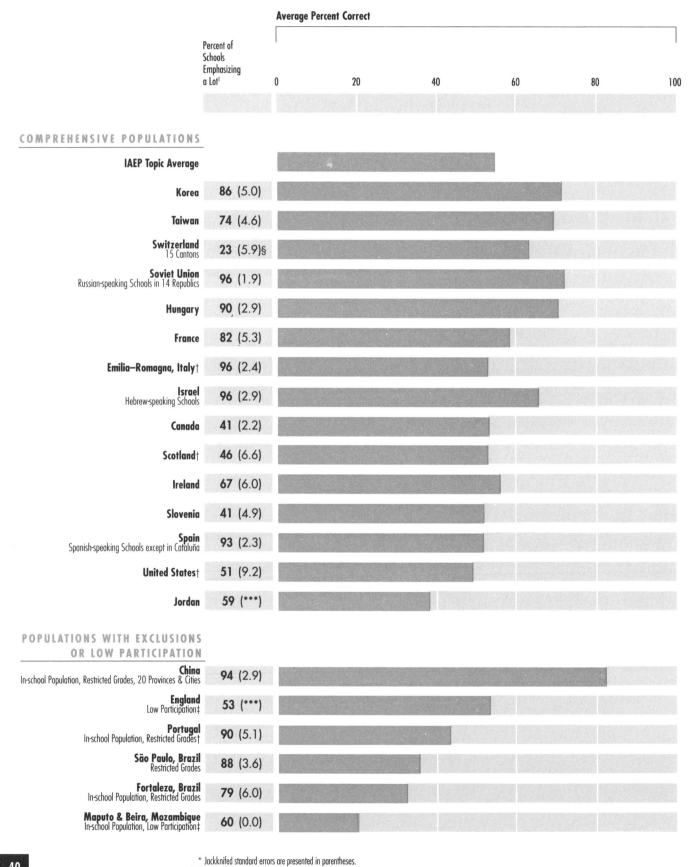

Average Percent Correct

Percent of Schools Emphasizing a Lot[1]

	Percent of Schools Emphasizing a Lot[1]
COMPREHENSIVE POPULATIONS	
IAEP Topic Average	
Korea	86 (5.0)
Taiwan	74 (4.6)
Switzerland 15 Cantons	23 (5.9)§
Soviet Union Russian-speaking Schools in 14 Republics	96 (1.9)
Hungary	90 (2.9)
France	82 (5.3)
Emilia–Romagna, Italy†	96 (2.4)
Israel Hebrew-speaking Schools	96 (2.9)
Canada	41 (2.2)
Scotland†	46 (6.6)
Ireland	67 (6.0)
Slovenia	41 (4.9)
Spain Spanish-speaking Schools except in Cataluña	93 (2.3)
United States†	51 (9.2)
Jordan	59 (***)
POPULATIONS WITH EXCLUSIONS OR LOW PARTICIPATION	
China In-school Population, Restricted Grades, 20 Provinces & Cities	94 (2.9)
England Low Participation‡	53 (***)
Portugal In-school Population, Restricted Grades†	90 (5.1)
São Paulo, Brazil Restricted Grades	88 (3.6)
Fortaleza, Brazil In-school Population, Restricted Grades	79 (6.0)
Maputo & Beira, Mozambique In-school Population, Low Participation‡	60 (0.0)

* Jackknifed standard errors are presented in parentheses.
*** Jackknifed standard errors are greater than 9.9.
† Combined school and student participation rate is below .80 but at least .70; interpret results with caution because of possible nonresponse bias.
‡ Combined school and student participation rate is below .70; interpret results with extreme caution because of possible nonresponse bias.
§ Results represent percent of classrooms in schools.
[1] IAEP School Questionnaires, Age 13.

In looking for ways to improve students' mathematics performance, more and more educators are focusing as much on the mathematical processes that students must use as on the content of the specific topics. Mathematics specialists in many countries are now recommending that teachers increasingly focus on process skills through problem-solving, communication, and reasoning tasks.[18]

In an attempt to reflect these emphases, IAEP participants decided to include questions at three levels of cognitive processing: **Conceptual Understanding, Procedural Knowledge,** and **Problem Solving.** In the age 13 assessment, about one-third of the questions fell into each of these categories.

Questions classified as Conceptual Understanding required students to exhibit an understanding of mathematical facts and concepts — for example, number facts; properties of measurement; geometry concepts; properties of charts, graphs, and tables; concepts of statistics and probability; and the conventions of algebraic expressions and equations. To complete Procedural Knowledge tasks, students had to apply knowledge and concepts in solving routine problems, typically following standard procedures taught in the classroom. Problem-Solving tasks required the application of several skills to a unique situation. These tasks typically had to be solved in multiple steps.

It is difficult to know exactly what processes students with differing backgrounds use to solve problems. A problem may require simple recall from a student who has studied the topic and may require problem-solving skills from another student who has had no experience with that type of task. Questions were assigned to the three process levels on the basis of expert judgment of typical approaches used by students at the target age levels.

FIGURE 2.12 presents the results for the two population groups for the three types of mathematical processes. Also reported is the percent of students in each location who agreed with the statements that "learning mathematics is mostly memorizing" and that "knowing how to solve a mathematics problem is as important as getting the right answer." This background information provides the students' perspectives on the importance of more routine mathematics skills versus problem solving.

---

[18] For example, in the United States, see *Curriculum and Evaluation Standards for School Mathematics*, Reston, VA, National Council of Teachers of Mathematics, 1989.

Mathematics, Age 13

Percentages of Students Agreeing with Characteristics of Mathematics and Average Percents Correct by Cognitive Process*
Part 1

FIGURE 2.12

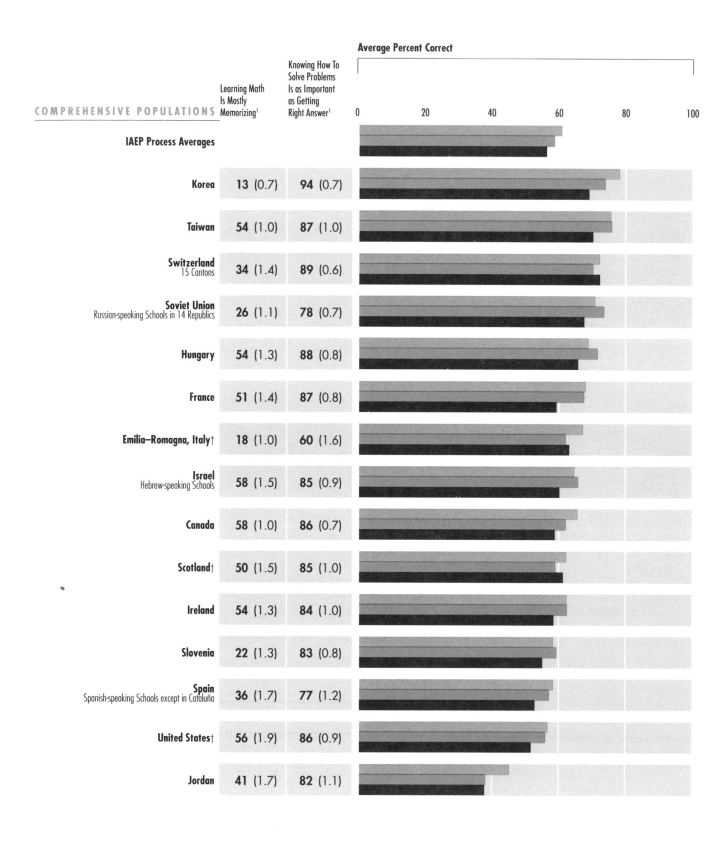

COMPREHENSIVE POPULATIONS	Learning Math Is Mostly Memorizing[1]	Knowing How To Solve Problems Is as Important as Getting Right Answer[1]
IAEP Process Averages		
Korea	13 (0.7)	94 (0.7)
Taiwan	54 (1.0)	87 (1.0)
Switzerland 15 Cantons	34 (1.4)	89 (0.6)
Soviet Union Russian-speaking Schools in 14 Republics	26 (1.1)	78 (0.7)
Hungary	54 (1.3)	88 (0.8)
France	51 (1.4)	87 (0.8)
Emilia–Romagna, Italy†	18 (1.0)	60 (1.6)
Israel Hebrew-speaking Schools	58 (1.5)	85 (0.9)
Canada	58 (1.0)	86 (0.7)
Scotland†	50 (1.5)	85 (1.0)
Ireland	54 (1.3)	84 (1.0)
Slovenia	22 (1.3)	83 (0.8)
Spain Spanish-speaking Schools except in Cataluña	36 (1.7)	77 (1.2)
United States†	56 (1.9)	86 (0.9)
Jordan	41 (1.7)	82 (1.1)

■ Conceptual Understanding
■ Procedural Knowledge
■ Problem Solving

* Jackknifed standard errors are presented in parentheses.
† Combined school and student participation rate is below .80 but at least .70; interpret results with caution because of possible nonresponse bias.
[1] IAEP Student Questionnaire, Age 13.

Mathematics, Age 13
Percentages of Students Agreeing with Characteristics of
Mathematics and Average Percents Correct by Cognitive Process*
Part 2

FIGURE 2.12

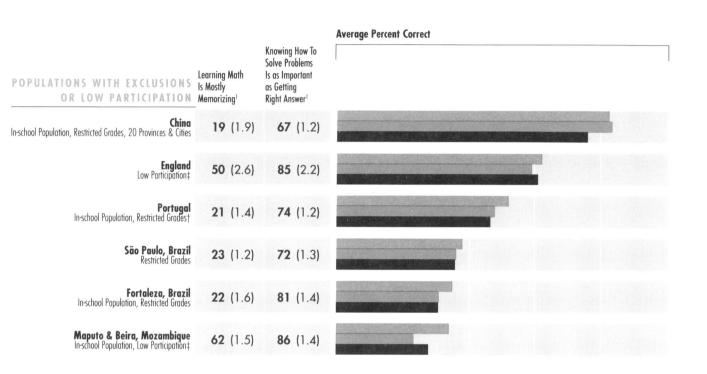

POPULATIONS WITH EXCLUSIONS OR LOW PARTICIPATION	Learning Math Is Mostly Memorizing[1]	Knowing How To Solve Problems Is as Important as Getting Right Answer[1]	Average Percent Correct
China In-school Population, Restricted Grades, 20 Provinces & Cities	19 (1.9)	67 (1.2)	
England Low Participation‡	50 (2.6)	85 (2.2)	
Portugal In-school Population, Restricted Grades†	21 (1.4)	74 (1.2)	
São Paulo, Brazil Restricted Grades	23 (1.2)	72 (1.3)	
Fortaleza, Brazil In-school Population, Restricted Grades	22 (1.6)	81 (1.4)	
Maputo & Beira, Mozambique In-school Population, Low Participation‡	62 (1.5)	86 (1.4)	

■ Conceptual Understanding
■ Procedural Knowledge
■ Problem Solving

* Jackknifed standard errors are presented in parentheses.

† Combined school and student participation rate is below .80 but at least .70; interpret results with caution because of possible nonresponse bias.

‡ Combined school and student participation rate is below .70; interpret results with extreme caution because of possible nonresponse bias.

[1] IAEP Student Questionnaire, Age 13.

In all populations, the vast majority of students (usually more than 75 percent) agreed that problem solving is important. Nevertheless, in 10 populations, about one-half of the students believed that learning mathematics is mostly memorizing. The pattern of responses does not coincide with high and low achievement. For example, most students from Korea and China (in-school population) did not view mathematics as a memorizing task, while many students from Taiwan and Hungary did.

The patterns of performance for all three process categories in the assessment generally match those for the mathematics assessment overall. The only exception is Maputo-Beira (in-school population), where students scored relatively higher in Conceptual Understanding and lower in Procedural Knowledge than they did overall.

The performance of the Canadian populations in each of the content and process categories, presented in FIGURE 2.13, mirrors their performance overall with only a few exceptions. Saskatchewan (French) performed better in Numbers and Operations compared to its performance overall; New Brunswick (English) scored relatively higher in Measurement than it did overall; and Quebec (French) demonstrated higher achievement in Geometry compared to its achievement overall. Like Canada as a whole, a number of provincial populations scored relatively higher in Data Analysis, Probability, and Statistics than they did overall: Alberta, Saskatchewan (English), Nova Scotia, Ontario (English), Manitoba (English), and Ontario (French). Also, five Canadian populations — Quebec (French), Alberta, Ontario (English), New Brunswick (English), and Ontario (French) — performed lower in Algebra and Functions compared to their performance on all mathematics questions. This pattern was also seen in Canada as a whole. The achievement levels of the Canadian populations in each of the process categories were relatively the same as their levels overall, except for New Brunswick (French) which scored lower in problem solving compared with its achievement on all mathematics questions.

Mathematics, Age 13
Average Percents Correct by Topic and Cognitive Process for Canadian Populations*

FIGURE 2.13

	Topics					Cognitive Processes		
	Numbers and Operations	Measurement	Geometry	Data Analysis, Probability, and Statistics	Algebra and Functions	Conceptual Understanding	Procedural Knowledge	Problem Solving
IAEP Averages	**61** (0.8)	**47** (1.2)	**62** (1.2)	**69** (0.9)	**54** (1.6)	**61** (0.8)	**58** (1.2)	**56** (0.9)
CANADIAN POPULATIONS								
Quebec French-speaking Schools	**72** (0.6)	**56** (1.0)	**78** (0.8)	**81** (0.6)	**58** (1.0)	**73** (0.7)	**68** (0.8)	**65** (0.8)
Saskatchewan French-speaking Schools	**74** (1.0)	**54** (1.3)	**69** (1.3)	**76** (1.2)	**62** (1.4)	**70** (1.2)	**69** (1.0)	**63** (1.1)
British Columbia	**69** (0.7)	**54** (0.9)	**70** (0.9)	**80** (0.7)	**60** (0.8)	**69** (0.7)	**68** (0.8)	**62** (0.7)
Quebec English-speaking Schools†	**69** (0.9)	**54** (1.1)	**71** (1.0)	**78** (1.0)	**60** (1.1)	**68** (0.9)	**67** (1.0)	**62** (1.0)
Alberta	**69** (0.7)	**54** (0.9)	**67** (0.8)	**80** (0.7)	**52** (0.9)	**68** (0.7)	**63** (0.8)	**61** (0.7)
Manitoba French-speaking Schools	**67** (0.7)	**49** (0.7)	**67** (0.8)	**75** (0.8)	**59** (0.7)	**65** (0.7)	**66** (0.7)	**58** (0.6)
Saskatchewan English-speaking Schools	**66** (0.6)	**50** (0.9)	**63** (1.2)	**78** (0.7)	**55** (0.8)	**64** (0.7)	**64** (0.8)	**57** (0.7)
New Brunswick French-speaking Schools	**65** (0.4)	**47** (0.5)	**65** (0.5)	**72** (0.5)	**54** (0.4)	**64** (0.4)	**63** (0.4)	**55** (0.4)
Nova Scotia	**63** (0.6)	**47** (0.8)	**64** (0.7)	**74** (0.7)	**54** (0.8)	**62** (0.6)	**60** (0.6)	**57** (0.6)
Newfoundland	**62** (0.6)	**45** (0.7)	**65** (0.9)	**72** (0.7)	**53** (0.6)	**62** (0.7)	**60** (0.7)	**54** (0.6)
Ontario English-speaking Schools	**62** (0.8)	**46** (0.9)	**63** (1.0)	**74** (0.8)	**50** (1.0)	**61** (0.8)	**59** (0.9)	**56** (0.8)
Manitoba English-speaking Schools	**63** (0.7)	**46** (0.9)	**58** (0.9)	**74** (0.9)	**51** (1.0)	**61** (0.8)	**59** (0.9)	**54** (0.7)
New Brunswick English-speaking Schools	**62** (0.5)	**51** (0.6)	**62** (0.6)	**71** (0.6)	**43** (0.6)	**61** (0.5)	**55** (0.6)	**56** (0.5)
Ontario French-speaking Schools	**58** (0.6)	**39** (0.7)	**59** (1.0)	**69** (0.7)	**45** (0.9)	**57** (0.7)	**54** (0.8)	**50** (0.6)

* Jackknifed standard errors are presented in parentheses.
† Combined school and student participation rate is below .80 but at least .70; interpret results with caution because of possible nonresponse bias.

The mathematics experts from all 20 countries agreed on the topics to be measured by the tests for 9- and 13-year-olds just as they did on the individual test questions that were included in the assessment. While the instruments were not perfectly aligned with any single country's curriculum, they were deemed to be appropriate for all.

Most IAEP countries still emphasize basic whole number operations at age 13. Many countries that emphasize geometry and algebra a lot performed well in those topics as well as in mathematics overall. Taiwan, a high performing population, is an exception; its schools do not emphasize geometry at this age level. Spain (except Cataluña), Portugal (restricted grades), São Paulo (restricted grades), and Fortaleza (restricted grades) all emphasize algebra a lot and yet are lower performers. The shift to more advanced content may suggest an effective strategy for challenging students, for presenting more interesting aspects of mathematics, and for underlining high expectations.

Classrooms

CHAPTER THREE

أُطْلُبُوا الْعِلْمَ مِنَ الْمَهْدِ إِلَى اللَّحْدِ

Seek knowledge from the
cradle to the grave.

The Hadith

In classrooms around the world, teachers apply their knowledge
and skills, employ a variety of teaching methods, make use of
available instructional materials, and organize their
students for learning. International comparative studies offer
unique opportunities to compare and contrast the ways in which
teachers do these things and to relate them to student performance. IAEP
collected information about some of these elements from the students who
participated in the study and from their school administrators.

The results reported in this chapter reflect the perceptions of those
students and administrators of their school situations. Responses of others
— for example, teachers or curriculum experts — might provide a
different picture of classrooms. Because the nature of schooling differs
from country to country — for example, the length of the school week, the
number of days of mathematics instruction each week, the ways various
instructional practices are used in the classroom — the student and school
background questions may take on different meanings from population to
population. Possible differences in interpretation are suggested in the
following discussion of results.

47

Teaching practices vary from country to country; in some instances, there is even greater variability among regions within a single country. In the hands of a gifted, caring teacher, the particular methods used may be immaterial. Nevertheless, educational experts often promote certain techniques as more effective than others. The descriptive data collected in IAEP highlight the variation in teaching practices across countries. Some of the results are summarized in FIGURE 3.1.

School administrators in most populations reported that their schools spent between 200 and 250 minutes a week (typically, 40 to 50 minutes a day) on mathematics instruction in the grade in which most 13-year-olds were enrolled. The average was more than 250 minutes a week in the Soviet Union (Russian-speaking schools) and more than 300 minutes a week in China (in-school population). Schools in Korea, Hungary, Ireland, Slovenia, Jordan, and England (low participation) spent less than 200 minutes a week on mathematics instruction.

Students in many countries regularly spent their instructional time listening to mathematics lessons. In 12 populations, more than half the students reported that they listened to their teacher give a mathematics lesson every day. The populations reporting less frequent use of teacher presentations were Korea, Hungary, Emilia-Romagna, Israel (Hebrew), Scotland, England (low participation), Portugal (restricted grades), São Paulo (restricted grades), and Fortaleza (restricted grades). In some participating countries, students did not necessarily have a mathematics class every day and some students probably interpreted "every day" as every school day while some may have interpreted "every day" as every mathematics class.

Another common classroom activity is to require students to work mathematics exercises on their own. While the most prevalent response for students in most locations was that they worked independently "several times a week," about one-half of the students in Switzerland (15 cantons), Canada, Scotland, Ireland, the United States, and Maputo-Beira (in-school population) indicated they did exercises on their own in mathematics class every day, as did about three quarters of the students in China (in-school population). In some locations, students did not necessarily receive instruction in mathematics every day, and students' interpretation of "every day" may have varied.

FIGURE 3.1

Mathematics, Age 13
Average Percents Correct and Teaching Practices*

COMPREHENSIVE POPULATIONS	Average Percent Correct	Average Minutes of Math Instruction Each Week[1]	Percent of Students Who Listen to Math Lesson Every Day[2]	Percent of Students Who Do Math Exercises by Themselves Every Day[2]	Percent of Students Who Solve Problems in Groups at Least Once a Week[2]	Percent of Students Who Take a Math Test or Quiz at Least Once a Week[2]	Percent of Students Who Spend 4 Hours or More on Math Homework Each Week[2]
Korea	73 (0.6)	179 (2.0)	32 (1.0)	17 (1.0)	28 (1.6)	28 (1.9)	33 (1.1)
Taiwan	73 (0.7)	204 (2.1)	64 (1.4)	32 (1.1)	38 (1.2)	87 (1.1)	24 (1.2)
Switzerland 15 Cantons	71 (1.3)	251 (3.9)§	60 (2.3)	47 (1.9)	47 (1.5)	40 (2.5)	15 (1.2)
Soviet Union Russian-speaking Schools in 14 Republics	70 (1.0)	258 (1.9)	62 (1.0)	40 (1.7)	54 (1.8)	52 (1.5)	33 (1.5)
Hungary	68 (0.8)	186 (2.3)	40 (1.4)	37 (1.6)	55 (1.6)	17 (1.3)	11 (0.7)
France	64 (0.8)	230 (1.8)	65 (1.3)	—	31 (1.2)	64 (1.3)	17 (1.3)
Emilia-Romagna, Italy†	64 (0.9)	219 (3.6)	33 (1.3)	10 (0.7)	78 (1.1)	19 (1.6)	27 (1.4)
Israel Hebrew-speaking Schools	63 (0.8)	205 (3.6)	5 (1.2)	12 (1.1)	48 (1.7)	36 (2.2)	17 (1.1)
Canada	62 (0.6)	225 (1.9)	51 (1.0)	50 (1.1)	40 (1.4)	53 (0.9)	15 (0.8)
Scotland†	61 (0.9)	210 (2.3)	23 (1.7)	48 (2.1)	27 (1.6)	17 (1.3)	4 (0.6)
Ireland	61 (0.9)	189 (2.2)	67 (1.7)	54 (1.5)	42 (1.6)	19 (1.5)	17 (1.3)
Slovenia	57 (0.8)	188 (4.3)	97 (0.6)	41 (1.4)	43 (1.5)	28 (1.5)	15 (0.9)
Spain Spanish-speaking Schools except in Cataluña	55 (0.8)	235 (3.3)	58 (1.4)	39 (1.6)	63 (1.5)	31 (1.7)	22 (1.3)
United States†	55 (1.0)	228 (5.6)	78 (1.4)	50 (2.7)	49 (2.4)	68 (2.1)	15 (1.3)
Jordan	40 (1.0)	180 (0.6)	62 (1.6)	34 (1.4)	83 (1.1)	68 (1.5)	14 (1.0)
POPULATIONS WITH EXCLUSIONS OR LOW PARTICIPATION							
China In-school Population, Restricted Grades, 20 Provinces & Cities	80 (1.0)	307 (***)	74 (2.0)	78 (1.6)	68 (2.1)	63 (2.2)	37 (1.8)
England Low Participation‡	61 (2.2)	190 (4.8)	17 (2.1)	21 (2.5)	44 (3.1)	28 (5.8)	6 (0.8)
Portugal In-school Population, Restricted Grades†	48 (0.8)	207 (2.7)	28 (1.2)	30 (1.6)	51 (1.6)	21 (1.8)	9 (0.8)
São Paulo, Brazil Restricted Grades	37 (0.8)	226 (7.3)	34 (2.0)	35 (1.4)	60 (1.5)	44 (1.5)	16 (1.2)
Fortaleza, Brazil In-school Population, Restricted Grades	32 (0.6)	230 (8.5)	26 (2.0)	31 (1.6)	69 (1.7)	56 (1.9)	18 (1.4)
Maputo & Beira, Mozambique In-school Population, Low Participation‡	28 (0.3)	217 (0.0)	63 (1.4)	62 (1.6)	79 (1.5)	94 (1.0)	11 (1.2)

* Jackknifed standard errors are presented in parentheses.
*** Jackknifed standard error is greater than 9.9.
† Combined school and student participation rate is below .80 but at least .70; interpret results with caution because of possible nonresponse bias.
‡ Combined school and student participation rate is below .70; interpret results with extreme caution because of possible nonresponse bias.
§ Results represent percent of classrooms in schools.
[1] IAEP School Questionnaire, Age 13.
[2] IAEP Student Questionnaire, Age 13.
—Information is not available.

ETS IAEP

More and more mathematics educators are recommending the use of group work as a method for developing problem-solving skills.[19] Nonetheless, this activity was practiced less frequently in IAEP countries than teacher presentation or independent work. The majority of students in only 10 populations said that they solved problems in small groups during mathematics class at least once a week. The practice was used most often in Emilia-Romagna, Jordan, and Maputo-Beira (in-school population).

Testing practices vary considerably from country to country. Some countries rely on short-answer and essay forms of testing, others use multiple-choice formats almost exclusively, and some administer tests on an irregular basis.[20] The IAEP results indicate that most participants were infrequent users of mathematics tests and quizzes. The exceptions are Taiwan and Maputo-Beira (in-school population), where between 85 and 95 percent of the students reported taking mathematics tests or quizzes at least once a week, and the Soviet Union (Russian-speaking schools), France, Canada, the United States, Jordan, China (in-school population), and Fortaleza (restricted grades), where at least 50 percent of the students reported being tested at least once a week.

Doing more homework is often cited by educators and parents as a means of improving academic performance. Many factors contribute to the effectiveness of homework as an instructional activity: the types of assignment, whether or not the homework is discussed in class, and whether or not it is graded.[21] IAEP results indicate that most students in most populations do not spend a great deal of time doing mathematics homework. The most common response of students in most participating countries was one hour or less each week. Only in Korea, and Israel (Hebrew) was the norm higher, two to three hours per week and in China (in-school population) the most common response was 4 hours or more each week. One-third or fewer students reported doing four hours or more of mathematics homework each week (at least 45 minutes a night), except in China (in-school population), where the percentage was 37.

[19] Neil Davidson, "Introduction and Overview," *Cooperative Learning in Mathematics*, Neil Davidson, Editor. Menlo Park, CA: Addision-Wesley Publishing Company, 1990.

[20] George F. Madaus and Thomas Kellaghan, *Student Examination Systems in the European Community: Lessons for the United States*. Contractors Report, Office of Technology Assessment, United States Congress, 1991.

[21] Herbert J. Walberg, Synthesis of Research on Time and Learning, *Educational Leadership*, *Vol. 45, No. 6*, March 1988.

The findings describing teaching practices highlight the variation in practices among countries and do not identify any particular practice that is common to all high-performing populations. On the contrary, in all cases, both high- and low-achieving populations had high values on all of the variables examined. This lack of strong interpretable patterns underlines the importance of examining other factors to understand differences in performance — for example, students' home environments, the countries' cultural factors, and the structure of their national education systems. These will be discussed in subsequent chapters.

While the information presented in FIGURE 3.1 does not show cross-population trends, it is possible to find more consistent relationships between classroom variables and mathematics achievement within individual participating countries. Analyses of this type are summarized in FIGURE 3.2. If the linear relationship between increasing levels of a particular variable and achievement within a population is positive, a "+" is shown; if the linear relationship is negative, a "–" is shown; and if a significant linear relationship does not exist, a "0" is shown.[22] For example, if the students in a particular population who spent more time on mathematics homework tended to do better on the assessment than their fellow students who spent less time, a "+" appears for the population in the homework column; if the students who worked in groups in mathematics class more frequently tended to do less well on the assessment than those who did so less frequently, a "–" appears in the group work column.

While for most factors, similar trends are seen in more than one-half of the participating countries, there are always at least one or two counter examples. In most populations, students reported relatively high frequencies of teacher presentation and independent work and lower frequencies of group work. Current research in the United States indicates that classroom instruction is often dominated by teacher lectures, traditional workbook and text book materials that is mostly drill-and-practice and that little time is left for students to participate actively in the learning enterprise.[23]

---

[22] These analyses did not look for curvilinear or other types of nonlinear trends that may be present in the data. The analyses tested for the presence of a statistically significant linear relationship between levels of the background variable and achievement. An estimated slope at least 2 standard errors (of the slope) larger than 0 was taken to indicate a positive relationship; a slope at least 2 standard errors less than 0 was taken to indicate a negative relationship; slopes less than 2 standard errors in absolute value were considered not to be statistically significant. More details of these analyses are provided in the Procedural Appendix, page 143, and the *IAEP Technical Report*.

[23] John Goodland, *A Place Called School*. New York: McGraw-Hill, 1984.
Iris R. Weiss, *Report of the 1985-86 National Survey of Science and Mathematics Education*. Research Triangle Park, NC: Research Triangle Institute, 1987.

FIGURE 3.2

Mathematics, Age 13
Relationship of Classroom Factors and
Average Percents Correct within Populations

COMPREHENSIVE POPULATIONS	Amount of Listening to Math Lessons[1]	Amount of Doing Math Exercises on Own[1]	Amount of Problem Solving in Groups[1]	Amount of Math Testing[1]	Amount of Time Spent on Math Homework[1]
Korea	+	+	−	−	+
Taiwan	+	+	+	+	+
Switzerland 15 Cantons	0	0	−	0	0
Soviet Union Russian-speaking Schools in 14 Republics	+	+	−	+	+
Hungary	+	+	−	−	+
France	0	NA	0	+	+
Emilia-Romagna, Italy†	0	0	+	0	0
Israel Hebrew-speaking Schools	+	+	−	−	+
Canada	−	+	−	+	0
Scotland†	−	+	−	−	0
Ireland	+	0	−	0	+
Slovenia	+	+	−	−	0
Spain Spanish-speaking Schools except in Cataluña	0	0	−	0	+
United States†	+	+	−	+	+
Jordan	+	0	0	−	+

POPULATIONS WITH EXCLUSIONS OR LOW PARTICIPATION					
China In-school Population, Restricted Grades, 20 Provinces & Cities	+	0	0	0	+
England Low Participation‡	0	+	−	0	0
Portugal In-school Population, Restricted Grades†	0	+	−	−	+
São Paulo, Brazil Restricted Grades	+	+	−	−	+
Fortaleza, Brazil In-school Population, Restricted Grades	0	+	−	−	+
Maputo & Beira, Mozambique In-school Population, Low Participation‡	0	0	−	+	−

+ Statistically significant positive relationship
− Statistically significant negative relationship
0 No statistically significant linear relationship
† Combined school and student participation rate is below .80 but at least .70; interpret results with caution because of possible nonresponse bias.
‡ Combined school and student participation rate is below .70; interpret results with extreme caution because of possible nonresponse bias.
[1] IAEP Student Questionnaire, Age 13.
NA Information is not available.

IAEP results indicate that teacher presentations and independent work are not negatively associated with performance within most populations. In more than one-half of the populations, performance is positively related with frequency of teacher presentation and independent work and negatively related to frequency of group work. The positive relationships between performance and teacher presentation and independent work may reflect the beneficial effects of more frequent mathematics instruction in general or of more frequent use of these specific practices. The negative relationship between performance and group work is harder to interpret because grouping is used for a variety of purposes, such as cooperative learning tasks or remedial work, and in some countries, grouping is only used infrequently.

The descriptive results suggest that testing was relatively infrequent among most IAEP participants, and even among those countries that use testing more frequently— Taiwan, the Soviet Union (Russian-speaking schools), France, Canada, the United States, Jordan, China (in-school population), Fortaleza (restricted grades), and Maputo-Beira (in-school population)—the relationship between testing and performance is not consistent. In some cases relationships are positive; in some, negative; and sometimes there are no discernable relationships.

In more than half the populations, time spent on mathematics homework is positively related with achievement. This is the case for most of the participating countries where between 20 and 40 percent of the students reported spending four hours or more on mathematics homework each week: Korea, Taiwan, the Soviet Union (Russian-speaking schools), Spain (except Cataluña), and China (in-school population). On the other hand, time on homework is not associated positively or negatively with achievement in Emilia-Romagna, where mathematics homework was quite prevalent.

Results about time spent on mathematics homework and mathematics performance, which are summarized in Figures 3.1 and 3.2, are provided in detail in FIGURE 3.3. This figure gives the percentage of students who reported spending various amounts of time on mathematics homework each week — 0 or 1 hour, 2 or 3 hours, 4 or more hours — and next to each category the average percent correct on the mathematics assessment is indicated by a bar.

The figure demonstrates that in the majority of the populations, achievement increased (i.e., the bars become longer) as time spent on mathematics homework each week increased. The increase is significant in 14 populations. The differences in the length of the bars shows the magnitude of the increase and the percentages of students in each category indicate how many students are represented in the increase.

Mathematics, Age 13

Percentages of Students Reporting Amounts
of Weekly Mathematics Homework and
Average Percents Correct by Homework Categories*

FIGURE 3.3

Part 1

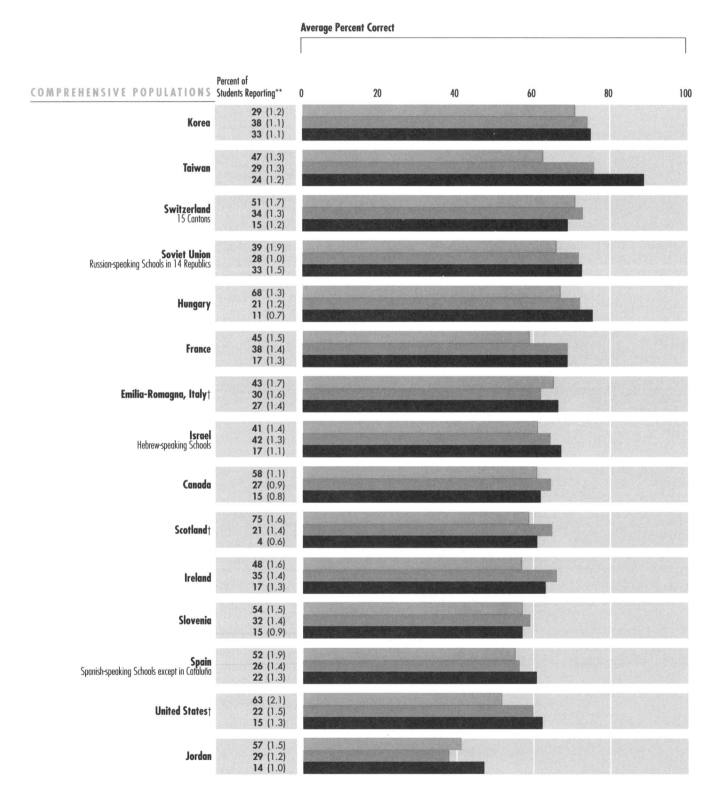

Average Percent Correct

COMPREHENSIVE POPULATIONS	Percent of Students Reporting**
Korea	29 (1.2) / 38 (1.1) / 33 (1.1)
Taiwan	47 (1.3) / 29 (1.3) / 24 (1.2)
Switzerland 15 Cantons	51 (1.7) / 34 (1.3) / 15 (1.2)
Soviet Union Russian-speaking Schools in 14 Republics	39 (1.9) / 28 (1.0) / 33 (1.5)
Hungary	68 (1.3) / 21 (1.2) / 11 (0.7)
France	45 (1.5) / 38 (1.4) / 17 (1.3)
Emilia-Romagna, Italy†	43 (1.7) / 30 (1.6) / 27 (1.4)
Israel Hebrew-speaking Schools	41 (1.4) / 42 (1.3) / 17 (1.1)
Canada	58 (1.1) / 27 (0.9) / 15 (0.8)
Scotland†	75 (1.6) / 21 (1.4) / 4 (0.6)
Ireland	48 (1.6) / 35 (1.4) / 17 (1.3)
Slovenia	54 (1.5) / 32 (1.4) / 15 (0.9)
Spain Spanish-speaking Schools except in Cataluña	52 (1.9) / 26 (1.4) / 22 (1.3)
United States†	63 (2.1) / 22 (1.5) / 15 (1.3)
Jordan	57 (1.5) / 29 (1.2) / 14 (1.0)

0 to 1 Hour
2 to 3 Hours
4 Hours or More

* Jackknifed standard errors are presented in parentheses.
** Percentages may not total 100 due to rounding
† Combined school and student participation rate is below .80 but at least .70; interpret results with caution because of possible nonresponse bias.

ETS IAEP

FIGURE 3.3

Mathematics, Age 13
Percentages of Students Reporting Amounts of Weekly Mathematics Homework and Average Percents Correct by Homework Categories*
Part 2

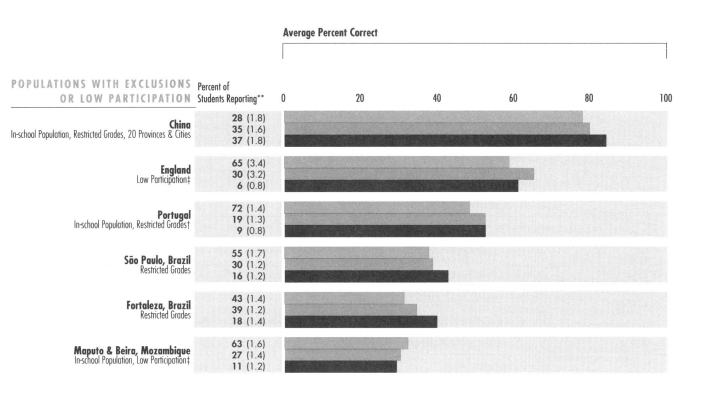

Average Percent Correct

POPULATIONS WITH EXCLUSIONS OR LOW PARTICIPATION	Percent of Students Reporting**	
China In-school Population, Restricted Grades, 20 Provinces & Cities	28 (1.8) 35 (1.6) 37 (1.8)	
England Low Participation‡	65 (3.4) 30 (3.2) 6 (0.8)	
Portugal In-school Population, Restricted Grades†	72 (1.4) 19 (1.3) 9 (0.8)	
São Paulo, Brazil Restricted Grades	55 (1.7) 30 (1.2) 16 (1.2)	
Fortaleza, Brazil Restricted Grades	43 (1.4) 39 (1.2) 18 (1.4)	
Maputo & Beira, Mozambique In-school Population, Low Participation‡	63 (1.6) 27 (1.4) 11 (1.2)	

0 to 1 Hour
2 to 3 Hours
3 to 4 Hours

* Jackknifed standard errors are presented in parentheses.
** Percentages may not total 100 due to rounding.
† Combined school and student participation rate is below .80 but at least .70; interpret results with caution because of possible non-response bias.
‡ Combined school and student participation rate is below .70; interpret results with extreme caution because of possible nonresponse bias.

For example, in Korea there is a moderate increase in performance for students who spent two to three hours weekly on mathematics homework (38 percent of the students), and an additional slight increase for students who spent four hours or more (33 percent of the students). In Taiwan, the increases were much greater for both groups of students, but fewer students spent these amounts of time on mathematics homework each week: 29 percent for two to three hours and 24 percent for four hours or more.

As the use of technology increases around the world, mathematics educators are advocating the use of calculators, computers, and hands-on activities in the mathematics classroom. The IAEP data presented in FIGURE 3.4, however, indicate that for most participating countries, these teaching materials were not yet a part of regular instruction.

Use of mathematics tools — counting blocks, geometric shapes, and geometric solids — to teach mathematics concepts is common in the elementary grades. However, the IAEP results suggest that these kinds of hands-on activities were used infrequently with 13-year-olds, not necessarily because they are inappropriate for older students but perhaps because materials are not available or because of time limitations. Only in Slovenia and Maputo-Beira (in-school population) did a majority of 13-year-old students report using mathematics tools at least once a week.

While in most populations, large percentages of students owned calculators, they did not always use them in school. Ownership of calculators was common in all countries except Korea, China (in-school population), and Maputo-Beira (in-school population), where less than 25 percent of the 13-year-olds had them. Use of calculators in school was very common in France, Scotland, and England (low participation), where more than 80 percent of students reported their use, but less so in the remaining participating countries. More than one-half of the students in 12 participating populations indicated that they never use a calculator in school.

As might be expected, computer use was even more infrequent than calculator use. The majority of students in 18 populations reported that they never use a computer for school work or homework. Only in France, Israel (Hebrew), and Slovenia did the majority of students report ever using a computer in this way. In almost all populations, school administrators reported having very few computers that 13-year-old students could use for school work. Only three populations had, on average, 20 or more computers in schools that students could use for instruction: Scotland, the United States, and England (low participation).

FIGURE 3.4

Mathematics, Age 13
Average Percents Correct and Teaching Materials*

COMPREHENSIVE POPULATIONS	Average Percent Correct	Percent of Students Who Work with Math Tools at Least Once a Week[1]	Percent of Students Who Have a Calculator[1]	Percent of Students Who Ever Use Calculators in School[1]	Percent of Students Who Ever Use Computers for School Work or Homework[1]	Average Number of Computers in School[2]
Korea	73 (0.6)	17 (1.0)	20 (1.1)	4 (0.5)	10 (0.8)	15 (1.5)
Taiwan	73 (0.7)	38 (1.2)	58 (1.3)	62 (1.0)	6 (0.7)	15 (1.2)
Switzerland 15 Cantons	71 (1.3)	36 (1.6)	85 (1.2)	51 (3.1)	25 (1.2)	4 (1.4)§
Soviet Union Russian-speaking Schools in 14 Republics	70 (1.0)	32 (1.7)	47 (5.0)	19 (2.1)	6 (0.8)	2 (0.4)
Hungary	68 (0.8)	43 (1.6)	87 (1.0)	71 (1.6)	31 (1.5)	6 (0.3)
France	64 (0.8)	42 (1.4)	98 (0.3)	94 (0.5)	57 (1.4)	13 (0.6)
Emilia-Romagna, Italy†	64 (0.9)	39 (1.4)	97 (0.4)	64 (2.1)	40 (2.3)	7 (0.7)
Israel Hebrew-speaking Schools	63 (0.8)	23 (1.5)	94 (0.7)	49 (2.3)	59 (1.7)	14 (1.1)
Canada	62 (0.6)	14 (0.8)	91 (0.5)	75 (1.3)	42 (1.1)	17 (0.8)
Scotland†	61 (0.9)	26 (1.4)	90 (0.8)	82 (1.2)	38 (1.5)	40 (2.8)
Ireland	61 (0.9)	13 (0.9)	58 (1.6)	25 (2.2)	13 (1.3)	9 (0.7)
Slovenia	57 (0.8)	63 (1.6)	86 (1.1)	46 (2.5)	61 (1.3)	5 (0.4)
Spain Spanish-speaking Schools except in Cataluña	55 (0.8)	39 (1.7)	86 (1.3)	45 (2.8)	12 (1.1)	3 (0.4)
United States†	55 (1.0)	18 (1.2)	89 (0.9)	54 (3.5)	37 (1.7)	24 (6.0)
Jordan	40 (1.0)	39 (1.8)	53 (1.9)	5 (0.8)	5 (0.6)	1 (0.4)

POPULATIONS WITH EXCLUSIONS OR LOW PARTICIPATION

China In-school Population, Restricted Grades, 20 Provinces & Cities	80 (1.0)	40 (1.7)	21 (2.9)	7 (1.1)	6 (0.9)	2 (0.7)
England Low Participation‡	61 (2.2)	16 (2.4)	93 (1.0)	90 (1.8)	44 (2.8)	26 (2.5)
Portugal In-school Population, Restricted Grades†	48 (0.8)	21 (1.3)	89 (1.1)	19 (1.9)	7 (1.1)	2 (0.5)
São Paulo, Brazil Restricted Grades	37 (0.8)	26 (1.3)	67 (1.6)	2 (0.4)	4 (0.5)	2 (0.7)
Fortaleza, Brazil In-school Population, Restricted Grades	32 (0.6)	41 (2.0)	39 (1.4)	4 (0.6)	3 (0.5)	0 (0.2)
Maputo & Beira, Mozambique In-school Population, Low Participation‡	28 (0.3)	70 (1.5)	21 (1.3)	5 (0.7)	13 (1.0)	0 (0.0)

* Jackknifed standard errors are presented in parentheses.
† Combined school and student participation rate is below .80 but at least .70; interpret results with caution because of possible nonresponse bias.
‡ Combined school and student participation rate is below .70; interpret results with extreme caution because of possible nonresponse bias.
§ Results represent percent of classrooms in schools.
[1] IAEP Student Questionnaire, Age 13.
[2] IAEP School Questionnaire, Age 13.

Two additional classroom variables are often studied by educational researchers: teacher background and classroom organization. The information IAEP collected from participating schools on these topics is presented in FIGURE 3.5.

School administrators were asked if students in the modal grade for 13-year-olds (typically grade 7 or 8) are taught by a person who teaches mathematics most or all of the time; in most populations, schools overwhelmingly responded "yes." The exceptions were Switzerland (15 cantons), Hungary, Emilia-Romagna, and Canada, where about 50 to 85 percent of the schools reported that the regular classroom teacher taught mathematics along with several other subjects. Schools also reported the percentage of seventh or eighth grade mathematics teachers who had taken some post-secondary mathematics courses other than courses in mathematics instruction. Advanced mathematics training was close to universal in Hungary and Slovenia. All or almost all schools in these populations indicated that all their mathematics teachers had had this type of preparation. More than half the schools in the Soviet Union (Russian-speaking schools), Scotland, Ireland, the United States, Jordan, England (low participation), São Paulo (restricted grades), and Fortaleza (restricted grades) reported that all of their mathematics teachers had taken at least some post-secondary level mathematics courses.

The efficacy of grouping students by ability is strenuously debated and grouping practices vary from country to country, as shown in Figure 3.5. While assigning students to mathematics classes by ability may give teachers an opportunity to gear their instruction to the specific achievement level of their students, it may also mean that some students are exposed only to lower-level content and skills while others are exposed to a more enriched curriculum.[24] Among IAEP participants, five countries were likely to organize mathematics classes on the basis of ability: Taiwan, Israel (Hebrew), Ireland, the United States, and England (low participation). More than half the schools in each of these locations reported this practice. The remaining countries organized their classes by ability with less frequency.

---

[24] Jeannie Oakes, *Unequal Opportunities: The Effects of Race, Social Class, and Ability Grouping and Access to Science and Mathematics Education.* Palo Alto, CA: The Rand Corp., 1989.

Jeannie Oakes, *Multiplying Inequalities: The Effects of Race, Social Class, and Ability Grouping on Students' Opportunity to Learn Mathematics and Science.* Santa Monica, CA: The Rand Corp., 1990.

COMPREHENSIVE POPULATIONS	Average Percent Correct	Percent of Schools Where Teacher Teaches Math Most or All the Time[1]	Percent of Schools Where All Math Teachers Have Taken Some Post-Secondary Math Courses[1]	Percent of Schools Where Math Classes are Based on Ability[1]
Korea	73 (0.6)	88 (5.2)	12 (7.2)	0 (0.0)
Taiwan	73 (0.7)	99 (1.2)	37 (7.2)	63 (7.6)
Switzerland 15 Cantons	71 (1.3)	25 (4.9)§	18 (4.5)§	18 (7.3)§
Soviet Union Russian-speaking Schools in 14 Republics	70 (1.0)	92 (2.9)	79 (7.9)	18 (3.0)
Hungary	68 (0.8)	53 (9.6)	100 (0.0)	0 (0.0)
France	64 (0.8)	91 (3.3)	30 (8.2)	27 (7.3)
Emilia-Romagna, Italy†	64 (0.9)	16 (4.3)	24 (5.4)	17 (4.7)
Israel Hebrew-speaking Schools	63 (0.8)	87 (4.0)	35 (8.4)	74 (7.2)
Canada	62 (0.6)	31 (1.4)	44 (2.0)	10 (1.3)
Scotland†	61 (0.9)	100 (0.0)	80 (4.5)	16 (4.1)
Ireland	61 (0.9)	71 (5.0)	53 (5.2)	67 (6.1)
Slovenia	57 (0.8)	99 (1.3)	96 (2.4)	2 (1.6)
Spain Spanish-speaking Schools except in Cataluña	55 (0.8)	82 (4.7)	48 (5.8)	3 (1.8)
United States†	55 (1.0)	95 (4.8)	76 (***)	56 (***)
Jordan	40 (1.0)	99 (0.7)	81 (6.2)	5 (2.6)

POPULATIONS WITH EXCLUSIONS OR LOW PARTICIPATION				
China In-school Population, Restricted Grades, 20 Provinces & Cities	80 (1.0)	91 (3.8)	45 (5.7)	3 (1.9)
England Low Participation‡	61 (2.2)	99 (1.4)	54 (***)	92 (4.7)
Portugal In-school Population, Restricted Grades†	48 (0.8)	98 (1.5)	20 (5.4)	6 (3.6)
São Paulo, Brazil Restricted Grades	37 (0.8)	99 (0.7)	78 (5.5)	15 (4.2)
Fortaleza, Brazil In-school Population, Restricted Grades	32 (0.6)	84 (4.6)	57 (4.3)	36 (6.3)
Maputo & Beira, Mozambique In-school Population, Low Participation‡	28 (0.3)	100 (0.0)	8 (0.0)	25 (0.0)

* Jackknifed standard errors are presented in parentheses.
*** Jackknifed standard errors are greater than 9.9.
† Combined school and student participation rate is below .80 but at least .70; interpret results with caution because of possible nonresponse bias.
‡ Combined school and student participation rate is below .70; interpret results with extreme caution because of possible nonresponse bias.
§ Results represent percent of classrooms in schools.
[1] IAEP School Questionnaire, Age 13.

WHAT WORKS IN THE CLASSROOM While classroom factors impact on student performance more directly than do home and societal variables, relationships between these variables and achievement were not consistent across the participating IAEP countries, reenforcing the notion that effective instructional practices may vary from culture to culture.

Generally, the results suggest that typical current practices — frequent use of teacher presentations and independent work — were effective. It is too early to tell if techniques that are now just being introduced into classrooms, such as working with small groups on problem solving, using mathematics tools, and using calculators and computers will make significant contributions in the future, once their implementation is perfected.

Students and Their Homes

CHAPTER FOUR

易學難精

**Most things are easy to learn
but hard to master.**

Chinese Proverb

The rhetoric of politicians and the realities faced by educators are often at odds with one another. The images of happy, loved, motivated children arriving at school ready to meet the challenges of the day conflict with the sometimes harsh realities of poverty, child abuse, drugs, and crime that also manage to pass through the schoolhouse door. Teachers and schools are asked to reconcile these conflicting views, to accept children with a wide range of abilities and readiness, and to transmit to them the knowledge, skills, traditions, and values held dear by the society.

To find out more about the background of the students in the assessment and to provide a broader context for the achievement results, IAEP collected descriptive information about the students themselves and their families. Some of the background questions were included because they tap some of the inevitable variation in social and economic advantage; others explored some of the ways in which families, rich and poor alike, may foster academic development. Finally, a number of questions examined how students spend some of their time outside of school, in ways that may enhance their in-school performance.

Information on the language spoken in the home, size of family, and the number of books in the home can provide indications of students' social and economic advantage as well as of other factors that might contribute more directly to their academic development. Language minority groups are often at a disadvantage within a dominant culture, and students from these families have the further handicap of receiving instruction in a language that is different from that which is spoken in the home. Size of family is often negatively correlated with disposable income, and students from large families may receive less individual attention from parents than those with fewer brothers and sisters. The number of books in the home is considered a general indicator of social and economic status and their presence also provides children opportunities for expanding their academic horizons.

The IAEP data related to these socioeconomic and academic factors are displayed in FIGURE 4.1. The percentages of language minority students participating in the assessment are low in all of the populations. A number of participants excluded language minority students from their samples or excluded geographic areas where large numbers of language minority students live. More than 10 percent of the students living in Switzerland (15 cantons), the Soviet Union (Russian-speaking schools), Emilia-Romagna, Israel (Hebrew), Canada, and Maputo-Beira (in-school population) reported that a different language from the one used in school was spoken at home. Some of these students had no choice but to attend schools where instruction is provided in the dominant language. Others could attend schools that teach in different languages and could choose an instructional program given in a language other than that spoken in their homes.

The IAEP results indicate that family size is relatively small in most industrialized nations. Only in Jordan and Maputo-Beira (in-school population) did large percentages of students indicate that they were part of families with four or more brothers or sisters, 88 percent in Jordan and 64 percent in Maputo-Beira (in-school population). Ireland is unusual among its European neighbors, with one-third of its students coming from large families.

Responses to the question on the number of books in the home also differed between more and less industrialized participating countries. Close to one-half of the students from Jordan, São Paulo (restricted grades), Fortaleza (restricted grades), and Maputo-Beira (in-school population) reported that they had fewer than 25 books at home. In most other IAEP populations, fewer than 25 percent of students fell into this category.

FIGURE 4.1

Mathematics, Age 13
Average Percents Correct and Home Characteristics*

	Average Percent Correct	Percent of Students					
COMPREHENSIVE POPULATIONS		Same Language Spoken at Home as at School[1]	Have 4 or More Brothers and Sisters[1]	Have Less Than 25 Books at Home[1]	Parents Want Them to Do Well in Math[1]	Talk with Someone at Home About Math Class[1]	Receive Help at Home with Math Homework[1]
Korea	73 (0.6)	97 (0.4)	19 (1.1)	24 (1.2)	92 (0.8)	52 (1.4)	53 (1.4)
Taiwan	73 (0.7)	—	12 (0.7)	35 (1.2)	90 (0.8)	74 (1.2)	51 (1.1)
Switzerland 15 Cantons	71 (1.3)	80 (1.4)	4 (0.6)	16 (1.1)	85 (1.1)	67 (1.2)	42 (1.3)
Soviet Union Russian-speaking Schools in 14 Republics	70 (1.0)	89 (2.3)	13 (1.9)	12 (1.8)	84 (0.8)	61 (1.4)	32 (1.3)
Hungary	68 (0.8)	99 (0.3)	3 (0.5)	10 (1.0)	93 (0.7)	85 (0.9)	80 (1.0)
France	64 (0.8)	94 (0.7)	11 (0.9)	24 (1.3)	86 (0.9)	67 (1.1)	53 (1.0)
Emilia-Romagna, Italy†	64 (0.9)	85 (1.3)	1 (0.4)	22 (1.1)	91 (0.9)	84 (1.1)	34 (1.4)
Israel Hebrew-speaking Schools	63 (0.8)	88 (0.8)	19 (1.8)	10 (0.8)	97 (0.4)	79 (1.1)	53 (1.4)
Canada	62 (0.6)	88 (1.0)	8 (0.5)	13 (0.8)	96 (0.3)	64 (1.0)	69 (1.1)
Scotland†	61 (0.9)	95 (0.5)	9 (0.9)	26 (1.7)	95 (0.6)	68 (1.3)	65 (1.7)
Ireland	61 (0.9)	97 (0.7)	33 (1.3)	24 (1.6)	94 (0.8)	70 (1.3)	61 (1.4)
Slovenia	57 (0.8)	95 (0.9)	3 (0.5)	19 (1.0)	87 (1.0)	84 (1.1)	62 (1.5)
Spain Spanish-speaking Schools except in Cataluña	55 (0.8)	91 (1.1)	11 (0.9)	19 (1.2)	90 (0.9)	82 (1.0)	58 (1.5)
United States†	55 (1.0)	94 (0.9)	18 (1.4)	17 (1.3)	96 (0.6)	67 (1.6)	74 (1.4)
Jordan	40 (1.0)	99 (0.3)	88 (1.1)	51 (1.7)	91 (0.9)	79 (1.2)	43 (1.3)
POPULATIONS WITH EXCLUSIONS OR LOW PARTICIPATION							
China In-school Population, Restricted Grades, 20 Provinces & Cities	80 (1.0)	97 (0.3)	11 (1.0)	26 (2.1)	81 (1.7)	85 (0.8)	37 (2.2)
England Low Participation‡	61 (2.2)	97 (0.5)	·8 (1.0)	15 (2.3)	94 (0.8)	74 (1.8)	65 (4.9)
Portugal In-school Population, Restricted Grades†	48 (0.8)	99 (0.3)	7 (1.0)	33 (1.8)	79 (1.2)	68 (1.3)	27 (1.5)
São Paulo, Brazil Restricted Grades	37 (0.8)	96 (0.8)	15 (1.2)	46 (1.9)	82 (1.1)	77 (1.4)	48 (1.8)
Fortaleza, Brazil In-school Population, Restricted Grades	32 (0.6)	97 (0.5)	32 (1.7)	48 (1.6)	89 (1.0)	76 (1.3)	46 (1.8)
Maputo & Beira, Mozambique In-school Population, Low Participation‡	28 (0.3)	82 (1.2)	64 (1.5)	55 (1.5)	85 (1.1)	89 (1.2)	65 (2.0)

* Jackknifed standard errors are presented in parentheses.
† Combined school and student participation rate is below .80 but at least .70; interpret results with caution because of possible nonresponse bias.
‡ Combined school and student participation rate is below .70; interpret results with extreme caution because of possible nonresponse bias.
[1] IAEP Student Questionnaire, Age 13.
—Information is not available

The home characteristics just discussed may be viewed as proxies for socio-economic indicators and also as variables that contribute to academic development. Parental involvement can have an important impact on a child's success in school regardless of the family's social or economic status. When asked if they thought their parents wanted them to do well in mathematics, almost all students in each population gave positive responses. Agreement ranged from 97 percent in Israel (Hebrew) to 79 percent in Portugal (restricted grades).

However, when students were asked if someone at home talked to them about their mathematics classes, the responses varied considerably from population to population. Only 52 percent of the Korean students indicated that their parents asked them about their mathematics classes, while 89 percent of the students from Maputo-Beira (in-school population) reported this type of parental interest.

Parents were more likely to ask their children about their mathematics classes than to help them with their homework. Parental help with homework was less prevalent in the Soviet Union (Russian-speaking schools), Emilia-Romagna, China (in-school population), and Portugal (restricted grades), with fewer than 40 percent of their students reporting this type of attention. Hungary was highest with 80 percent of its students indicating that their parents helped them with homework.

RELATIONSHIP OF HOME CHARACTERISTICS AND MATHEMATICS PERFORMANCE

The descriptive data about home characteristics show some predictable variation between industrialized and non-industrialized countries and contribute to an understanding of low performance among some of the non-industrialized countries.

These trends are further substantiated when home characteristics are examined in relationship to achievement within individual populations. FIGURE 4.2 provides this type of analysis. For each population, it indicates with pluses, minuses, and zeros whether the relationship between increasing levels of a particular home-related variable and mathematics achievement is positive, negative, or not related in a linear fashion to a statistically significant degree.

The importance of socioeconomic factors is confirmed by the within-population results. Mathematics achievement is positively related with number of books in the home in all but one participating population and is negatively related to family size in 15 populations.

FIGURE 4.2

Mathematics, Age 13
Relationship of Home Characteristics and Average Percents Correct within Populations

COMPREHENSIVE POPULATIONS	Number of Brothers and Sisters[1]	Number of Books in Home[1]	Parents' Wanting Student to Do Well in Math[1]
Korea	−	+	+
Taiwan	−	+	+
Switzerland 15 Cantons	−	+	0
Soviet Union Russian-speaking Schools in 14 Republics	−	+	0
Hungary	−	+	0
France	−	+	0
Emilia-Romagna, Italy†	0	+	0
Israel Hebrew-speaking Schools	−	+	0
Canada	−	+	+
Scotland†	0	+	+
Ireland	0	+	+
Slovenia	−	+	0
Spain Spanish-speaking Schools except in Cataluña	−	+	0
United States†	0	+	+
Jordan	0	+	+

POPULATIONS WITH EXCLUSIONS OR LOW PARTICIPATION			
China In-school Population, Restricted Grades, 20 Provinces & Cities	−	+	+
England Low Participation‡	−	+	0
Portugal In-school Population, Restricted Grades†	−	+	0
São Paulo, Brazil Restricted Grades	−	+	−
Fortaleza, Brazil In-school Population, Restricted Grades	−	+	0
Maputo & Beira, Mozambique In-school Population, Low Participation‡	0	0	0

+ Statistically significant positive relationship
− Statistically significant negative relationship
0 No statistically significant linear relationship
† Combined school and student participation rate is below .80 but at least .70; interpret results with caution because of possible nonresponse bias.
‡ Combined school and student participation rate is below .70; interpret results with extreme caution because of possible nonresponse bias.
[1] IAEP Student Questionnaire, Age 13.

The data about parents are more difficult to interpret. Interest in their children's academic performance was fairly universal among parents in all of the participating countries. The level of parental involvement was high in some high-performing countries, such as Hungary but not always. Korean students, for example, reported relatively low levels of mathematics-related discussion at home and help with mathematics homework. Within individual populations, parental attitudes toward mathematics was positively related with achievement in only eight instances.

STUDENTS' OUT-OF-SCHOOL ACTIVITIES While education is often cited as the dominant responsibility of school-aged children, young people actually spend much more of their time outside of school. Some of this out-of-school activity is clearly directed at furthering academic development — for example, doing homework and leisure reading. However, time spent watching television may or may not be supportive of learning. IAEP asked students how much time they spent in these non-school activities and probed their attitudes toward mathematics as a subject area. These descriptive results are presented in FIGURE 4.3.

While reading for fun is not on the face of it directly related to mathematics performance, consistent readers tend to be high achievers in many academic areas. The percentages of students reporting reading for fun almost every day varied across participating countries. The lowest percentage of daily readers was in Korea, 11 percent, and the highest percentage in Switzerland (15 cantons), 51 percent.

Populations varied more in the amount of time students spent doing homework across all school subjects each day. The most common response of students in a majority of IAEP populations was one hour or less of homework each school day across all school subjects. In eight populations, one-half or more of students reported doing two or more hours of homework each day. Students from Emilia-Romagna spent the most time doing homework, with close to 80 percent reporting two hours or more of homework daily.

Some television programming is clearly targeted at developing the academic abilities of children, and some countries provide more of this type of television than do others. However, for many students, the content of the television watched has little academic value and consumes valuable hours that could be devoted to activities requiring more intellectual effort. Among all but two of the populations, the most common response of students was two to four hours of television viewing each school day. Sixty-five percent of the Chinese students (in-school population) reported watching one hour or no television on a daily basis, probably reflecting the fact that many of these students had only limited access to television. Just over 50 percent of the students from France reported watching one hour or less of television each day.

FIGURE 4.3

Mathematics, Age 13
Average Percents Correct and Home Activities*

COMPREHENSIVE POPULATIONS	Average Percent Correct	Percent of Students Who Read for Fun Almost Every Day[1]	Percent of Students Who Spend 2 Hours or More on All Homework Every Day[1]	Percent of Students Who Watch Television 5 Hours or More Every Day[1]	Percent of Students Who Have Positive Attitudes towards Math[1,2]
Korea	73 (0.6)	11 (0.8)	41 (1.7)	11 (0.9)	71 (1.3)
Taiwan	73 (0.7)	19 (1.2)	41 (1.3)	10 (0.7)	79 (0.9)
Switzerland 15 Cantons	71 (1.3)	51 (1.1)	20 (1.3)	7 (0.8)	85 (1.1)
Soviet Union Russian-speaking Schools in 14 Republics	70 (1.0)	47 (1.3)	52 (1.6)	17 (1.0)	76 (1.8)
Hungary	68 (0.8)	44 (1.2)	58 (1.3)	13 (1.0)	85 (0.8)
France	64 (0.8)	40 (1.2)	55 (1.6)	5 (0.7)	81 (1.0)
Emilia-Romagna, Italy†	64 (0.9)	47 (1.3)	79 (1.3)	5 (0.7)	86 (0.9)
Israel Hebrew-speaking Schools	63 (0.8)	40 (1.7)	50 (1.9)	20 (1.2)	90 (0.8)
Canada	62 (0.6)	38 (0.9)	27 (1.0)	14 (0.7)	94 (0.4)
Scotland†	61 (0.9)	38 (1.5)	14 (1.1)	24 (1.3)	91 (0.7)
Ireland	61 (0.9)	41 (1.3)	63 (1.9)	9 (0.9)	88 (1.0)
Slovenia	57 (0.8)	42 (1.2)	28 (1.7)	4 (0.5)	83 (1.0)
Spain Spanish-speaking Schools except in Cataluña	55 (0.8)	36 (1.3)	64 (1.5)	10 (0.8)	89 (1.0)
United States†	55 (1.0)	28 (1.3)	29 (1.8)	20 (1.7)	90 (1.1)
Jordan	40 (1.0)	24 (1.3)	56 (2.0)	7 (0.8)	77 (1.5)

POPULATIONS WITH EXCLUSIONS OR LOW PARTICIPATION					
China In-school Population, Restricted Grades, 20 Provinces & Cities	80 (1.0)	28 (1.5)	44 (1.8)	7 (0.5)	79 (2.1)
England Low Participation‡	61 (2.2)	41 (3.2)	33 (2.8)	14 (2.2)	91 (1.2)
Portugal In-school Population, Restricted Grades†	48 (0.8)	44 (1.8)	30 (1.6)	11 (1.0)	84 (1.1)
São Paulo, Brazil Restricted Grades	37 (0.8)	33 (1.5)	45 (1.9)	19 (1.2)	83 (1.0)
Fortaleza, Brazil In-school Population, Restricted Grades	32 (0.6)	41 (1.3)	48 (1.8)	21 (1.5)	86 (1.1)
Maputo & Beira, Mozambique In-school Population, Low Participation‡	28 (0.3)	41 (1.6)	42 (1.8)	20 (1.2)	88 (1.0)

* Jackknifed standard errors are presented in parentheses.
† Combined school and student participation rate is below .80 but at least .70; interpret results with caution because of possible nonresponse bias.
‡ Combined school and student participation rate is below .70; interpret results with extreme caution because of possible nonresponse bias.
[1] IAEP Student Questionnaire, Age 13.
[2] Attitudes towards math is a composite score based on responses to four attitude questions.

IAEP

At the other extreme, 20 percent or more of 13-year-olds from Israel (Hebrew), Scotland, the United States, Fortaleza (restricted grades), and Maputo-Beira (in-school population) indicated they watch five hours or more of television each school day and 19 percent of their peers from São Paulo (restricted grades) and 17 percent from the Soviet Union (Russian-speaking schools) also reported heavy television viewing.

ATTITUDES TOWARD MATHEMATICS   Students bring to school certain attitudes toward education in general and toward specific school subjects. These attitudes contribute to, and are a product of, academic success. Students who approach a school subject enthusiastically are more likely to do well in that subject; conversely, students who succeed in a content area are more likely to develop positive attitudes toward it.

Students in the assessment were asked to what extent they agreed with the following statements:

- *Mathematics is useful in solving everyday problems.*
- *It is important to know some mathematics in order to get a good job.*
- *I am good at mathematics.*
- *My parents want me to do well in mathematics.*

Their responses were combined to form an index of attitudes toward mathematics; students were categorized as generally expressing positive, negative, or neutral attitudes.

As shown in Figure 4.3, the majority of 13-year-olds in participating countries expressed positive attitudes toward mathematics, with 90 percent or more of the students from Israel (Hebrew), Canada, Scotland, the United States, and England (low participation) giving favorable responses. Curiously, fewer students from a number of high-performing populations — for example, Korea, Taiwan, the Soviet Union (Russian- speaking schools), and China (in-school population) — exhibited positive attitudes toward mathematics, but still, between 70 and 80 percent gave positive responses to these questions. Students from Jordan, a lower performing group, also fit into this range.

RELATIONSHIP OF HOME ACTIVITIES AND MATHEMATICS PERFORMANCE
An examination of the relationship between home activities and mathematics performance within populations confirms the importance of how students spend their time outside of school. For each population, FIGURE 4.4 indicates with pluses, minuses, and zeros whether the relationship between achievement and increasing levels of a particular home-activity variable is positive, negative, or not related in a linear fashion to a statistically significant degree.

FIGURE 4.4

Mathematics, Age 13
Relationship of Home Activities and Average Percents Correct within Populations

COMPREHENSIVE POPULATIONS	Amount of Leisure Reading[1]	Amount of Time Spent on All Homework[1]	Amount of Time Spent Watching Television[1]	Students' Attitudes Towards Math[1,2]
Korea	+	O	−	+
Taiwan	+	+	−	+
Switzerland 15 Cantons	O	O	O	O
Soviet Union Russian-speaking Schools in 14 Republics	+	+	O	+
Hungary	+	+	−	O
France	+	+	−	O
Emilia-Romagna, Italy†	+	+	O	+
Israel Hebrew-speaking Schools	O	+	O	+
Canada	+	−	−	+
Scotland†	+	+	−	+
Ireland	+	+	−	O
Slovenia	+	O	O	O
Spain Spanish-speaking Schools except in Cataluña	+	+	−	O
United States†	+	O	−	+
Jordan	O	+	O	+

POPULATIONS WITH EXCLUSIONS OR LOW PARTICIPATION				
China In-school Population, Restricted Grades, 20 Provinces & Cities	+	O	O	O
England Low Participation‡	+	+	−	+
Portugal In-school Population, Restricted Grades†	O	O	+	O
São Paulo, Brazil Restricted Grades	O	+	+	O
Fortaleza, Brazil In-school Population, Restricted Grades	−	+	O	O
Maputo & Beira, Mozambique In-school Population, Low Participation‡	O	O	O	+

+ Statistically significant positive relationship
− Statistically significant negative relationship
O No statistically significant linear relationship
† Combined school and student participation rate is below .80 but at least .70; interpret results with caution because of possible nonresponse bias.
‡ Combined school and student participation rate is below .70; interpret results with extreme caution because of possible nonresponse bias.
[1] IAEP Student Questionnaire, Age 13.
[2] Attitudes towards math is a composite score based on responses to four attitude questions.

There is a positive relationship between leisure reading and mathematics achievement in 14 populations. Time spent on homework across all school subjects is positively related to performance in 13 populations, and the amount of time spent watching television is negatively related in 10 populations. Positive student attitudes toward mathematics are related to higher mathematics performance in 11 populations.

Results about time spent watching television and mathematics performance, which are only summarized in Figures 4.3 and 4.4, are provided in detail in FIGURE 4.5. This figure gives the percentage of students who reported spending various amounts of time watching television each day — 0 to 1 hour, 2 to 4 hours, 5 or more hours — and next to each category, those students' average percent correct on the mathematics assessment is indicated by a bar.

The figure demonstrates that in many populations, achievement decreased (i.e., the bars become shorter) as time spent watching television each day increased. The decrease was significant in 10 populations. The differences in the length of the bars show the magnitude of the decrease, and the percentages of students in each category indicate how many students are represented in the decrease. For example, in Korea, performance decreased substantially among students who watched two to four hours of television each day (65 percent of the students) and again among students who watched five hours or more each day (11 percent of the students). It is also possible to see from the bar patterns that the relationship between time spent watching television daily and mathematics performance is positively related in two populations: Portugal (restricted grades) and São Paulo (restricted grades).

Mathematics, Age 13

Percentages of Students Reporting Amounts
of Daily Television Viewing and Average Percents
Correct By Television Viewing Categories*

FIGURE 4.5

Part 1

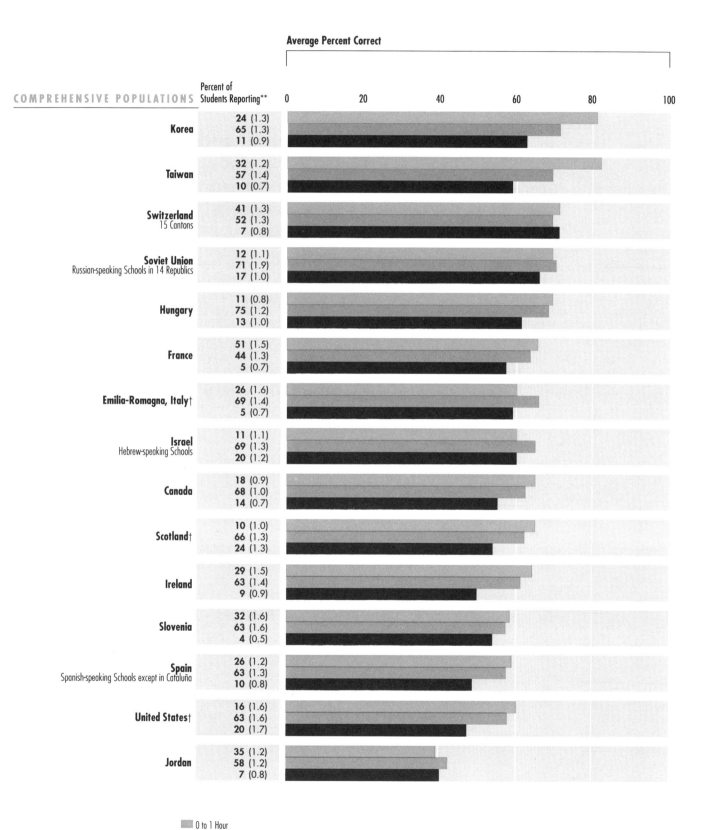

Average Percent Correct

COMPREHENSIVE POPULATIONS	Percent of Students Reporting**	
Korea	24 (1.3)	
	65 (1.3)	
	11 (0.9)	
Taiwan	32 (1.2)	
	57 (1.4)	
	10 (0.7)	
Switzerland 15 Cantons	41 (1.3)	
	52 (1.3)	
	7 (0.8)	
Soviet Union Russian-speaking Schools in 14 Republics	12 (1.1)	
	71 (1.9)	
	17 (1.0)	
Hungary	11 (0.8)	
	75 (1.2)	
	13 (1.0)	
France	51 (1.5)	
	44 (1.3)	
	5 (0.7)	
Emilia-Romagna, Italy†	26 (1.6)	
	69 (1.4)	
	5 (0.7)	
Israel Hebrew-speaking Schools	11 (1.1)	
	69 (1.3)	
	20 (1.2)	
Canada	18 (0.9)	
	68 (1.0)	
	14 (0.7)	
Scotland†	10 (1.0)	
	66 (1.3)	
	24 (1.3)	
Ireland	29 (1.5)	
	63 (1.4)	
	9 (0.9)	
Slovenia	32 (1.6)	
	63 (1.6)	
	4 (0.5)	
Spain Spanish-speaking Schools except in Cataluña	26 (1.2)	
	63 (1.3)	
	10 (0.8)	
United States†	16 (1.6)	
	63 (1.6)	
	20 (1.7)	
Jordan	35 (1.2)	
	58 (1.2)	
	7 (0.8)	

Legend:
- 0 to 1 Hour
- 2 to 4 Hours
- 5 Hours or More

* Jackknifed standard errors are presented in parentheses.
** Percentages may not total 100 due to rounding
† Combined school and student participation rate is below .80 but at least .70; interpret results with caution because of possible nonresponse bias.

Mathematics, Age 13

Percentages of Students Reporting Amounts
of Daily Television Viewing and Average Percents
Correct By Television Viewing Categories*

FIGURE 4.5

Part 2

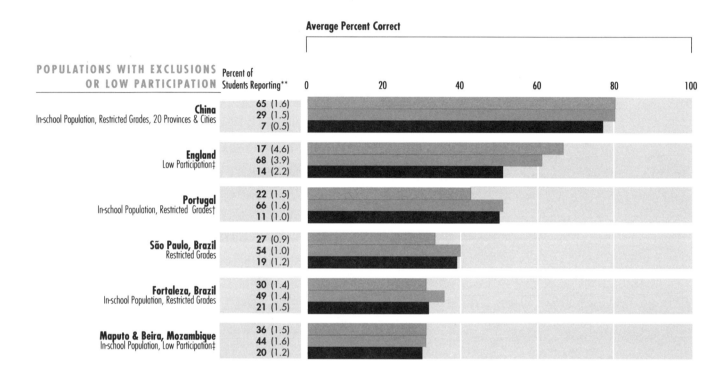

Average Percent Correct

POPULATIONS WITH EXCLUSIONS OR LOW PARTICIPATION	Percent of Students Reporting**	0	20	40	60	80	100
China In-school Population, Restricted Grades, 20 Provinces & Cities	65 (1.6) 29 (1.5) 7 (0.5)						
England Low Participation‡	17 (4.6) 68 (3.9) 14 (2.2)						
Portugal In-school Population, Restricted Grades†	22 (1.5) 66 (1.6) 11 (1.0)						
São Paulo, Brazil Restricted Grades	27 (0.9) 54 (1.0) 19 (1.2)						
Fortaleza, Brazil In-school Population, Restricted Grades	30 (1.4) 49 (1.4) 21 (1.5)						
Maputo & Beira, Mozambique In-school Population, Low Participation‡	36 (1.5) 44 (1.6) 20 (1.2)						

- 0 to 1 Hour
- 2 to 4 Hours
- 5 Hours or More

  * Jackknifed standard errors are presented in parentheses.
 ** Percentages may not total 100 due to rounding.
  † Combined school and student participation rate is below .80 but at least .70; interpret results with caution because of possible nonresponse bias.
  ‡ Combined school and student participation rate is below .70; interpret results with extreme caution because of possible nonresponse bias.

IAEP

The factors influencing learning are not restricted to school variables. Family and out-of-school activity play an important role in promoting in-school success. Some aspects of home life, such as number of books in the home and family size, are often cited as indicators of social and economic advantage and in IAEP these variables are related to mathematics achievement in predictable ways. These factors help explain low performance in some non-industrialized countries, but do not suggest why some countries appear to succeed in spite of difficult conditions. Perhaps parental involvement, which can influence a child's academic performance regardless of a family's socioeconomic status, is another element that should be considered. Significant amounts of parental involvement were found in some high-performing IAEP populations but not in others.

What students do with their time after school seems to be another important home factor that affects academic performance. In many IAEP populations, high mathematics performance was associated with large amounts of time spent on leisure reading and mathematics homework and small amounts of time spent watching television. Trends were not consistent across all populations, however, which suggests once again that these factors may operate differently from culture to culture.

SWITZERLAND *March 22, 1991*

It was snowing. And it should have been. We drove right into a Christmas card.

We got to the small French city the way you get anywhere in Switzerland; by climbing over a mountain. At 1,000 meters, our hill was not "serious" in Swiss terms, but these were only the Juras, not the Alps. It was a 45-minute drive from the lake at Neuchâtel.

The secondary school was steel and glass and obvious among all the other traditional buildings. The thirty-year-old math teacher who welcomed us warmly was an Ernest Hemingway look-alike, with a large bushy mustache. Affable and pleasant, he was nonetheless worried that some of the students about to take the test had been transported from other schools that morning and would therefore, "not feel at home," during this important event.

The classroom, large, bright, and airy, with clinical desks and chairs, featured an enormous poster of a sweaty Sylvester Stallone on the front wall. The rear wall bulletin board was covered with pictures of sports teams, action shots of soccer plays, and a couple of pages from the Sports Illustrated swimsuit edition.

Outside the wall of windows, the snow was falling heavily on the hillside forest across the street. As the assessment began, I concentrated on my quality-control checklist.

"Were directions read VERBATIM?" The Swiss never do anything by the book. At least not by someone else's book. But, he covered the essentials more than adequately. "Did the Coordinator start on time?" What a question! The National Observatory by which Switzerland sets the official time for all of its clocks and watches is 10 kilometers from here.

A hand goes up. A student asks a question. The teacher responds with a Gallic shrug. The manual says nothing about Gallic shrugs and they can be powerfully expressive. What to do?

The teacher whispers to me that this kind of test [multiple-choice] is OK once in a while, but if given too often, it could affect the way teachers teach. I agree with him. All of the students finish before time is called and declare victory.

After the event, the students crowd around to ask questions.

"Is this the kind of test Americans take?" "Yes. And this month your colleagues in London, Budapest, and Taipei are answering these very same questions. "Sans blagues!" [No kidding!] "Where do you live?" "Near New York City." "Wow, really? Can I come and visit you?" "When will we know the results?"

Most of them will graduate from this school to the technical institute next door. A few may go on to be engineers. Most will spend their lives in this canton.

At the end, each of the 26 walks over to shake my hand and say, "Merci, Monsieur." These 13-year-olds thanked me for the privilege of taking a test! On the way back, the National Coordinator explained how each and every canton does its own thing (curriculum, test books, examinations, and teacher certification). We stopped to see an enormous statue of a Reformation hero, who devoted his life to breaking statues. There's a lesson there, somewhere.

ETS Quality Control Observer

Countries and Their Education Systems

CHAPTER FIVE

במקום תושה תשכין חכמה

Where there is learning,
there is wisdom.

Hebrew Saying

While it is difficult to tie global differences in social, cultural, and economic frameworks to the mathematics performance of students, these factors clearly play a role in determining the characteristics of education systems. Each country makes decisions about the education of its citizens and the roles schools play in strengthening the national identity and economy. These choices are rooted in the physical, demographic, and socioeconomic characteristics of the country as well as in its it values and cultural traditions.

COUNTRY CHARACTERISTICS The countries participating in IAEP represent a broad range of physical, demographic, and socioeconomic characteristics: large and small, homogeneous and heterogeneous, urban and rural, and rich and poor. Some of these characteristics are presented in FIGURE 5.1; these data reflect the participating countries in their entirety and not just the republics, provinces, or cities that were sampled in the survey.

While most of these country characteristics are not directly related to the achievement of 13-year-old students, they provide an important context for understanding the relative performance of participants. China, the Soviet Union, and the United States are the largest populations involved in IAEP with about 1.1 billion, 300 million, and 250 million people, respectively. Alongside these giants stand the 2 million citizens of Slovenia, 3 million of Jordan, 3.5 million of Ireland, and 4.5 million of Israel. Clearly, large and small countries face different problems in the administration of national educational programs.

The degree of a country's cultural homogeneity influences how educational programs are formulated and implemented. Eleven of the participating countries have populations that are dominated by a single ethnic group: Korea, Hungary, France, Italy, Scotland, Ireland, Slovenia, Jordan, China, England, and Portugal. Similarities in language, religion, and values tend to reflect ethnic homogeneity. More than 10 percent of the population in the remaining countries comes from one or more ethnic minority groups.

Most of the participating countries are urbanized with industrialized economies. All but three of the countries' populations are at least 50 percent urban. China, Portugal, and Mozambique are still predominantly rural, which must influence their orientation toward education.

Among participants, variation in national wealth, as measured by per-capita gross national product (in U.S. dollars), is startling and can sometimes explain and sometimes confuse our understanding of differences in mathematics performance. Among the poorest countries are Mozambique, the lowest-performing population, and China, the highest-performing population. In per-capita terms, the wealthiest country is Switzerland, followed by the United States, Canada, and France.

Some countries compensate for limited resources by spending a greater share of their wealth on education. Among the IAEP countries, Israel spends the greatest percent of gross national product on education, more than 10 percent. China spends the smallest percentage, less than three percent.

Statistics indicate that literacy rates are high in all IAEP countries except in Mozambique, where more than 80 percent of the adult population is still categorized as illiterate. Jordan, China, Portugal, and Brazil are the only other countries with sizable pockets of illiteracy, ranging between 15 and 30 percent.

FIGURE 5.1

Mathematics, Age 13
Average Percents Correct and Country Characteristics*

COMPREHENSIVE POPULATIONS	Average Percent Correct	Population (in Thousands)[1]	Ethnic Homogeneity (90 Percent or More from One Group)[1]	Percent Urban[1]	Per Capita Gross National Product (U.S. $)[2]	Percent of Gross National Product Spent on Education[2]	Percent Literate[1]
Korea	**73** (0.6)	42,793	Yes	70	3,883	4.5	93
Taiwan	**73** (0.7)	20,221	No	74	4,355	3.6	92
Switzerland 15 Cantons	**71** (1.3)	6,756	No	60	27,693	4.8	100
Soviet Union Russian-speaking Schools in 14 Republics	**70** (1.0)	290,122	No	66	8,728	7.0	99
Hungary	**68** (0.8)	10,437	Yes	62	2,490	5.7	99
France	**64** (0.8)	56,647	Yes	73	16,419	6.1	99
Emilia-Romagna, Italy†	**64** (0.9)	57,512	Yes	65	13,814	4.0	97
Israel Hebrew-speaking Schools	**63** (0.8)	4,666	No	89	8,882	10.2	92
Canada	**62** (0.6)	26,620	No	76	17,309	7.4	96
Scotland†	**61** (0.9)	5,094	Yes[3]	92[3]	10,917[3]	5.2[3]	100[3]
Ireland	**61** (0.9)	3,509	Yes	57	7,603	6.7	100
Slovenia	**57** (0.8)	1,948	Yes[4]	74[4]	7,233[4]	3.4[4]	99[4]
Spain Spanish-speaking Schools except in Cataluña	**55** (0.8)	39,618	No	76	8,078	3.2	93
United States†	**55** (1.0)	251,394	No	77	19,789	7.5	96
Jordan	**40** (1.0)	3,169	Yes	70	1,527	7.1	77
POPULATIONS WITH EXCLUSIONS OR LOW PARTICIPATION							
China In-school Population, Restricted Grades, 20 Provinces & Cities	**80** (1.0)	1,133,683	Yes	26[5]	356	2.7	73
England Low Participation‡	**61** (2.2)	47,536	Yes[3]	92[3]	10,917[3]	5.2[3]	100[3]
Portugal In-school Population, Restricted Grades†	**48** (0.8)	10,388	Yes	30	3,740	4.4	84
São Paulo, Brazil Restricted Grades	**37** (0.8)	150,368	No	75	2,245	3.3	81
Fortaleza, Brazil In-school Population, Restricted Grades	**32** (0.6)	150,368	No	75	2,245	3.3	81
Maputo & Beira, Mozambique In-school Population, Low Participation‡	**28** (0.3)	15,696	No	13	113	—	17

* Jackknifed standard errors are presented in parentheses.
† Combined school and student participation rate is below .80 but at least .70; interpret results with caution because of possible nonresponse bias.
‡ Combined school and student participation rate is below .70; interpret results with extreme caution because of possible nonresponse bias.
[1] *1991 Britannica Book of the Year.* Chicago: Encyclopedia Britannica, Inc, 1991. Data reflect entire country.
[2] *P.C. Globe.* Tempe, AZ: P.C. Globe, Inc., 1990. Data reflect entire country.
[3] Data are for United Kingdom.
[4] *Annual Statistical Report of Slovenia,* Central Statistics Office, Ljubljana, Slovenia, 1990.
[5] National Population Census Office, *Major Figures of the Fourth National Population Census of China.* Beijing: China Statistical Publishing House, 1991.
— Information is not available.

Basic descriptive characteristics illustrate some of the grave problems that developing countries such as Jordan, Brazil, and Mozambique face in the education of their young people. The data, however, fail to explain why some poor, non-industrialized countries manage to achieve phenomenal success in education and why some rich and powerful nations fail to perform at the same high levels.

EDUCATION SYSTEMS Differences in country characteristics are often translated into differences in education systems. Predominantly urban countries are more likely to have large schools and large classes. Countries with strong centralized governments tend to centralize educational policy as well. Poor countries have higher incidences of problems in their schools, such as overcrowding, inadequate facilities, and not enough textbooks. Some of these characteristics of education systems are summarized in FIGURE 5.2.

Although countries vary with respect to the age at which children are required to start school, in most IAEP countries, children are six years old when they begin compulsory schooling. Children in Scotland and England start first grade earlier, at the age of five, and those in the German part of Switzerland, parts of the Soviet Union, Slovenia, parts of China, Brazil, and Mozambique do not start until age seven. Countries also vary in terms of the availability of nursery schools and kindergartens and the degree of academic content in these programs. Furthermore, since academic development often proceeds along with physical and mental maturation, one cannot assume that, by age 9 or 13, students who started school at age seven are two years behind those who started at age five.

Likewise, one must also be careful in comparing countries with respect to the number of days in the school year. In many locations, festivals, sports events, and other non-academic activities are integrated into the school-year calendar. Trying to get a more precise measure of time spent on school activities, IAEP asked school administrators to indicate the number of days specifically devoted to student instruction in the school year. The results are reported in FIGURE 5.2. Variation among participating countries is evident in this indicator as well. The average for most populations is from 175 to 199 days a year. France, Ireland, and Portugal (restricted grades) provide fewer than 175 days of instruction annually. The average in China (in-school population) is dramatically higher (251 days), and Korea, Taiwan, Switzerland (15 cantons), Emilia-Romagna, and Israel (Hebrew) report averages from 200 to 224 days a year.

FIGURE 5.2

Mathematics, Age 13
Average Percents Correct and Education Systems*

COMPREHENSIVE POPULATIONS	Average Percent Correct	Age Start School[1]	Average Days of Instruction in Year[2]	Average Minutes of Instruction in School Each Day[2]	Average Class Size for Modal Grade[2]	National Curriculum[1]	Percent of Schools with One or More Serious Problems[2]
Korea	73 (0.6)	6	222 (0.4)	264 (2.4)	49 (0.7)	Yes	24 (4.9)
Taiwan	73 (0.7)	6	222 (2.5)	318 (6.9)	44 (0.6)	Yes	10 (2.8)
Switzerland 15 Cantons	71 (1.3)	6 or 7	207 (3.2)§	305 (7.4)§	18 (0.7)§	No	11 (3.5)§
Soviet Union Russian-speaking Schools in 14 Republics	70 (1.0)	6 or 7	198 (2.1)	243 (2.6)	22 (1.1)	Yes	72 (5.1)
Hungary	68 (0.8)	6	177 (1.5)	223 (1.3)	27 (0.8)	Yes	32 (4.2)
France	64 (0.8)	6	174 (1.7)	370 (3.4)	25 (0.6)	Yes	29 (4.9)
Emilia-Romagna, Italy†	64 (0.9)	6	204 (0.5)	289 (5.0)	21 (1.9)	Yes	18 (5.1)
Israel Hebrew-speaking Schools	63 (0.8)	6	215 (2.2)	278 (6.5)	32 (0.7)	Yes	46 (6.7)
Canada	62 (0.6)	6	188 (0.2)	304 (0.8)	25 (0.3)	No	13 (1.3)
Scotland†	61 (0.9)	5	191 (0.9)	324 (2.3)	24 (0.7)	Yes	23 (4.0)
Ireland	61 (0.9)	6	173 (0.9)	323 (4.4)	27 (0.7)	Yes	39 (5.8)
Slovenia	57 (0.8)	7	190 (1.5)	248 (2.5)	25 (0.4)	Yes	50 (5.3)
Spain Spanish-speaking Schools except in Cataluña	55 (0.8)	6	188 (2.3)	285 (3.2)	29 (0.7)	Yes	33 (5.0)
United States†	55 (1.0)	6	178 (0.4)	338 (5.0)	23 (1.3)	No	5 (2.2)
Jordan	40 (1.0)	6	191 (1.6)	260 (2.9)	27 (1.5)	Yes	63 (5.3)

POPULATIONS WITH EXCLUSIONS OR LOW PARTICIPATION							
China In-school Population, Restricted Grades, 20 Provinces & Cities	80 (1.0)	6.5 or 7	251 (2.1)	305 (7.1)	48 (0.8)	Yes	43 (6.3)
England Low Participation‡	61 (2.2)	5	192 (1.8)	300 (4.4)	22 (1.7)	Yes	24 (8.3)
Portugal In-school Population, Restricted Grades†	48 (0.8)	6	172 (1.1)	334 (6.5)	25 (0.8)	Yes	56 (7.9)
São Paulo, Brazil Restricted Grades	37 (0.8)	7	181 (0.2)	271 (9.3)	38 (1.8)	No	60 (4.6)
Fortaleza, Brazil In-school Population, Restricted Grades	32 (0.6)	7	183 (1.1)	223 (9.8)	32 (2.1)	No	62 (5.3)
Maputo & Beira, Mozambique In-school Population, Low Participation‡	28 (0.3)	7	193 (0.0)	272 (0.0)	51 (0.0)	Yes	92 (0.0)

* Jackknifed standard errors are presented in parentheses.
† Combined school and student participation rate is below .80 but at least .70; interpret results with caution because of possible nonresponse bias.
‡ Combined school and student participation rate is below .70; interpret results with extreme caution because of possible nonresponse bias.
§ Results represent percent of classrooms in schools.
[1] IAEP Country Questionnaire. Data reflect entire country.
[2] IAEP School Questionnaire, Age 13.

To obtain a full picture of instructional time, one needs also to know the number of minutes spent on instruction each school day, excluding time spent for homeroom, lunch, recess, study hall, or moving from class to class. Most IAEP countries devote, on average, about 240 to 360 minutes (four to six hours) to instruction each day. France spends the most time on instruction, 370 minutes daily. Two populations provide less than 240 minutes daily: Hungary and Fortaleza.

While large class sizes do not hinder many types of instruction, they do limit opportunities for individual attention, group work, and hands-on activities. School administrators in 10 populations indicated that the average class size for the grade in which most 13-year-olds are enrolled is from 25 to 34 students. Schools in Switzerland (15 cantons), the Soviet Union (Russian-speaking schools), Emilia-Romagna, Scotland, the United States, and England (low participation) have smaller classes, ranging from 15 to 24 students. Very large classes of 45 or more students are the norm in Korea, China (in-school population), and Maputo-Beira (in-school population), while classes average from 35 to 44 students in Taiwan and São Paulo (restricted grades).

Four IAEP countries encourage local or regional control over curricular matters: Switzerland (15 cantons), Canada, the United States, and Brazil, which does not set the education programs for São Paulo and Fortaleza. Within this group, the United States is actively discussing centralization.

The remaining countries have a national curriculum. In England (low participation), the centralization of educational goals and objectives is only two years old. In the other countries, a strong national ministry of education is a long-established tradition.

School administrators were asked to what extent they face problems of overcrowded classrooms, inadequate facilities and maintenance, shortages of textbooks and other educational materials. Student absenteeism and lack of discipline and vandalism of school property were also surveyed. Their responses to eight questions listing these problems were combined into an index of serious problems. In only seven populations did at least one-half of the schools report one or more serious problems: the Soviet Union (Russian-speaking schools), Slovenia, Jordan, Portugal (restricted grades), São Paulo (restricted grades), Fortaleza (restricted grades), and Maputo-Beira (in-school population).

NO SINGLE SOLUTION Education systems vary from country to country but not necessarily in patterns that explain high and low mathematics achievement. It does not seem to matter greatly whether students begin school early or late, and while some high-performing countries have a longer school year or a longer school day, these characteristics were also present among some low-achieving groups as well. While no one would advocate the benefits of increasing class size, several education systems demonstrated success despite large class sizes. Finally, some countries succeed while others do not, in some cases, in spite of serious problems in school.

ITALY March 20, 1991

The elementary school was in an industrial suburb of Bologna. The kids were playing outside as well as in a very large open reception area right inside the front door. Excited voice-noises were magnified many times in this substantial echo chamber. An old, black-cassocked priest was collecting disciples for a class in religion.

A handsome, young principal greeted us enthusiastically and led us through the chaos toward a room upstairs. As we proceeded, strident soprano voices shouted "Ciaó, Direttore" (Hi, Principal)! Each greeting was responded to with a smile, a wave, a pat on a head, a caress on a face.

As the National Coordinator parted groups of children to create a passage for use, she stooped to kiss and hug, indiscriminately, these complete strangers. All of this with an easy casualness that caused no serious interruption in our fast-paced conversation concerning the new education legislation and its affect on the building arrangement.

Thirty-four 9-year-olds from three different schools were arriving and being seated quietly after locating their name tags, previously put on each desk. Three teachers facilitated the process. Booklets were passed out, instructions read, and questions solicited. Questions were answered, tasks begun, a little girl left the room to tend to something she should have thought of earlier.

At the end of the test, the teachers handed out beautifully wrapped candies as a reward. At my request, the children were asked for reactions to the experience. Hands went up and were individually recognized: "Bello! (Nice)," "Facile (Easy)," "Divertente (Fun)."

The feelings were unanimous and enthusiastic.

We said goodbye as the kids streamed through the door — a confusion of hand shakes, pats, "Grazie's" and "Ciaó's." A quiet moment was spent with the teachers, one of whom was vocal and emphatic that no group of human beings, especially her children, should be put through such a dehumanizing experience.

My observation to the National Coordinator about how pleasantly surprised I was to see all the easy demonstrations of affection between students and teachers elicited her own surprised reaction.

"But why not? The children must know that they are most important and that they are loved. They must feel secure or they cannot learn. A school is a family!" Neat idea!

I had promised the children of San Felipo that I would tell the world about them.

This is a start.

ETS Quality Control Observer

Performance of 9-Year-Olds

CHAPTER SIX

What we first learn we best ken.

Scottish Proverb

Fourteen of the 20 countries participated in an optional assessment of 9-year-olds. Some countries sampled students from the entire age cohort within a defined population and others excluded some segments of the age-eligible population or had low school and student participation rates. The results for these two sets of populations are reported separately as comprehensive populations and populations with exclusions or low participation.

OVERALL MATHEMATICS PERFORMANCE The average percent correct and distribution of scores for each population are presented in FIGURE 6.1. The green bars indicate the average percents correct and take into account the imprecision of these estimates due to sampling. When the bars overlap with one another, as they do in many cases, performance is not significantly different.

Mathematics, Age 9

FIGURE 6.1

Distribution of Percent Correct Scores by Country*

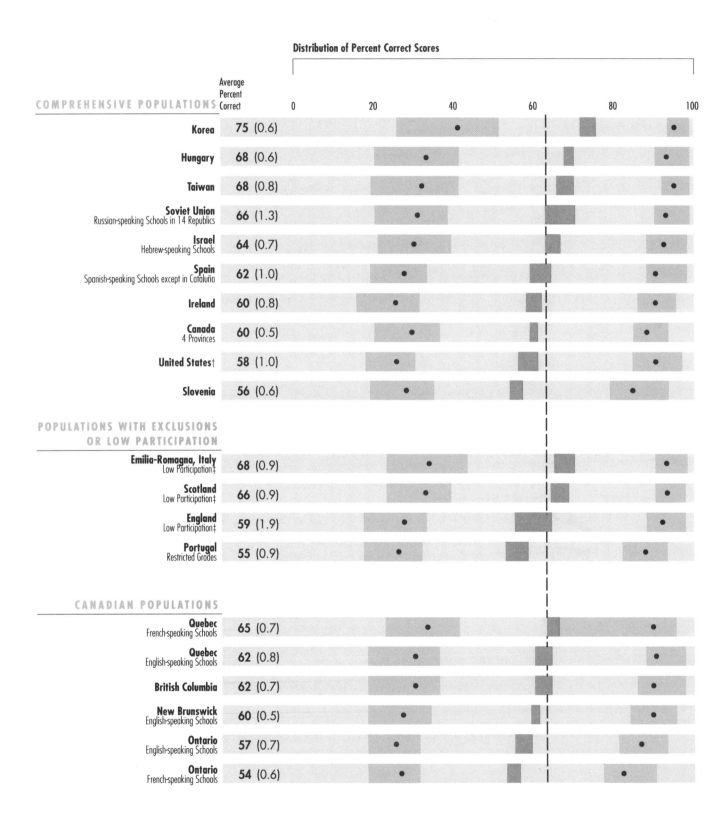

Distribution of Percent Correct Scores

COMPREHENSIVE POPULATIONS	Average Percent Correct		0	20	40	60	80	100
Korea	75	(0.6)						
Hungary	68	(0.6)						
Taiwan	68	(0.8)						
Soviet Union — Russian-speaking Schools in 14 Republics	66	(1.3)						
Israel — Hebrew-speaking Schools	64	(0.7)						
Spain — Spanish-speaking Schools except in Cataluña	62	(1.0)						
Ireland	60	(0.8)						
Canada — 4 Provinces	60	(0.5)						
United States†	58	(1.0)						
Slovenia	56	(0.6)						

POPULATIONS WITH EXCLUSIONS OR LOW PARTICIPATION

Emilia-Romagna, Italy — Low Participation‡	68	(0.9)						
Scotland — Low Participation‡	66	(0.9)						
England — Low Participation‡	59	(1.9)						
Portugal — Restricted Grades	55	(0.9)						

CANADIAN POPULATIONS

Quebec — French-speaking Schools	65	(0.7)						
Quebec — English-speaking Schools	62	(0.8)						
British Columbia	62	(0.7)						
New Brunswick — English-speaking Schools	60	(0.5)						
Ontario — English-speaking Schools	57	(0.7)						
Ontario — French-speaking Schools	54	(0.6)						

Average percent correct with simultaneous confidence interval controlling for all possible comparisons among comprehensive populations, populations with exclusions or low participation, and Canadian populations.

● Bullet is 5th and 95th percentile. ▨ are 1st to 10th percentiles and 90th to 99th percentiles.

┊ IAEP Average

* Jackknifed standard errors are presented in parentheses.

† Combined school and student participation rate is below .80 but at least .70; interpret results with caution because of possible nonresponse bias.

‡ Combined school and student participation rate is below .70; interpret results with extreme caution because of possible nonresponse bias.

Ⓔ︎Ⓢ︎ IAEP

The shaded bars indicate the range of scores for the best students (those in the 90th through the 99th percentiles) and the range of scores for the lowest-performing students (those in the first through the 10th percentiles). The average percents correct for students in the 5th and 95th percentiles are marked by bullets within the shaded bars.[25]

The range of average percents correct across the 14 comprehensive populations and populations with exclusions or low participation at age 9 is 20 points and in all of these populations, some students performed very well and others performed poorly. The difference between the highest and lowest performing groups was much greater at age 13, but when considering just those populations that participated in assessments at both age levels, the difference was only 25 points.

The average score across the comprehensive populations and populations with exclusions or low participation, represented by a vertical dashed line, is 63 percent correct.[26] Nine-year-olds in the Soviet Union (Russian-speaking schools), Israel (Hebrew), Spain (except Cataluña), and England (low participation) performed about at the IAEP average.

The highest-scoring population was Korea, with an average percent correct of 75. Other populations performing above the IAEP average, from highest to lowest, were Hungary, Taiwan, Emilia-Romagna (low participation), and Scotland (low participation). As the overlapping bars on the figure illustrate, performance of these four groups is essentially the same.

The remaining populations scored below the IAEP average. These included, in order of average percent correct, Ireland, Canada (4 provinces), the United States, Slovenia, and Portugal (restricted grades) and in many instances, when sampling error is taken into account, their performance levels are equivalent.

Three Canadian populations scored at the IAEP average: Quebec (French), Quebec (English), and British Columbia. The remaining Canadian populations performed below the average: New Brunswick (English), Ontario (English), and Ontario (French). The range of scores for the Canadian populations is only 11 points and in many cases performance is equivalent from one population to another.

---

[25] Performance of students at the very bottom of the distribution (the lowest 1 percent) and at the very top (the highest 1 percent) are not represented on the figure because very few students fall into these categories and their performance cannot be estimated with precision.

[26] The IAEP average is the unweighted average of the scores of the comprehensive populations, populations with exclusions or low participation, and Canadian populations. An unweighted average was chosen to describe the midpoint because it is not influenced by the differential weights of very large and very small populations.

Achievement reflects the percent correct on 61 questions. Responses to one question included in the assessment were removed from the results after a series of data analysis steps determined it was not functioning the same way across all populations.[27]

MATHEMATICS PERFORMANCE BY GENDER The patterns of performance for males and females at age 9, shown in FIGURE 6.2, are not the same as those seen at age 13. The advantage of boys over girls is not evident in as many comprehensive populations and populations with exclusions or low participation at this age. Only in Korea, Israel (Hebrew), and Emilia-Romagna (low participation) did boys aged 9 significantly outperform girls. Performance levels of boys and girls was about the same in each of the Canadian populations.

The country results were not always consistent at the two age levels. While there were no gender differences at age 9 in Spain (except Cataluña), Ireland, and Canada,[28] boys scored significantly higher than girls in these three countries at age 13. The reverse is true in Korea and Israel (Hebrew). Here, boys had significantly higher mathematics achievement at age 9 but performed about the same as girls at age 13. In Emilia-Romagna (low participation), the pattern is consistent; boys displayed significantly higher performance at both age levels.

Figure 6.2 also indicates that most students in most populations agreed that mathematics is equally appropriate for boys and girls. As was seen at age 13, only in Korea did significant numbers of students view mathematics as gender linked. Here, 25 percent thought mathematics was more for boys and 27 percent thought it was more for girls.

---

[27] See the Procedural Appendix, pp. 142-143, and the *IAEP Technical Report* for a detailed discussion of cluster and differential item functioning analysis.

[28] Fewer Canadian provinces participated in the 9-year-old assessment, so the groups are not strictly comparable at the two ages.

Mathematics, Age 9
Percentages of Students Reporting Math Is Equally Appropriate for Boys and Girls and Average Percents Correct by Gender*

FIGURE 6.2

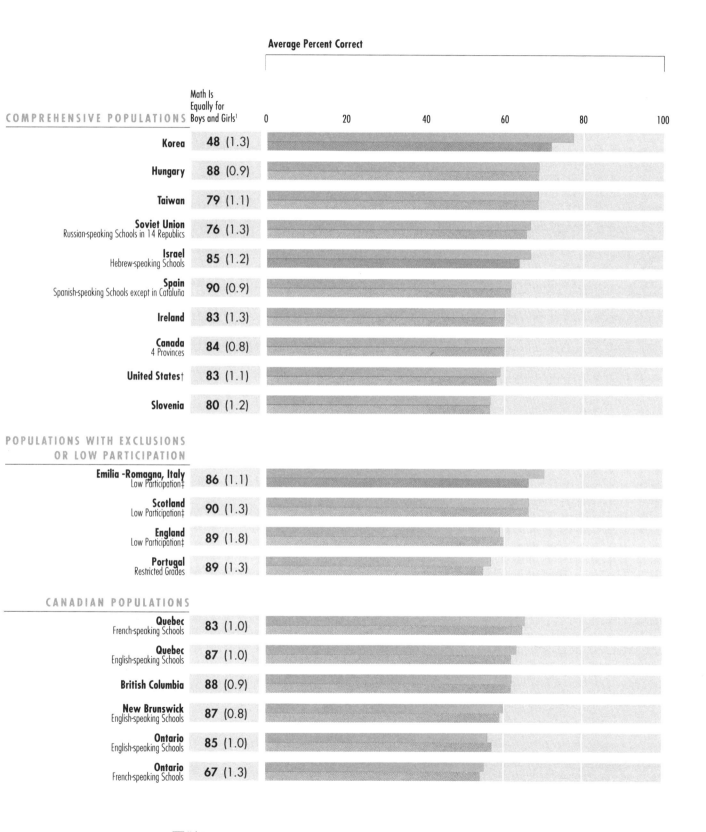

	Math Is Equally for Boys and Girls[1]	Average Percent Correct
COMPREHENSIVE POPULATIONS		
Korea	48 (1.3)	
Hungary	88 (0.9)	
Taiwan	79 (1.1)	
Soviet Union Russian-speaking Schools in 14 Republics	76 (1.3)	
Israel Hebrew-speaking Schools	85 (1.2)	
Spain Spanish-speaking Schools except in Cataluña	90 (0.9)	
Ireland	83 (1.3)	
Canada 4 Provinces	84 (0.8)	
United States†	83 (1.1)	
Slovenia	80 (1.2)	
POPULATIONS WITH EXCLUSIONS OR LOW PARTICIPATION		
Emilia -Romagna, Italy Low Participation‡	86 (1.1)	
Scotland Low Participation‡	90 (1.3)	
England Low Participation‡	89 (1.8)	
Portugal Restricted Grades	89 (1.3)	
CANADIAN POPULATIONS		
Quebec French-speaking Schools	83 (1.0)	
Quebec English-speaking Schools	87 (1.0)	
British Columbia	88 (0.9)	
New Brunswick English-speaking Schools	87 (0.8)	
Ontario English-speaking Schools	85 (1.0)	
Ontario French-speaking Schools	67 (1.3)	

Males
Females
Statistically significant differences between groups at the .05 level.
* Jackknifed standard errors are presented in parentheses.
† Combined school and student participation rate is below .80 but at least .70; interpret results with caution because of possible nonresponse bias.
‡ Combined school and student participation rate is below .70; interpret results with extreme caution because of possible nonresponse bias.
[1] IAEP Student Questionnaire, Age 9.

 IAEP

Summaries of mathematics performance just begin to describe the variation that exists from country to country. Of more importance to educators is a description of performance in the various mathematics content areas that are taught in school. While initial analyses of the IAEP data confirm that questions across all topics can be legitimately summarized without masking important differences between countries, results by topic categories do show some variation.[29]

The results for students age 9 are presented for five topics, which are listed in FIGURE 6.3 along with the number of questions in each category. Three quarters of the questions used a multiple-choice format and the remaining questions required students to write their answers on lines provided.

FIGURE 6.3

Mathematics, Age 9:
Numbers of Questions by Topic

Numbers and Operations	Measurement	Geometry	Data Analysis, Statistics and Probability	Algebra and Functions	Total
32	9	6	8	6	61

The performance of the comprehensive populations and populations with exclusions or low participation in each of the five topics is presented in FIGURE 6.4. The populations are listed in order of overall performance across all mathematics questions. The bars show the IAEP average across all comprehensive populations and populations with exclusions or low participation as well as the average percents for each population in each topic category.

In general, the relative performance of the two population groups in each of the topics mirrors their overall achievement in mathematics. This is evident by the fact that the bars that represent the topic averages for the populations generally follow the same pattern as the wide bars that represent overall averages presented in Figure 6.1.

---

[29] A country-by-topic interaction analysis using Hartigan and Wong's K-Means cluster analysis technique indicates that the differences in performance from topic to topic do not confound the main effects of overall performance. This means that the relative performance of countries would remain essentially the same if a group of items from a particular topic or topics were removed from the overall summary measure. More details of this analysis are provided in the Procedural Appendix, p. 142 and in the *IAEP Technical Report*.

The patterns of performance were examined to see if the achievement of a population in a particular topic area was different from its overall achievement and some exceptions were identified. Since the average difficulty levels of the questions in the various topics and across all topics differ, performance was examined in relative terms: by comparing the difference between a population's topic average and the IAEP topic average with the difference between the population's overall average and the IAEP overall average.[30]

The performance of comprehensive populations and populations with exclusions or low participation in Numbers and Operations, which constituted about 50 percent of the assessment, was relatively the same as that across all mathematics questions. In Measurement, 15 percent of the assessment, students from Korea and Spain (except Cataluña) scored lower relative to their overall performance. Ten percent of the assessment was devoted to Geometry questions and in this category, Canada (4 provinces), Slovenia, and England (low participation) performed better compared with their performance across all mathematics questions and Emilia-Romagna (low participation) and Israel (Hebrew) performed less well in relation to their performance in general. Performance of populations varied from the norm the most in the area of Data Analysis, Statistics, and Probability — about 15 percent of the assessment. While the questions in this topic were relatively easy, these skills are not always taught to students at this age level, which may explain why students in some populations scored high on these items and others scored low. Four populations performed better in this category compared with their scores overall — Canada (4 provinces), the United States, Scotland (low participation), and England (low participation) — and four performed relatively less well than they did overall — Hungary, Soviet Union (Russian-speaking schools), Israel (Hebrew), and Slovenia. In Algebra and Functions — 10 percent of the assessment — 9-year-olds from Hungary, Israel (Hebrew), and Slovenia had comparatively higher scores than their overall level of achievement, while Emilia-Romagna (low participation) achieved at relatively lower levels in this area than it did overall.

---

[30] For these analyses of achievement by topics, populations are cited as deviating from their normal pattern if the difference between their deviation from the mean for the topic and their deviation from the overall mean is twice the standard error of the difference between these deviations or greater. Further details of these analyses are provided in the Procedural Appendix, p. 143, and the *IAEP Technical Report*.

FIGURE 6.4

Mathematics, Age 9
Average Percents Correct by Topic

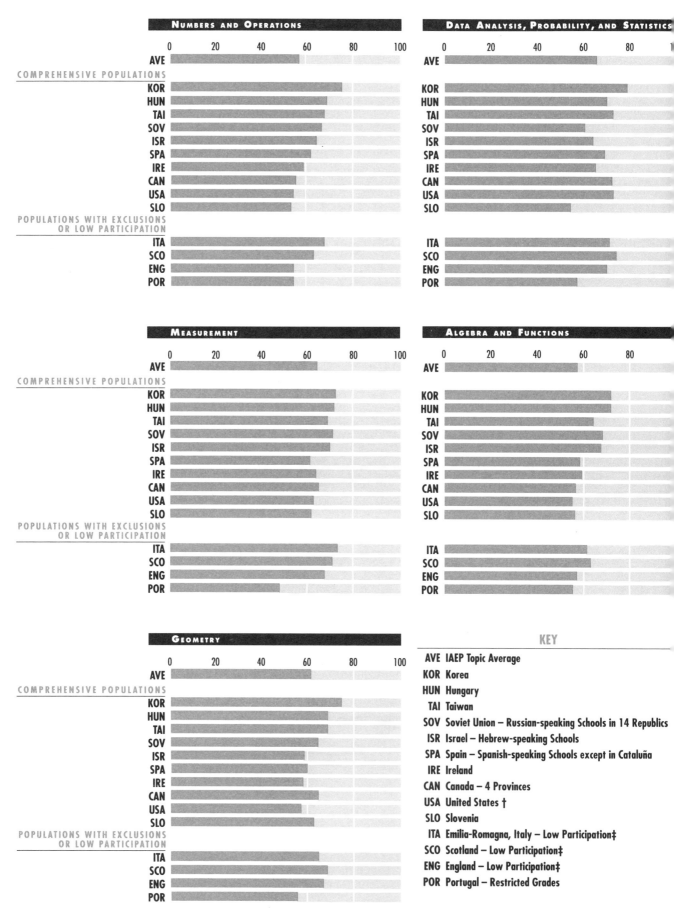

KEY

AVE	IAEP Topic Average
KOR	Korea
HUN	Hungary
TAI	Taiwan
SOV	Soviet Union – Russian-speaking Schools in 14 Republics
ISR	Israel – Hebrew-speaking Schools
SPA	Spain – Spanish-speaking Schools except in Cataluña
IRE	Ireland
CAN	Canada – 4 Provinces
USA	United States †
SLO	Slovenia
ITA	Emilia-Romagna, Italy – Low Participation‡
SCO	Scotland – Low Participation‡
ENG	England – Low Participation‡
POR	Portugal – Restricted Grades

† Combined school and student participation rate is below .80 but at least .70; interpret results with caution because of possible nonresponse bias.
‡ Combined school and student participation rate is below .70; interpret results with extreme caution because of possible nonresponse bias.

In addition to the five topics, results are presented for three categories of mathematics processes: Conceptual Understanding, Procedural Knowledge, and Problem Solving. The performance of comprehensive populations and populations with exclusions or low participation in each process area, shown in FIGURE 6.5, in almost all cases follows the same pattern as their overall performance in mathematics. The only exception is Taiwan, where students scored better in Procedural Knowledge questions and less well on Problem Solving questions compared with their overall achievement levels.

FIGURE 6.5

Mathematics, Age 9
Average Percents Correct by Cognitive Process

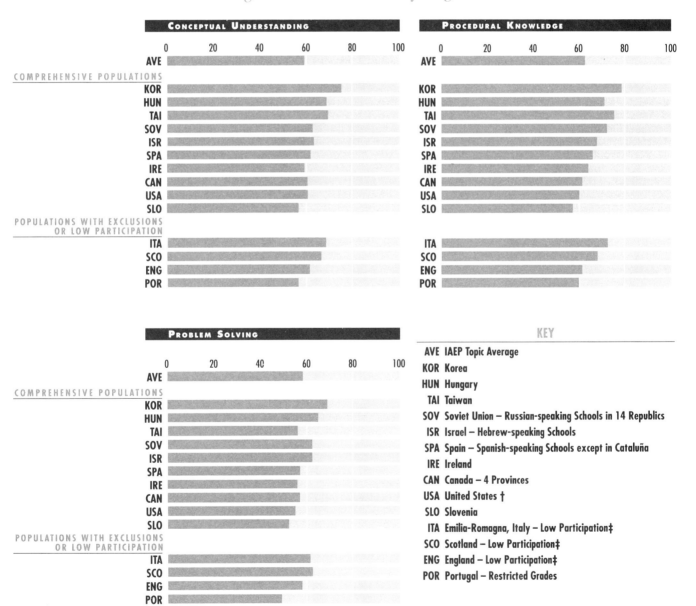

KEY

AVE IAEP Topic Average
KOR Korea
HUN Hungary
TAI Taiwan
SOV Soviet Union – Russian-speaking Schools in 14 Republics
ISR Israel – Hebrew-speaking Schools
SPA Spain – Spanish-speaking Schools except in Cataluña
IRE Ireland
CAN Canada – 4 Provinces
USA United States †
SLO Slovenia
ITA Emilia-Romagna, Italy – Low Participation‡
SCO Scotland – Low Participation‡
ENG England – Low Participation‡
POR Portugal – Restricted Grades

† Combined school and student participation rate is below .80 but at least .70; interpret results with caution because of possible nonresponse bias.
‡ Combined school and student participation rate is below .70; interpret results with extreme caution because of possible nonresponse bias.

The performance of the Canadian populations in the various topic and process categories shown in FIGURE 6.6 also was fairly consistent. The most exceptions occur in the topic of Data Analysis, Statistics, and Probability, where all Canadian populations performed relatively better than they did overall. In addition, 9-year-olds from Ontario (French) performed less well in Numbers and Operations, better in Geometry, and less well on Procedural Knowledge compared with their overall achievement. Their peers in Quebec (French) scored relatively higher in Geometry than they did overall. Students from British Columbia and New Brunswick (English) performed less well in Algebra and Functions compared to their overall scores.

Mathematics, Age 9
Average Percents Correct by Topic and Cognitive Process for Canadian Populations*

FIGURE 6.6

	Topics					Cognitive Processes		
	Numbers and Operations	Measurement	Geometry	Data Analysis, Probability, and Statistics	Algebra and Functions	Conceptual Understanding	Procedural Knowledge	Problem Solving
IAEP Topic Averages	61 (1.1)	67 (0.8)	64 (1.0)	68 (1.0)	62 (1.2)	63 (0.9)	67 (1.0)	58 (1.0)
CANADIAN POPULATIONS								
Quebec French-speaking Schools	59 (0.8)	68 (0.7)	73 (0.7)	77 (0.7)	64 (0.8)	65 (0.6)	66 (0.9)	62 (0.8)
British Columbia	59 (0.8)	67 (0.7)	62 (1.0)	72 (0.8)	57 (0.7)	62 (0.7)	64 (0.8)	59 (0.7)
Quebec English-speaking Schools	59 (0.9)	69 (0.7)	64 (0.9)	73 (0.7)	58 (0.8)	64 (0.8)	64 (0.8)	59 (0.8)
Ontario English-speaking Schools	52 (0.8)	63 (0.7)	60 (0.9)	70 (0.7)	52 (0.7)	58 (0.7)	58 (0.8)	54 (0.7)
New Brunswick English-speaking Schools	56 (0.6)	66 (0.5)	63 (0.5)	69 (0.6)	55 (0.5)	61 (0.4)	61 (0.6)	56 (0.6)
Ontario French-speaking Schools	48 (0.6)	60 (0.7)	62 (0.7)	68 (0.7)	55 (0.6)	56 (0.6)	54 (0.6)	52 (0.7)

* Jackknifed standard errors are presented in parentheses.

Collecting background information from 9-year-olds is a challenge. Children at this age often do not understand difficult questions and cannot make fine distinctions in their responses. For these reasons the IAEP assessment asked only a few questions about their home and school experiences. Also, because the educational environment varies from country to country, students may interpret questions in different ways.

Many of the answers of 9-year-olds mirror the responses of their 13-year-old schoolmates. Information obtained about the language spoken in the home, family size, and number of books in the home is essentially the same at both ages. The differences that do occur may be due to misunderstandings by some of the younger students.

Asked about classroom activities, 9-year-olds' responses suggested that these students, like their older colleagues, spend more time working exercises on their own than doing hands-on activities. As shown in FIGURE 6.7, in almost all populations, about 40 to 70 percent of the students indicated that they often did independent work, while only 10 to 30 percent reported that they often used mathematics tools, such as counting blocks, geometric shapes, or geometric solids. Fewer Korean and Portuguese students reported doing independent work often (23 and 32 percent, respectively).

Participating countries differed with respect to organizational practices in the classroom. Some were much more likely than others to group students by ability within mathematics classes. Most of the schools in Scotland (low participation), 78 percent, reported that they use ability groups in mathematics, and between 40 and 60 percent of the schools in Korea, Hungary, the Soviet Union (Russian-speaking schools), Ireland, Canada (4 provinces), Slovenia, England (low participation), and Portugal (restricted grades) also said they follow this organizational practice. The large majority of schools in the remaining countries use heterogenous grouping in mathematics classes.

The responses to IAEP student questionnaires indicate that the out-of-school activities of 9-year-olds differ somewhat from those of their older schoolmates. Nine-year-olds were more likely to read books for fun, to watch more television, and to spend less time doing homework than 13-year-olds. A major portion of young students, about 40 to 60 percent, indicated that they read for fun almost every day in all countries except Korea and Taiwan, where only about one quarter reported daily leisure reading.

FIGURE 6.7

Mathematics, Age 9
Average Percents Correct and Classroom and Home Activities*

COMPREHENSIVE POPULATIONS	Average Percent Correct	Percent of Students Who Do Math Exercises by Themselves Often[1]	Percent of Students Who Work With Math Tools Often[1]	Percent of Schools Where Students Are Grouped by Ability within Math Class[2]	Percent of Students Who Read For Fun Almost Every Day[1]	Percent of Students Who Spend 2 Hours or More on Homework Every Day[1]	Percent of Students Who Watch Television 5 Hours or More Every Day[1]
Korea	75 (0.6)	23 (1.0)	11 (1.0)	49 (5.3)	25 (1.2)	22 (1.1)	9 (0.7)
Hungary	68 (0.6)	69 (1.0)	20 (1.0)	50 (9.8)	50 (1.6)	25 (1.4)	16 (1.2)
Taiwan	68 (0.8)	47 (1.3)	30 (1.1)	4 (2.0)	29 (1.3)	31 (1.2)	8 (0.8)
Soviet Union Russian-speaking Schools in 14 Republics	66 (1.3)	62 (1.2)	21 (1.0)	43 (5.7)	63 (1.3)	31 (1.3)	18 (0.7)
Israel Hebrew-speaking Schools	64 (0.7)	42 (1.5)	21 (1.2)	36 (6.4)	57 (1.4)	35 (1.5)	24 (1.1)
Spain Spanish-speaking Schools except in Cataluña	62 (1.0)	60 (1.7)	23 (1.7)	17 (4.1)	55 (1.4)	29 (1.8)	17 (1.4)
Ireland	60 (0.8)	51 (1.6)	14 (1.1)	51 (6.1)	45 (1.4)	18 (1.5)	23 (1.5)
Canada 4 Provinces	60 (0.5)	48 (1.0)	13 (0.6)	45 (3.2)	48 (0.8)	13 (0.6)	22 (0.8)
United States†	58 (1.0)	44 (1.5)	19 (1.3)	32 (7.6)	45 (1.5)	20 (1.2)	26 (1.6)
Slovenia	56 (0.6)	61 (1.4)	20 (1.3)	50 (5.1)	63 (1.5)	15 (1.1)	8 (0.6)

POPULATIONS WITH EXCLUSIONS OR LOW PARTICIPATION

	Average Percent Correct	Percent of Students Who Do Math Exercises by Themselves Often[1]	Percent of Students Who Work With Math Tools Often[1]	Percent of Schools Where Students Are Grouped by Ability within Math Class[2]	Percent of Students Who Read For Fun Almost Every Day[1]	Percent of Students Who Spend 2 Hours or More on Homework Every Day[1]	Percent of Students Who Watch Television 5 Hours or More Every Day[1]
Emilia-Romagna, Italy Low Participation‡	68 (0.9)	42 (2.1)	18 (1.3)	25 (4.9)	51 (1.9)	17 (1.5)	9 (0.8)
Scotland Low Participation‡	66 (0.9)	48 (1.5)	13 (1.5)	78 (7.0)	43 (1.6)	4 (0.6)	23 (1.5)
England Low Participation‡	59 (1.9)	47 (2.8)	18 (1.5)	59 (7.3)	51 (2.6)	9 (1.2)	23 (2.0)
Portugal Restricted Grades	55 (0.9)	32 (2.1)	17 (1.7)	53 (5.8)	60 (2.2)	20 (1.7)	20 (1.5)

* Jackknifed standard errors are presented in parentheses.
† Combined school and student participation rate is below .80 but at least .70; interpret results with caution because of possible nonresponse bias.
‡ Combined school and student participation rate is below .70; interpret results with extreme caution because of possible nonresponse bias.
[1] IAEP Student Questionnaire, Age 9.
[2] IAEP School Questionnaire, Age 9.

The norm for time spent on all homework by 9-year-olds in most all populations was one hour or less for all school subjects on a typical school day. Heavy concentration on homework at age 9 was very rare in Scotland (low participation) and England (low participation), with fewer than 10 percent reporting two hours or more nightly. About a third of the students in Taiwan, the Soviet Union (Russian-speaking schools), and Israel (Hebrew) spent at least two hours on homework a night at age 9.

About one-half of the students in almost all participating countries typically reported watching two to four hours of television each day. Heavy television viewing, five hours or more daily, was more prevalent at age 9 than among older students. Heavy television viewing was most prevalent in Israel (Hebrew), Ireland, Canada, the United States, Scotland (low participation), and England (low participation), where about one quarter of the 9-year-olds watched television five hours or more each day.

The relationships between mathematics performance and classroom and home factors at age 9, shown in FIGURE 6.8, confirm many of the findings at age 13. However, as at age 13, the results are not always consistent across all populations and some counter examples are also evident. In Figure 6.8, the pluses, minuses, and zeros indicate whether the relationship between achievement and increasing levels of a particular background variable for each population is positive, negative, or not related in a linear fashion to a statistically significant degree.

The descriptive data indicate that 9-year-olds tended to spend more time doing mathematics exercises on their own and less time working with counting blocks, geometric shapes, and geometric solids, and for the majority of IAEP populations, mathematics performance is positively related to doing independent work and negatively related to using mathematics tools. Since little time is typically spent in using mathematics tools, it is too early to tell if hands-on instructional activities can be used successfully to build mathematics skills.

The relationships between out-of-school activities and achievement are not as consistent at age 9 as at age 13. Nine-year-olds spent more time than their older schoolmates reading for fun and those who read more often performed better on the mathematics assessment. This was true in 12 populations. However, the amount of time 9-year-olds spend doing homework across all school subjects appears to be unrelated to mathematics performance in more than half of the participating countries at age 9, perhaps because homework is not prevalent at that age. Spending more time watching television is also unrelated to achievement for eight populations, negatively related to achievement in five, and positively related to achievement in one.

Mathematics, Age 9
Relationship of Classroom and Home Factors and
Average Percents Correct within Populations

FIGURE 6.8

COMPREHENSIVE POPULATIONS	Amount of Doing Math Exercises on Own[1]	Amount of Working With Math Tools[1]	Amount of Leisure Reading[1]	Amount of Time Spent on All Homework[1]	Amount of Time Spent Watching Television[1]
Korea	+	O	+	O	−
Hungary	+	−	+	O	−
Taiwan	+	+	+	+	−
Soviet Union Russian-speaking Schools in 14 Republics	+	−	+	O	O
Israel Hebrew-speaking Schools	O	−	+	+	+
Spain Spanish-speaking Schools except in Cataluña	O	O	+	O	O
Ireland	+	−	+	+	O
Canada 4 Provinces	+	−	+	−	−
United States†	+	−	+	O	O
Slovenia	O	−	O	O	−

POPULATIONS WITH EXCLUSIONS OR LOW PARTICIPATION					
Emilia-Romagna, Italy Low Participation‡	O	−	+	−	O
Scotland Low Participation‡	O	−	+	−	O
England Low Participation‡	+	−	+	O	O
Portugal Restricted Grades	−	O	O	O	O

+ Statistically significant positive relationship
− Statistically significant negative relationship
O No statistically significant linear relationship
† Combined school and student participation rate is below .80 but at least .70; interpret results with caution because of possible nonresponse bias.
‡ Combined school and student participation rate is below .70; interpret results with extreme caution because of possible nonresponse bias.
[1] IAEP Student Questionnaire, Age 9

Collecting data at two ages allows populations to compare levels of performance of equivalent samples on equivalent assessment tasks. In mathematics, a set of 14 questions covering a range of mathematical topics and processes were administered to both age groups.

The average percents correct across the common items are presented for each age group in each participating population in FIGURE 6.9. The differences in scores at the two age levels is typically 20 to 30 percentage points. The smallest differences are seen for students from the higher-performing populations of Korea and Emilia-Romagna (low participation) — each with a 22-point spread — and the largest, for students from the lower-performing population of Slovenia with a 32-point spread. This probably reflects the fact that there is more room for growth among lower-achieving groups.

The sample questions shown in FIGURE 6.10 give three examples of tasks that most 13-year-olds can do and most 9-year-olds cannot.[31] It is not surprising that younger students do not understand the correspondence between common and decimal fractions required to answer the first sample problem. The second example demonstrates a routine numbers problem, but it requires the student to work with numbers provided in a graphic form. Apparently, this application of basic skills makes the task difficult for 9-year-olds. The last sample problem requires the students to formulate and solve a simple algebraic expression. This is a higher level problem-solving task that may be familiar to 13-year-olds but would be an unusual task for their younger schoolmates.

---

[31] The difficulty level for the sample questions is an unweighted average of the item percents correct across the comprehensive populations and populations with exculsions or low participation.

FIGURE 6.9

Mathematics, Ages 9 and 13
Average Percents Correct for Common Questions*

COMPREHENSIVE POPULATIONS	Age 9	Age 13	Difference
Korea	**60** (0.7)	**82** (0.7)	22
Hungary	**54** (0.8)	**80** (0.6)	26
Taiwan	**51** (0.8)	**78** (0.6)	27
Soviet Union Russian-speaking Schools in 14 Republics	**54** (1.5)	**81** (0.8)	27
Israel Hebrew-speaking Schools	**52** (0.9)	**79** (0.7)	27
Spain Spanish-speaking Schools except in Cataluña	**50** (1.0)	**74** (0.7)	24
Ireland	**44** (0.9)	**74** (0.8)	30
Canada 4 Provinces	**45** (0.5)	**76** (0.5)	31
United States†	**46** (1.1)	**71** (1.1)	25
Slovenia	**41** (0.7)	**73** (0.7)	32

POPULATIONS WITH EXCLUSIONS OR LOW PARTICIPATION			
Emilia-Romagna, Italy Low Participation‡	**55** (1.1)	**77** (0.9)	22
Scotland Low Participation‡	**48** (0.9)	**74** (0.8)	26
England Low Participation‡	**44** (1.9)	**74** (1.9)	30
Portugal Restricted Grades	**41** (1.0)	**68** (1.0)	27

* Jackknifed standard errors are presented in parentheses.
† Combined school and student participation rate is below .80 but at least .70; interpret results with caution because of possible nonresponse bias.
‡ Combined school and student participation rate is below .70; interpret results with extreme caution because of possible nonresponse bias.

FIGURE 6.10

Mathematics, Ages 9 and 13:
Sample Test Questions

IAEP Item Average   Age 9: 41%
   Age 13: 82%

Which of the following decimals is equal to $\frac{9}{10}$?

A 0.1
B 0.3
Ⓒ 0.9
D 9.0

IAEP Item Average   Age 9: 39%
   Age 13: 77%

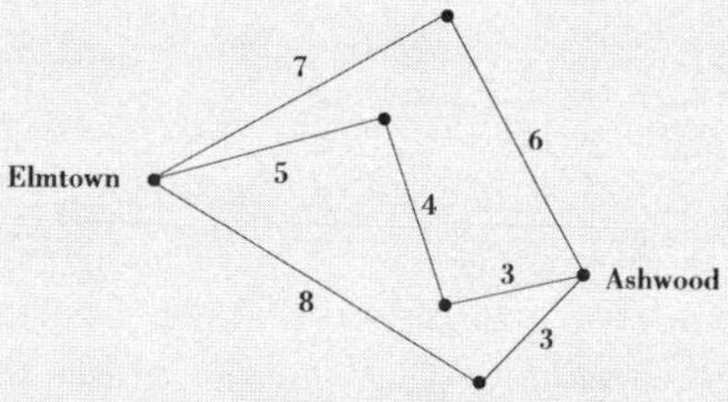

The figure above shows three different routes
between two places, measured in miles.
How long is the shortest of these routes?

Answer: _____ **11** _____ miles

IAEP Item Average   Age 9: 41%
   Age 13: 75%

The total weight of three suitcases is 28 pounds.
The weight of Terri's suitcase is as much as the
weight of the other two suitcases together.
What is the weight, in pounds, of Terri's suitcase?

A 13
Ⓑ 14
C 15
D 22

During the primary school years, students are taught whole-number operations and are introduced to the basic concepts of measurement, geometry, charts and graphs, and functional relationships. While the range of mathematics performances among participating countries is not as great as it is at age 13, some populations clearly out-performed others.

In the classroom, 9-year-olds tended to spend more time doing mathematics exercises on their own than they spent working with mathematics tools and the amount of time spent on independent work is positively associated with mathematics achievement. At home, these children tended to spend more time reading for fun and watching television and less time doing homework across all school subjects than their 13-year-old counterparts.

A Final Word

The task of reporting the achievement results in mathematics from 20 countries as diverse as China, the Soviet Union, the United States, Switzerland, Israel, Brazil, and Mozambique is a challenge and a unique opportunity. Because it only makes sense to interpret academic performance of such a varied group of populations within the educational and cultural context of each participant, achievement data have been presented together with descriptive information about curriculums, classrooms, home environments, and country characteristics.

While it would have been satisfying to see clear distinctions between the characteristics of high- and low-performing countries, the data rarely suggest a universal answer to the question of what factors contribute to effective schooling and high performance. While consistent relationships between certain background characteristics and achievement were often noted for a majority of populations, counter examples were almost always present. And perhaps this is one of the important findings of the study: factors that impact academic performance interact in complex ways and operate differently in different cultures and education systems.

The second important finding relates to the actual levels of achievement that were documented. The IAEP results provide educators, policymakers, and parents with a view of what students in 20 countries know and can do at ages 9 and 13. Unfortunately, the IAEP data may lead some individuals to focus on the academic horse race, and others will decide that all comparisons are unfair. Still, international comparative achievement data can provide a picture of educational accomplishment that expands the value of national findings. As policymakers attempt to set goals and standards for their own young citizens, it can be instructive to know what levels of achievement are *possible* as demonstrated by the performance of students in other societies.

The Participants

The thrust of this report has been to put achievement results into context. Results have been displayed and discussed together with background information about the curriculum, classroom practices, students' home environments, and the characteristics of the society and education system of each participating country. These presentations of results have, in some instances, identified factors that are characteristic of high- or low-performing populations. But in many cases, the data have reinforced the notion that many of these variables operate differently from country to country and cannot be interpreted in the same way in all cultures.

Then what does make a difference in performance levels from country to country? The answer must lie in a deeper understanding of the interactions among the variables that were studied and in a recognition of the significance of other factors that cannot be assessed in a survey project such as IAEP. Among these are historical traditions, cultural values, systems of reward, expectations, and motivation, which are most profitably studied using methods of observation and interview and reported in the form of verbal descriptions rather than data tables and graphs.

IAEP attempted to capture some of these difficult-to-measure qualities in a country questionnaire completed by project directors. Most of the questions asked for descriptive responses as opposed to multiple-choice or numerical answers. The following short summaries of each country drew upon those descriptions and describe some of the factors that are difficult to quantify.

These short descriptions can only highlight some of the unique characteristics and current challenges that each country faces and, different topics are addressed for each situation. Typical themes include: demographic characteristics, cultural values, educational systems, the role of testing, and current educational reform movements.

A separate, follow-up study will conduct a series of ethnographic studies of several of these environments in an attempt to describe, rather than quantify, the qualities of these societies that motivate parents and students to value learning and to seek knowledge. Its results will be published in 1993.

BRAZIL

No. of 13-year-olds in country	3,383,600
% of 13-year-olds in IAEP frame	3%
Per Capita GNP (US $)	$2,245
% of GNP spent on education	3.3%

One of the largest countries in the world, with an area over 8.5 million square kilometers and a population of 150 million, it presents some problems which are typical of developed countries and others which are common to underdeveloped regions. In spite of its expanse and of the influence of different ethnic groups (Europeans, Africans, and Asians), it has managed, throughout its history, to maintain its linguistic unity in spite of its cultural diversity.

Regular education in Brazil consists of pre-school, for children under 7, which is not compulsory, elementary school from 7 to 14 years of age, and secondary school from 15 to 18 years of age. Access to higher education is achieved by means of highly selective examination.

The complexity of the education system presents problems as in almost all Latin American countries. The major national concern in elementary school is a cycle of repeating grades culminated by students dropping out. Even in the first grade, 52 percent of the students fail to complete the requirements. Failure rates are particularly high in grades 4 through 7. Although elementary school is available to all, it only reaches 87 percent of the 30 million children between the ages of 7 and 14. The great majority of children do not manage to finish the eight years of schooling required by law. The illiteracy rate, which was 26.0 percent in 1980 dropped to 18.8 percent in 1989; the largest pockets of illiteracy occur in the northeastern part of Brazil (36.5 percent).

Another current problem concerns the training of 1.2 million teachers for elementary school. Approximately 230,000 teachers, mainly in the rural and poorer areas, do not have formal teacher training .

There is great concern over investment in the various levels of the educational system. Constitutionally, the federal government must invest 18 percent of its national budget in education. While many state and municipal governments must invest 25 percent each of their budgets, some municipal governments are already investing up to 30 or 40 percent because they consider education an important national challenge.

CANADA

No. of 13-year-olds in country	361,600
% of 13-year-olds in IAEP frame	94%
Per Capita GNP (US $)	$17,309
% of GNP spent on education	7.4%

An enormous land mass occupying well over one-half of the North American continent, Canada's population of 26.5 million includes more than 6.5 million whose primary language is French. About 15 percent of the total population are "New Canadians," immigrants who have recently arrived from Asia, Europe, Central and South America, and Africa. This significant population of students who speak different languages and who reflect different cultures represents a major challenge to the educational system.

Each of the 10 provinces has its unique demographics, its own distinctive economy, which range from rural agricultural to highly developed industrial and financial centers and its own traditions. Canada refers to itself as a mosaic, an apt description.

Each province considers education to be its own responsibility and not that of the federal government. Nine of the 10 provinces (except for Prince Edward Island, population 130,000) participated in IAEP and each of the nine provincial ministers of education agreed to having its results become part of an all-Canada statistic.

Descriptions of each province's educational priorities can be found on pages 118 through 123.

CHINA

No. of 13-year-olds in country	18,474,000
% of 13-year-olds in IAEP frame	38%
Per Capita GNP (US $)	$356
% of GNP spent on education	2.7%

About 74 percent of the Chinese population lives in rural areas. Although great attention is paid to education, the conditions in many schools are not suitable for specific subject instruction, especially for science education.

Children start school at 6.5 or 7 years of age and a few of them have preschool education. Nine years of compulsory education are divided into 6 years of primary school and 3 years of middle school. Students may enter 3 years of senior middle school (general or vocational), if they pass a highly competitive entrance test.

All students have to take at least one test for each subject at the end of each semester. Groups of students from China regularly attend international competitions in chemistry, physics, and mathematics (the International Mathematics Olympics) and perform with distinction.

The current curricula were designed in 1982. Since the intense entrance tests competition places a heavy burden on students, a reform of school practice is underway. The goals of the reform are: to reduce or eliminate some non-basic knowledge from textbooks and to supplement basic vocational knowledge in middle school.

ENGLAND

No. of 13-year-olds in country	591,900
% of 13-year-olds in IAEP frame	96%
Per Capita GNP (US $)	$10,917
% of GNP spent on education	5.2%

England, the largest of the four countries that comprise the United Kingdom, has a population of 47.5 million. About 92 percent of its people live in cities and towns and England is one of the most densely populated countries in the world. About 2 million English people are from ethnic minority communities with Asian or African-Caribbean origins.

All but a small percentage of schools are maintained by governmental authorities. Under the new Education Reform Act of 1988, schools may seek permission to remove themselves from the control of local authority and can be funded directly by the Department of Education and Science. The Education Reform Act of 1988 also introduced a national curriculum which specifies for separate subject areas, "attainment targets" at 10 different levels and requires testing of all students at ages 7, 11, 14, and 16. Vocational education is also receiving more prominence.

The goal of education is to develop fully the potential and abilities of all individuals. Overall, current educational policies have sought to raise standards at all levels of ability, increase parental choice, make higher education more widely accessible and more responsive to the needs of the economy, and, generally, to the needs of a multi-ethnic society.

FRANCE

No. of 13-year-olds in country	771,700
% of 13-year-olds in IAEP frame	98%
Per Capita GNP (US $)	$16,419
% of GNP spent on education	6.1%

A recent law governing education, enacted in 1989, reaffirms the tradition that elementary schools should give priority attention to the development of the basic skills of reading, writing, and mathematics. These are viewed as essential in order to pursue higher levels of academic achievement. It is anticipated that by the year 2,000, 80 percent of the students will reach their senior year of secondary school (12th grade).

It is a widely held belief that today's youth are less well educated than their predecessors. In the view of many, the present educational system places too much emphasis on studies of the classics with insufficient stress on pre-professional and scientific preparation. This criticism is leveled at both secondary and post-secondary institutions.

Free, public education is considered to be a right of all children regardless of socioeconomic conditions and faithful attendance is a civic responsibility. Access to a university education is obtained through success at the Baccalaureat examination after secondary studies. A successful student may select from most of the universities except medical and special advanced institutions which have further entrance requirements.

Today's teachers, once highly regarded, are accorded much less prestige, even though their recruitment criteria and training are still very rigorous. There are many other career options for competent university graduates especially those skilled in mathematics and the sciences.

School funding is shared by the national government (65 percent), the local community (20 percent), industry (5 percent), and families (10 percent). The curriculum goals are set at the national level but local schools and teachers have increasing freedom to plan the sequence and methodology of instruction. Families are increasingly involved in their children's education and most families help with homework and course selection.

No. of 13-year-olds in country	152,000
% of 13-year-olds in IAEP frame	99%
Per Capita GNP (US $)	$2,490
% of GNP spent on education	5.7%

An industrialized country of close to 10.5 million people (97 percent of which are ethnic Hungarian), Hungary has a long and successful history of valuing education and schooling. Culture and education have always enjoyed high esteem throughout the society.

Like many other Eastern European countries, Hungary is emerging aggressively from Marxist frameworks. Indeed, its efforts to radically change education during the 1980s created as much confusion as it did new direction.

Traditionally, Hungary has had a strong, centralized, and controlled system. Changes in educational legislation and policy in 1985 and 1989 have opened the system to new groups of stakeholders: teachers, unions, employers, and parents. There are strong differences of opinion and debates are underway, but the movement is clearly toward western ideas. Severe budget constraints are slowing the pace of reform and change.

The priorities of the emerging system have been set: changing the foreign language requirements from Russian to other languages, introducing a "new moral basis for learning" that aims at higher education standards and competition, strengthening local control of education, and encouraging and supporting religious institutions.

No. of 13-year-olds in country	70,130
% of 13-year-olds in IAEP frame	93%
Per Capita GNP (US $)	$7,603
% of GNP spent on education	6.7%

Ireland is a small country of 3.5 million people, where agriculture and food production are vital components of its economy. Over the past thirty years the industrial and technological sectors have grown in importance so that today, more than one-half of the population resides in urban areas.

About 55 percent of 4 year olds and 99 percent of 5 year olds are enrolled in primary school. Education is compulsory between the ages of 6 and 15. At age 18, the student enrollment decreases to 40 percent.

Education is centralized and all primary-school teachers follow a common set of curriculum guidelines. In 1971, there was a move to a child-centered curriculum and guidelines were established for all subjects. Mathematics occupies an important role in the curriculum, but science is taught as part of Social and Environmental Studies, and does not receive as much emphasis.

For post-primary schools, the department of education prescribes curricula for a broad range of subjects that lead to public examination — the Junior Certificate after three years and the Leaving Certificate after two additional years.

The teaching profession is highly regarded in Ireland. Students entering teacher-education programs have traditionally been among the most able. There are limited opportunities for advancement, however, and there is concern at the growing imbalance between males and females in the teaching force.

The goal of the educational system is to provide young people with the necessary skills and academic preparation for further personal development, for working life, for leisure, and for living in the community.

ISRAEL

No. of 13-year-olds in country	91,900
% of 13-year-olds in IAEP frame	71%
Per Capita GNP (US $)	$8,882
% of GNP spent on education	10.2%

Israel's short history is a record of rapid and constant change. Its Jewish population is increasing rapidly due to the regular arrival of large numbers of immigrants. The total population of 4.5 million is about 18 percent Arabic. Currently there is a surplus of highly trained people in the society.

The chief goals of Israel's educational policy are the closing of the educational gaps among various segments of the population, promoting social integration, raising the general level of achievement to strengthen the productive sectors of the economy, and promoting Jewish-Zionist consciousness.

The differences among schools in socioeconomic status and scholastic achievement are relatively high and issues of equity, equality, and excellence are currently under discussion. Compensatory extracurricular activities are provided to more than 30 percent of the student population from disadvantaged backgrounds.

All children are legally bound to attend school from ages five to 15. More than 90 percent of the children aged three and four are enrolled in preschool programs. More than 50 percent of the high-school students are enrolled in vocational, technological, and comprehensive secondary education. Others are enrolled in academic education. At age 18, anyone who passes entrance examinations may attend universities. Loans and financial aid are available for higher education, especially to those from poor backgrounds.

Reforms are geared toward decentralization, free choice for parents, and increased community involvement.

No. of 13-year-olds in country	669,600
% of 13-year-olds in IAEP frame	6%
Per Capita GNP (US $)	$13,814
% of GNP spent on education	4.0%

Italy has only been a country for slightly more than 130 years. It is still going through the process of becoming a single society. Although the cultural backgrounds of the various regions are different, the national media have had a strong homogenizing effect.

Economic development is most successful in the northern third of the country where Emilia-Romagna is located and is least evident in the South. About 65 percent of the population lives and works in cities. Even though a host of new values have changed the way people think, certain cultural traditions are still important, as evidenced by the importance of extended families, cooperative societies, and volunteer charitable organizations.

School learning continues to be held in high respect since school certificates and degrees provide access to good jobs and careers. The school system is centralized at the national level but legislation is being considered that will increase the financial and organizational autonomy of local schools. There is a good network of well-equipped vocational and technical schools.

Elementary school teachers increasingly participate in in-service training but this is much less common among secondary school faculty members. The main objective of the fairly strong teachers' associations is to protect their autonomy and areas of responsibility.

The primary school's program is relatively new, established in 1985, and the middle school curriculum, installed in 1979, has been kept current. Secondary schools are being encouraged to conduct research and to use innovative instructional practices. The current economic crisis imposes severe limitations on what is possible, but the concern about future international competition is a constant stimulus for educational improvement. Public schools are under public pressure to improve the quality of general education, to delay student specialization, and to increase counseling services.

JORDAN

No. of 13-year-olds in country	83,000
% of 13-year-olds in IAEP frame	96%
Per Capita GNP (US $)	$1,527
% of GNP spent on education	7.1%

Jordan is a fast-developing country of about 3 million, mostly Moslems with a small percentage of Christians. About 70 percent of the population is accommodated in urban areas.

Education policy is strictly centralized and uniform for the whole country. Since 1964, the aim of the national education system has been to integrate elements of Arabic and Western thought, technology, and scientific development. It also aims at helping every student grow intellectually, socially, physically, and emotionally in order to become an ideal citizen, capable of self-support and of making a positive contribution to society. Focus is centered on the diversification of secondary education (academic and vocational) and on in-service teacher training. School enrollment at the various educational levels has become one of the highest in the world.

However, the quantitative expansion has been at the expense of quality. The ever-increasing use of technology in all aspects of life has prompted a new, 10-year Education Reform Plan (1989-1999). The plan aims at producing graduates equipped with high-quality general education geared towards problem solving, critical thinking, analytical skills, and the ability to apply information in creative and productive ways in order to give Jordan the skill- and knowledge-intensive workforce it needs to develop its domestic technological capacity and to maintain its competitive advantage in the region-wide labor market.

Basic education has been extended to 10 years. Graduates can continue into higher education after passing the General Secondary Education examination.

KOREA

No. of 13-year-olds in country	811,700
% of 13-year-olds in IAEP frame	97%
Per Capita GNP (US $)	$3,883
% of GNP spent on education	4.5%

Korea is an increasingly industrialized nation of 43 million people with a growing economy and a highly centralized government. The population, which is homogeneous in both language and ethnic origins, is growing at a slower pace than in the 1950s and is more than 90 percent literate.

The Education Act of 1948 stipulates that the purpose of education is to "enable every citizen to perfect his personality, uphold the ideals of universal fraternity, develop a capability for self-support in life, and enable him to work for the development of a democratic state and for the common prosperity of all humankind."

Curriculum and instructional reforms in the 1970s decreed that lectures and textbooks be supplemented by multiple-learning materials and extensive use of radio and television programs. Diagnostic tests and student workbooks guide student activity to mastery.

Middle school students study mathematics and science four hours per week in each subject the first year, then three to four hours per week during the second and third years. There are generally 40 to 55 students in a classroom with teachers rather than students rotating rooms.

No. of 13-year-olds in country	422,600
% of 13-year-olds in IAEP frame	1%
Per Capita GNP (US $)	$113
% of GNP spent on education	—

Mozambique's population of 15.5 million is predominantly African. Its African people can be divided into roughly 10 different cultural groups, the largest of which, the Makuo-Iowo, has been heavily influenced by Arab cultural traditions including the Moslem faith. The very small non-African group is largely Portuguese.

Before 1970, most schooling was in the hands of missionaries and the curriculum was heavily influenced by Portuguese history and culture. At that time, it was estimated that only 2 percent of the indigenous population had completed four years of primary education.

Education is now seen as an important vehicle for social change and schooling is linked closely to economic development and political needs. In 1977, education was second only to defense in the national budget.

Elementary school lasts four years and there are three types of secondary schools: lyceum, technical, and agricultural/vocational. The schools' curricula include a substantial amount of health education. Agricultural training is conducted both in schools and on farming sites since learning to grow crops is a national priority.

A shortage of trained teachers has presented Mozambique with a formidable challenge. To fill the need, the government established regional training centers in 1975 where graduates of six years of primary schooling were given six months of teacher training. Teachers typically instruct two different groups of students each day, one in the morning and one in the afternoon.

No. of 13-year-olds in country	151,400
% of 13-year-olds in IAEP frame	68%
Per Capita GNP (US $)	$3,740
% of GNP spent on education	4.4%

Fifteen percent of the Iberian peninsula is home to Portugal's 10.5 million citizens. With historical roots in the Roman, Moslem, and Christian cultures, Portugal has recently joined the European Economic Community (EEC) and is becoming an industrialized country.

Since 1974, in response to the growing demand for secondary education, the country has made energetic and creative efforts to increase the literacy levels of its population through an enormous school literacy program and through the improvement of adult basic education courses.

Nine years of schooling are compulsory for all children. Secondary schools provide optional programs that are predominantly vocational or academic. After their secondary education, students can either enter the work force or go on to universities.

Assessment of student achievement in basic and secondary education is the responsibility of the schools and is accomplished through continuous and final assessments. If students do not attain the necessary results, they are required to repeat a grade level. There are no national examinations.

The ministry of education is responsible for pedagogic, administrative, financial, and disciplinary control of all primary and secondary schools. Since 1987, important measures have been instituted to decentralize, and as a consequence, the schools' autonomy has been increased.

Pre-primary and elementary teachers are trained during a three- or four-year course that includes practice teaching. Secondary-school teachers must hold university degrees in their areas of specialization. There are programs in place to complete the training of uncertified teachers.

The new educational policy envisions the modernization of the country to enable it to meet the challenges of participation in the EEC.

SCOTLAND

No. of 13-year-olds in country	62,100
% of 13-year-olds in IAEP frame	99%
Per Capita GNP (US $)	$10,917
% of GNP spent on education	5.2%

Scotland's tradition of support for a strong and broad educational system is a proud one. There are 750,000 pupils in its primary and secondary schools who are required to continue their education until age 16. Ninety percent of them are in comprehensive schools.

Educational policy is the responsibility of the Scottish education department and 12 local education authorities. Evaluation of the education system is the major responsibility of Her Majesty's Inspectors of Schools, who routinely report on educational institutions.

School teachers are trained for at least four years at the post-secondary level and are traditionally respected members of society, though some feel they are less valued today than in the past. School size ranges widely in terms of number of pupils. There are many very small primary schools reflecting the sparse population in certain parts of the country. A recent development has been the introduction of local school boards, which include both parent and teacher representatives.

A major curriculum and assessment development program is underway for ages 5 through 14 following the successful introduction of new certificate examinations for all pupils at age 16. The emphasis in these examinations and in other assessments is on valid measurement of all relevant knowledge and skills by means of written tests, as well as practical and project work.

SLOVENIA

No. of 13-year-olds in country	30,243
% of 13-year-olds in IAEP frame	97%
Per Capita GNP (US $)	$7,233
% of GNP spent on education	3.4%

Located at the juncture of three major European cultures, Germanic, Romance, and Slavic, Slovenia's educational system for centuries followed Germanic traditions. This pattern abruptly changed during the 19th century occupation by Napoleon's forces and again in 1918 when Slovenia merged with other nations to become Yugoslavia. The first transformation was characterized by Romance influences and the second introduced a Byzantine flavor.

The end of World War II brought with it a Soviet influence in all areas of Slovenia's life, including education. During that time, a number of scholars devoted a great deal of energy to liberalizing those stringent educational concepts and practices.

Education is a strong value among Slovenia's homogeneous and largely Roman Catholic population, and schooling is mandatory until age 15. The objectives of elementary and secondary education include basic and higher-level skills as well as moral values and employment preparation.

Teachers at all levels of education are required to have university degrees and at the secondary level are specialists in their subjects. Teachers are now able to select their own teaching materials and textbooks from local and international sources. Currently there is no national testing or assessment program.

THE SOVIET UNION

No. of 13-year-olds in country	4,485,000
% of 13-year-olds in IAEP frame	60%
Per Capita GNP (US $)	$8728
% of GNP spent on education	7.0%

Until September 1991, the Soviet Union was comprised of 15 republics, with a population of 290 million people of many different cultures and languages. New structures and relationships unfolded as the year drew to a close.

For a long time, almost all schools in the country had one common curriculum and common textbooks were provided to schools for all subjects. Secondary education was characterized by strenuous curriculum requirements and was reserved for students of strong academic ability. Since 1988, the standards for secondary education have been adjusted so that the main goals are now to provide all students a strong basic education, and to develop their personalities and creativity. Also, the years of compulsory education have been reduced from 11 to 9 years.

Instruction in the higher levels of knowledge and skills is provided only for those planning university careers. Higher education is open to all who can pass difficult entrance examinations. Achievement is viewed as the result of diligence, persistence, and intelligence.

Public opinion is that the Soviet Union has too many university graduates whose training is not considered of high quality. The trend is to improve the quality of graduates and to reduce their numbers.

SPAIN

No. of 13-year-olds in country	573,900
% of 13-year-olds in IAEP frame	80%
Per Capita GNP (US $)	$8,078
% of GNP spent on education	3.2%

Spain's 39.5 million people are unevenly distributed throughout the country. During the past decade, its demographics have changed significantly as a declining birth rate has resulted in an increasing percentage of retired workers within the society. The workforce has moved from agricultural, to industrial, and currently is moving to the service sectors of the economy. One of the country's severest problems is a high unemployment rate, especially among the young. This has resulted in higher expectations for better educated and better trained graduates from educational institutions.

The most striking feature of the educational scene in Spain today is the deliberate transfer of responsibility for education to the autonomous communities. A vital issue is the liberation of educational institutions from excessive rules and regulations and the encouragement of local community support and involvement. In 1990 the new federal education law established the sharing of authority and funding of public education by the federal government and the autonomous communities. Its provisions take effect in 1992.

The national administration defines the content of the curriculum for all Spanish schools. However, there are no national examinations; schools evaluate achievement in their own way. Those who wish to teach at any level in the public or private school systems must have a university degree and appropriate pedagogical training.

Education is highly valued in the culture and many families privately fund a variety of educational enrichment activities for their children.

No. of 13-year-olds in country	73,800
% of 13-year-olds in IAEP frame	76%
Per Capita GNP (US $)	$27,693
% of GNP spent on education	4.8%

A small country of 7 million in the heart of Europe, Switzerland is made up of 26 democratic and independent cantons. Sixty-five percent of its population speak German, 18 percent speak French, 10 percent speak Italian, and less than 1 percent, Romansch. The remaining people speak other languages. The economy is moving from an industrial- to a service-centered base. Not currently part of the European Economic Community (EEC), the country is wrestling with decisions about its own future. Because of its political structure, a national decision must reflect the combined wishes of the 26 cantons.

Each canton makes its own decisions concerning educational policy, teacher certification, curriculum, instructional materials, and standards. Regional ministries of education are tiny and act by convening groups of teachers and administrators and reaching consensus on issues affecting schooling. Schools tend to be small and local and are often administered by a senior teacher rather than by a full-time director.

There is growing concern over the level of preparation being provided their young citizens (only 11 percent go on to universities) as they face direct competition from their peers in neighboring countries.

No. of 13-year-olds in country	392,000
% of 13-year-olds in IAEP frame	100%
Per Capita GNP (US $)	$4,355
% of GNP spent on education	3.6%

Taiwan is a mountainous, prosperous, and industrialized nation of 20 million people, 85 percent of whom are Taiwanese and 14 percent mainland Chinese.

Education is highly valued and centralized. All schools use the same set of textbooks. While basic facilities such as laboratories, computers, and instructional materials are readily available, educational experts in Taiwan feel they are not properly used in most schools. Teachers are highly regarded and there is no shortage of mathematics and science teachers.

After-school academic-enrichment programs are popular for secondary school students. Most parents provide strong home support for school programs and regularly pay for extra educational materials.

An important educational goal is to develop a sense of dignity in students by building their confidence in subjects in which they have shown potential. About one quarter of the students leave school for employment at about age 15. The others who pass competitive national entrance examinations go on for technical education or university training.

No. of 13-year-olds in country	3,451,000
% of 13-year-olds in IAEP frame	98%
Per Capita GNP (US $)	$19,789
% of GNP spent on education	7.5%

In the United States, public education extends through grade 12 and about three in four students graduate from high school at the expected time; about 90 percent earn their secondary diplomas by their early 20s. Half of high-school graduates enter college, and about one in four will eventually enter the full-time labor force with a four-year college degree.

At present, the nation is engaged in a concerted effort to raise educational achievement in a system that is highly decentralized. Educational authority for elementary and secondary education exists at the state level and is decentralized considerably beyond that level to about 15,000 local school districts.

The nation's 50 governors and the president have recently established six goals for education to be reached by the year 2000. One such goal is to be *Number 1* in the world in mathematics and science by that year.

The United States has been involved in an educational reform effort for more than a decade. This effort, stimulated by the report of a national Educational Excellence Commission, is being carried out by governors and legislators; mathematics particularly has been a target for improvement. However, the National Assessment of Educational Progress (NAEP), through regular assessments for more than 20 years, has found no sustained improvement in mathematics and science for that period, although there has been a recovery from declines in proficiency during the 1970s.

There are currently under discussion significant changes toward a more centralized system including voluntary national curricula, a national test, and achievement standards. Adoption of these features would constitute a major shift in the United States' educational policy.

These radical departures from traditional practice are being considered and promoted because of concerns about the country's ability to compete successfully in an increasingly technological global market place.

ALBERTA   Alberta is a resource-rich province with a multicultural population of approximately 2.4 million. About 80 percent of the people live in urban centers.

All children in Alberta are entitled to public education and are required to attend school until age 16. The province supports two major school systems in Alberta: public and Catholic. Approximately 20 percent of all students attend Catholic schools.

The provincial government has primary responsibility for education and curricula but shares it with local school boards. Since 1982, student learning has been monitored through a provincial assessment program for students in grades 3, 6, and 9. Provincial examinations, which count for 50 percent of a student's final grade in selected twelfth-grade courses, have been in place since 1984. School boards are responsible for the instructional needs of their students and for individual student progress. The system strives to achieve equity, excellence, and effectiveness in meeting its students' needs.

Alberta is keen on ensuring that its students are adequately prepared to live happily and productively in an international marketplace. Its citizens consider international comparisons, such as IAEP, an important indicator of how well this goal is being achieved.

BRITISH COLUMBIA   Geographically, British Columbia is Canada's third largest province and has a population of about 3 million. Greater Vancouver is home to 50 percent of the population with another 20 percent residing in the towns and cities of the extreme southwest.

British Columbia's society is becoming increasingly diverse. Twenty years ago, immigrants were easily integrated into a Eurocentric education system. Today, special school programs are needed to integrate Asian students into the schools.

The ministry of education, which is responsible for overall funding and direction of the system, plays a leading role both in the development and maintenance of curriculum and educational standards. Local boards of trustees are responsible for distribution of funding, hiring of teachers, and delivery of programs and services.

British Columbia's education system, spurred by the recommendations of the latest Royal Commission, is undergoing considerable — and very exciting — change. Based upon principles concerning the nature of learning, the curriculum and assessment process is learner-focused rather than subject matter-focused. Educational change is well underway, with significant momentum and support.

The purpose of the British Columbia school system is to enable students to develop their individual potential and to acquire the knowledge, skills, and attitudes needed to contribute to a healthy society and a prosperous and sustainable economy.

MANITOBA Sixty percent of this large province's 1 million people live in or near the capital city of Winnipeg. Brandon, the next largest city, has only 40,000 inhabitants.

All students have access to free public education until the age of 21 and attendance is compulsory until age 16. The goals of elementary education are to develop basic skills as well as to introduce students to family and societal values, while secondary schools focus on academic and vocational preparation and the development of critical thinking skills.

Curriculua are designed at the provincial level by committees that develop content descriptions and scope and sequence patterns across grades. Local adaptations are allowed but textbooks and other instructional materials are approved at the provincial level. Evaluation is the responsibility of local faculties but periodic provincial subject matter examinations are administered to 12th graders.

Teachers, who are required to have a university degree, are fairly well regarded and paid on a scale similar to other professionals. There is some concern that some of the many ethnic groups in the province are not represented among Manitoba teachers. Elementary school faculty are more child-focused while secondary teachers are more discipline-oriented. Family participation in school activities varies according to parents' educational and socioeconomic status. Pressure on students to work hard depends upon parental values.

Compared with other Canadian provinces New Brunswick is relatively small in terms of its physical size (72,515 square kilometers). It has a population of 727,000, of which almost half resides in urban areas.

New Brunswick is Canada's only officially bilingual province where about 64 percent of the total population classify themselves as English-speaking and 32 percent claim French as their first language. The remaining 4 percent are bilingual or speak different languages at home.

The provincial government finances all public schools. The curriculum is prescribed and authorized by the ministry of education. The province's schools and school boards are operated on the basis of language. There are 27 English-speaking districts and 15 French-speaking districts with a combined total of 415 schools. Those now entering the teaching profession in New Brunswick must complete a four-year degree program.

Education is deemed necessary for economic self-reliance and human development. Serious efforts are being made to improve and enhance public schooling. Just recently, a provincially financed, full-day kindergarten program was introduced for 5-year-olds. In the near future, the release of a provincially sponsored study dealing with excellence in education is expected to initiate dialogue among all the stakeholders in public education.

NEWFOUNDLAND Newfoundland includes the island portion and a large territory on the mainland of Canada known as Labrador. Although the province is geographically large, it has a small population of just more than 500,000. The total school population, Kindergarten through grade 12, is approximately 125,000 and is decreasing rapidly because of a low birth rate and continuous emigration.

The language of instruction in almost all schools is English. There is a small population of French-speaking natives and immigrants in the province, but 98 percent of those assessed are English-speaking.

Although Newfoundland's per-pupil expenditure is among the lowest in Canada, education is highly valued and the province commits 11.5 percent of its gross national product to it, the highest percentage of the 10 provinces.

The province has a centralized curriculum and the teacher population is well educated. A system of provincial examinations sets the standard for graduation from secondary school, and an assessment program to evaluate strengths and weaknesses in the basic skills areas has been in place for more than a decade.

Although the province was not totally satisfied with its performance on the IAEP testing, the trends of its own testing programs has shown continuous improvement. This gradual improvement gives a real sense of optimism about Newfoundland's education system, and it is felt that good assessment programs with measures of accountability will further improve its education system.

NOVA SCOTIA Nova Scotia is a small province with a total area of 54,400 square kilometers and a population of approximately 895,000. Close to half the population is of British origin and about 6 percent is French. The rest of the population includes sizable groups of Germans, Dutch, Blacks and Native people. Forestry, fishing, mining, construction and agriculture make up a major part of the economy along with service and tourist sectors.

Nova Scotia has many connections with the traditions and values of the British Isles. Education was of particular concern to the settlers, many of whom were from educated British families. Shortly after their arrival they set up schools to ensure the education of their children. The Acadian French also have a significant population and have maintained their culture and language.

All children in Nova Scotia are entitled to a free public school education to the age of 21, and attendance is compulsory from the age of 6 to 16. The provincial government has overall responsibility for the elementary and secondary schools, with 21 local school boards handling the operations of the schools. Funding is allocated on a formula basis with both provincial and local input.

Teacher training is provided at a provincially run teachers' college and at universities. All institutions have supervised practicums as part of their training programs.

Academic, vocational, and technical programs are available to meet the needs of the population. Promotion and placement are a responsibility of local school boards and no central examination system is used. The province does, however, have provincially developed achievement tests at grades 5, 9, and 12 to monitor curriculum throughout the province. These assessment instruments are not used for promotion purposes.

The province is in the process of reviewing curriculum offerings and of developing new guidelines for credit requirements for high school completion and issuance of graduation credentials.

In Ontario, education is the shared responsibility of the ministry of education and the local school boards. The ministry establishes the goals of education, provides broad curriculum guidelines, approves textbooks, establishes requirements for diplomas and certificates for both teachers and students, and distributes operating grants to school boards. It is the responsibility of local school boards to deliver education programs and services to their students.

All permanent residents of Ontario between the ages of 6 and 15 are required by law to attend school. Approximately 2 million students are enrolled in elementary or secondary schools. Instruction in Ontario's schools is offered in either English or French. In 1990-91, close to 98,000 students received their education with French as the language of instruction.

The last decade has seen a significant increase in immigration, and about two-thirds of these new children start school with a first language other than English or French. To serve the needs of the various cultural communities, all newcomers are given the opportunity to take courses in English or French as a second language. Elementary school students are given the opportunity to learn about the language and customs of their home country through the Heritage Languages Program.

Elementary schools attempt to shape a child's attitude toward learning and provide the basic skills and motivation for secondary studies. Secondary schools (grades 9 to 12) offer a wide variety of courses to prepare students for post-secondary education or employment.

The ministry of education does not administer any province-wide examinations. The only school examinations are those given to measure students' readiness for selected academic courses and these are reviewed by the ministry to improve the consistency of evaluation practices across the province.

Quebec has a population of almost 7 million people. The largest linguistic groups are the Francophones (nearly 85 percent) and the Anglophones (more than 12 percent). School attendance is compulsory for all youth from age 6 to 16. Access to the public school system — six years of elementary education, five years of secondary education — is free for all students.

The ministry of education determines the programs of study and the rules governing the organization of educational services and approves textbooks. It also administers compulsory examinations at the end of secondary school.

All elementary and secondary teachers must hold a university degree and are required to follow the same programs of study, although they have a choice of teaching methods and materials. They also have a major part of the responsibility for the summative evaluation of their students' learning.

For the next three years, the ministry's plan of action identifies the following priorities: reduction of the school drop-out rate, consolidation of vocational education reforms and of the improvements that have occurred in general education.

SASKATCHEWAN   Saskatchewan, officially a province of Canada since 1905, has a population of about 1 million. Approximately one-third of the province's people live in the two urban centers of Regina and Saskatoon. Forty-four percent of the province's students are enrolled in rural areas. Ethnic diversity is a feature of Saskatchewan. In addition to the Native people, the province's ethnic makeup reflects waves of immigration from various parts of the world.

Enrollments in kindergarten through grade 12 in publicly funded schools (public and Catholic) are estimated at 200,000 with approximately 10,000 students enrolled in French language schools and French Immersion programs. The department of education issues official curriculum guides and lists of appropriate teaching resources. Alternative English and French programs are offered at the secondary level. The department of education administers provincial examinations in 18 subject areas for grade 12 students. However, only students of non-accredited teachers are obliged to take them.

The curriculum and instruction review process of the 1980s resulted in a new core curriculum. A variety of provincial initiatives in the areas of student, program, and curriculum evaluation are also being undertaken.

IAEP is the first international study in which Saskatchewan has participated in recent years. Comparative information from the project will be valuable to the province's educational community and to the public at large.

Procedural Appendix

The second International Assessment of Educational Progress (IAEP), conducted in 1991, is an international comparative study of the mathematics and science skills of samples of 9- and 13-year-old students from 20 countries. The first IAEP in 1988 provided results on the mathematics and science achievement of 13-year-olds from six countries: Canada (which conducted separate surveys in four provinces), Ireland, Korea, Spain, the United Kingdom, and the United States.[32]

The IAEP applies a technology developed for a United States project, the National Assessment of Educational Progress (NAEP), which has conducted national surveys of the educational achievement of United States' students for more than 20 years. Using reliable and uniform scientific procedures, NAEP has obtained comprehensive educational achievement data and reported trends over time on student performance. Since 1983, Educational Testing Service (ETS) has administered NAEP as well as related projects, including IAEP.

IAEP was designed to collect and report data on what students know and can do, on the educational and cultural factors associated with achievement, and on students' attitudes, backgrounds, and classroom experiences. By utilizing existing NAEP technology and procedures, the time and money required to conduct these international comparative studies was reduced and many interested countries were able to experiment with these innovative psychometric techniques.

After the first international assessment, interest from representatives of several foreign countries prompted ETS staff to develop a proposal for a second international assessment that sought to expand upon the 1988 experience. This second project was a four-part survey: a main assessment of 13-year-olds' performance in mathematics and science; an assessment of 9-year-olds' performance in mathematics and science; an experimental, performance-based assessment of 13-year-olds' ability to use equipment and materials to solve mathematics and science problems; and a short probe of the geography skills and knowledge of 13-year-olds. All countries participated in the main assessment of 13-year-olds; participation in the other assessment components was optional.

---

[32] Archie E. Lapointe, Nancy A. Mead, and Gary W. Phillips, *A World of Differences. An International Assessment of Mathematics and Science.* Princeton, NJ: Educational Testing Service, 1989.

The IAEP project was asked to provide separate, state-level results for the state of Colorado, which opted to assess its 9- and 13-year-old students in mathematics, science, and geography. The results described in this report, however, include performance statistics only for the United States as a whole and for participants from the other 19 countries. The results from the Colorado state project will be reported in a separate publication.

Each participating country was responsible for carrying out all aspects of the project, including sampling, survey administration, quality control, and data entry using standardized procedures that were developed for the project. Several training manuals were developed for the IAEP project. These comprehensive documents, discussed with participants during several international training sessions, explained in detail each step of the assessment process.[33]

The second International Assessment of Educational Progress is supported financially by the National Science Foundation and the U.S. Department of Education's National Center for Education Statistics for the expenses of overall coordination, sampling, data analysis, and reporting. The Carnegie Corporation provided additional funds to cover the travel expenses of some of the participants who could not meet the financial burdens of traveling to the project's coordination and training meetings, held in Canada, England, France, Hong Kong, and the United States. Decisions concerning the design and implementation of the project were made collaboratively by the representatives of the provinces and countries involved in the survey. The National Academy of Sciences' Board on International Comparative Studies in Education reviewed plans for IAEP at several stages of its development and made suggestions to improve the technical quality of the study. The board is responsible for reviewing the soundness of the technical procedures of international studies funded by federal agencies of the U.S. government.

DEVELOPING THE ASSESSMENT The IAEP assessment was developed through a consensus-building process that involved curriculum and measurement experts from each of the participating countries and provinces. As models, several existing NAEP frameworks were reviewed by participants and evaluated as to their appropriateness for their own countries' curriculums. Together, the participants then adapted the NAEP frameworks to reflect an international consensus of subject-specific topics and cognitive processes that they believed reasonably reflected curriculums being implemented in their own school systems.[34]

Once the participants had agreed upon common frameworks and the relative emphases that would be placed on each topic and cognitive process category of the assessment, more than one-half submitted test items from their countries' own assessment programs that they felt were appropriate and met the requirements of the IAEP assessment. Many questions from the United States' NAEP assessments were included as well. These items, more than 1,500, were then distributed to each country and each was evaluated and rated for its quality, relevance to the framework, and appropriateness for that country's culture and curricula. The items with the highest ratings across all countries were placed into a pool of acceptable questions from which a subset was selected and pilot-tested in all of the participating provinces and countries.[35]

---

[33] See the *IAEP Technical Report* for a full discussion of the standardized assessment procedures.

[34] See *The 1991 IAEP Assessment: Objectives for Mathematics, Science, and Geography* for a full discussion of the development of the frameworks and selection of questions.

[35] One participant, Slovenia, joined the project after the pilot testing had been completed.

All questions for the IAEP assessment were screened by subject-matter experts and subjected to ETS editorial and sensitivity review procedures to detect any potential bias or lack of sensitivity to any particular student group. In non-English-speaking countries, each question was translated into the appropriate language and then checked for accuracy by language experts at ETS. The IAEP assessment included 13 separate language groups among the 20 countries. All countries made minor adaptations to the items, such as changing mathematical notations (e.g., decimals points to commas), units of measurement (yards to meters), and the names of people, places, and types of plants and animals to reflect local usage. These adaptations did not alter the psychometric nature or content of the assessment questions.

In the final administration of the assessment, about 70 cognitive test questions or items were selected for each subject area and for each age level. Each assessment contained a range of questions that measured achievement of the objectives developed by the participants. The mathematics portion of the assessment for both 9- and 13-year- olds contained about one quarter constructed-response questions requiring students to generate and write their own answers, while the remaining questions required students to select from several response choices. All of the science and geography items used a multiple-choice format.

FIGURE A.1 describes the percentage distributions of questions for 9- and 13-year-old students by topic and cognitive process. The target percentages of questions within each category were established at the onset of the project. The final numbers and percentages of questions within each topic and process category represent final decisions after examination of the results of pilot-testing in the participating countries. After final data collection, responses for each question were analyzed to ensure the results could be summarized accurately for all populations. At that time, some questions were removed from the summary statistics as indicated in a later section.

Because it is particularly instructive to policymakers and educators to interpret achievement results in context, IAEP developed three separate background questionnaires including one each for the student, the school, and the country. These asked various questions about resources within the school and at home, curricular emphases, instructional practices, as well as other school and non-school factors that may influence learning. In addition, a limited set of subject-specific background questions asked students for information about the mathematics, science, and geography instruction they received and probed their own attitudes about these subjects. In this report, the answers to background questions are examined along with student performance — for example, the relationship between how much television students report watching and their performance on the IAEP assessment. Since IAEP was designed to collect only a limited amount of background information from students at one point in time, these analyses cannot be used to establish cause-and-effect relationships, which may be impacted by a great number of variables.

Some of the countries asked other background questions in addition to those required by the project in order to evaluate issues relevant to their own cultures. These additional items appeared at the end of the commonly agreed-upon questions.

Percentage Distributions of Questions for 9- and
13-Year-Olds by Mathematics Topic and Cognitive Process**

TOPICS	Ages	Target Percentage of Questions	Actual Number of Questions	Actual Percentage of Questions
Numbers and Operations	9	50	32	52
	13	30	28	37
Measurement	9	15	9	15
	13	15	13	17
Geometry	9	15	6	10
	13	20	11	14
Data Analysis, Statistics, and Probability	9	10	8	13
	13	15	9	12
Algebra and Functions	9	10	7	11
	13	20	15	20

PROCESS AREAS				
Conceptual Understanding	9	35	25	40
	13	33	25	33
Procedural Knowledge	9	35	22	35
	13	33	27	36
Problem Solving	9	30	15	24
	13	33	24	32

** Percentages may not total 100 due to rounding.

ASSESSMENT DESIGN   At each age level, two separate booklets, one for each subject area in the main assessment, were prepared. At age 13, the mathematics and science booklets also included a small number of geography items for countries that chose to assess geography. At each age, students were administered either a mathematics or a science booklet. The administration instructions and procedures for both the mathematics and science assessments were identical and permitted sampled students at a particular school to be assessed together in a single 90-minute session.

At age 9, each assessment booklet was composed of five parts called "blocks": four 15-minute blocks of cognitive questions followed by an untimed block of background questions. For age 13, students were administered four 15-minute blocks of cognitive questions, followed by 7 minutes of background questions. Those countries assessing geography also administered a final block that included 7 1/2 minutes of geography items, followed by 2 1/2 minutes of geography-related background questions at the end of the assessment.

In each subject area, one common block, "an overlap block," asked 9- and 13-year-old students to respond to the same set of items. This overlap block permitted IAEP to compare performance at the two age levels. (At age 13, the overlap block contained a few additional questions at the end of the block.)

The test questions in each block were arranged in easy-to-more-difficult order and reflected a broad range of content and cognitive processes based on the frameworks described earlier.

In order to minimize the possible effects of fatigue on final results, the cognitive blocks were administered in two different sequences. Students from one-half of the schools in each country answered the four cognitive blocks sequentially (Part 1, Part 2, Part 3, Part 4) followed by the background questions (Part 5). Students in the other half of the schools responded to the four cognitive blocks in a different order (Part 3, Part 4, Part 1, Part 2) followed by the background questions (Part 5). Countries that opted for the geography assessment administered this block (Part 6) last in all schools.

SAMPLING   The sampling design for the IAEP survey called for representative samples of 3,300 students from about 110 schools in each participating country at each age level. Three countries — Brazil, Korea, and Mozambique — which begin the school year in March, conducted the survey in September 1990. The remaining 17 countries conducted the assessment during an equivalent period in the school year, in March 1991. School samples were drawn from public and private elementary and secondary schools. Samples of 9-and 13-year-old students were drawn from those born during calendar years 1981 and 1977, respectively. Students assessed in Brazil and Korea were six months older (born between July 1, 1976 and June 30, 1977) because they were assessed six months earlier.

The IAEP sample design was a two-stage, stratified, cluster design. The first-stage sampling units were usually individual schools, but in some instances, consisted of two or more small schools (i.e., school clusters). Typically, 110 schools or school clusters were selected with probability proportionate to the estimated number of age-eligible students in the school. At the second stage of sampling, a list of age-eligible students was prepared for each sampled school. A systematic sample of 30 to 35 students was typically drawn from each school and one-half of the sampled students were assigned the mathematics assessment and the remaining half, the science assessment. Thus, each country typically assessed 1,650 students in each subject area at each age level.

Each participating country had the option of selecting its own samples of schools and students or of having Westat, Inc., a sampling and survey design subcontractor for the project, select the samples. Five participants, including Korea, Mozambique, Ontario, Quebec, and the United States, opted to have Westat select their samples. Countries and provinces that elected to select their own samples were trained in the use of specially designed computer software created for this purpose.

Most of the participants used the IAEP design and software. Special circumstances in some of the participating countries necessitated the development and use of alternative sampling procedures. Their designs, sampling procedures, and final weights were reviewed and approved by Westat. For example, China and the Soviet Union used a three-stage sample (first selecting primary sampling units, PSUs, consisting of defined geographic areas) because centralized lists of school enrollments for the entire country do not exist. In England and Switzerland, the need to sample whole classrooms meant that alternative within-school sampling procedures using classrooms as sampling units had to be designed and implemented.[36]

---

[36] The sample designs used by each participant are described in detail in the *IAEP Technical Report*.

Some countries drew samples from virtually all children in the appropriate age group and others confined their assessments to specific geographic areas, language groups, or grade levels. The definition of populations often coincided with the structure of school systems, political divisions, and cultural distinctions. All countries limited their assessment to students in school, which for some, meant excluding significant numbers of age-eligible children.

In Brazil, two separate samples of 13-year-olds were drawn, one each from the cities of São Paulo and Fortaleza. In Mozambique, a single sample of 13-year-olds was drawn across two cities, Maputo and Beira.

In Canada, nine out of 10 provinces drew separate samples of 13-year-olds and five of these drew separate samples of English-speaking and French-speaking schools, for a total of 14 separate samples. Taken together, these samples represent 94 percent of the 13-year-olds in Canada. Four Canadian provinces — six separate samples — participated in the 9-year-old assessment, representing 74 percent of the children that age in Canada. The assessment of native English-speaking students who were enrolled in French immersion programs (where they receive all or most of their instruction in French) was not handled in a consistent way across the provinces. In Manitoba and Saskatchewan they were a part of the French samples and assessed in French. In Alberta, British Columbia, Newfoundland, Nova Scotia, and Quebec they were part of the English samples and assessed in English. In Ontario, French-immersion students were part of the English sample and some schools assessed these students in English and others assessed them in French.

The characteristics of the sampling frame of each of the participating countries at each age level are documented in FIGURES A.2 and A.3.

The first four columns of Figures A.2 and A.3 indicate the representativeness of the sampling frames. The first column provides the number of age-eligible children in the country. The second and third columns give the estimated percentages of age-eligible children included in the sampling frame for the country as a whole and for the defined population. If the defined population is the whole country, these two percentages are the same. If the population is limited to a specific region or language group, the percentage in the third column reflects the coverage of the sampling frame within those defined limits.

Age 9
Sampling Frame

	No. of Age-eligible Children in Country[1]	Estimated Percent of Age-eligible Children in Country Included in the Sampling Frame	Estimated Percent of Age-eligible Children in Defined Population Included in the Sampling Frame	Percent of Age-eligible Children in School[2]	No. of Schools in Sampling Frame	Estimated No. of Age-eligible Students in School Frame	Estimated No. of Age-eligible Students Represented by Study
Canada[3]	364,000	74	97	96 – 99.6	5,595	267,797	238,295
England	625,400[4]	97	97	100	15,715	571,091	553,543[2]
Hungary	125,700	99	99	97.8	2,609	159,649	122,651
Ireland	65,700	94	94	99.8	2,619	66,609	60,040
Israel	98,000	71	93	98.5	1,045	61,927	52,344
Italy	599,700	4	98	99.0	290	31,680	25,794
Korea	809,800	95	95	98.9	4,990	804,500	762,161
Portugal	137,200	81	81	100	7,818	110,352	120,701
Scotland	64,900	98	98	100	2,054	64,919	63,308
Slovenia	29, 279[5]	97	97	96.1	399	28,572	26,870
Soviet Union	4,645,000[6]	63	99	—	52,178	2,822,700	2,258,384
Spain	482,100	80	96	100	9,983	436,399	397,972
Taiwan	409,000[7]	97	97	98	1,754	387,021	379,881
United States	3,660,000[8]	97	97	98.9	70,405	3,460,234	3,069,620[4]

— Information is not available.
[1] *1988 Demographic Yearbook*, Fortieth Issue, New York: United Nations, 1990.
[2] Estimates were provided by project director from available data.
[3] Details of the sampling frames of the individual Canadian populations are provided in the *IAEP Technical Report*.
[4] Including Wales.
[5] *Annual Statistical Report of Slovenia*, Ljubljana, Slovenia: Central Statistics Office, 1990.
[6] Counts are based on the 1989 census.
[7] *Education Statistics of the ROC*, Taipei: Ministry of Education, 1989.
[8] *Current Population Reports, Population Estimates and Projections*, Series p. 25, No. 1045. Washington, DC: U.S. Department of Commerce, n.d..

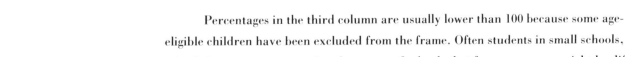

Percentages in the third column are usually lower than 100 because some age-eligible children have been excluded from the frame. Often students in small schools, schools in remote areas, or in other types of schools that for some reason might be difficult to assess have been excluded. In some cases, students in particular grades have been excluded. Also, since the sample is school-based, children who do not attend schools have been excluded, and the magnitude of this exclusion is indicated in the fourth column, the percentage of age-eligible children attending school. If the estimated percentage of age-eligible children in the defined population included in the sampling frame (column 3) is below 90 percent, the frame is not considered to be representative of the target-age population and results from these samples are presented as a special group of populations with exclusions and low participation.

	No. of Age-eligible Children in Country[1]	Estimated Percent of Age-eligible Children in Country Included in the Sampling Frame[2]	Estimated Percent of Age-eligible Children in Defined Population Included in the Sampling Frame[2]	Percent of Age-eligible Children in School[3]	No. of Schools in Sampling Frame	Estimated No. of Age-eligible Students in School Frame	Estimated No. of Age-eligible Students Represented by Study
Brazil, São Paulo	3,383,600	3	80	92	1,565	126,053	97,652
Brazil, Fortaleza	3,383,600	<1	56	85	388	13,861	13,612
Canada[4]	361,600	94	95	94 – 100	5,555	345,827	310,274
China	18,474,000	38	45	51	60,790	7,117,960	6,388,601
England	591,900[5]	96	96	100	5,078	515,000	504,590
France	771,700	98	98	99.7	6,678	661,728	672,764
Hungary	152,000	99	99	97.8	2,609	159,649	149,647
Ireland	70,130	93	93	99.8	1,002	71,512	63,791
Israel	91,900	71	90	95.5	651	66,777	55,348
Italy	669,600	6	98	98.2	391	38,127	36,817
Jordan	83,000	96	96	98.5	1,462	77,947	74,290
Korea	811,700	97	97	95.9	2,258	709,903	671,867
Mozambique	422,600	1	25	25.5	13	6,322	4,988
Portugal	151,400	68	68	86.1	1,364	110,992	149,228
Scotland	62,100	99	99	100	458	60,265	55,398
Slovenia	30,243[6]	97	97	95.4	407	28,150	26,640
Soviet Union	4,485,000[7]	60	99	—	49,491	2,619,300	2,374,694
Spain	573,900	80	96	100	9,663	524,567	440,322
Switzerland	73,800	76	92	100	classes only	52,819	52,726
Taiwan	392,000[8]	100	100	90	669	346,619	338,249
United States	3,451,000[9]	98	98	99.0	73,769	3,518,390	3,028,386

— Information is not available.

[1] *1988 Demographic Yearbook,* Fortieth Issue, New York: United Nations, 1990.

[2] Estimates were provided by project director from available data.

[3] Estimates for Fortaleza, Brazil, China, Mozambique, and Portugal take into account the age-eligible children who have dropped out of school; estimates for the other populations (those with at least 90 percent of age-eligible children in school) do not take into account age-eligible children who have dropped out.

[4] Details of the sampling frames of the individual Canadian populations are provided in the *IAEP Technical Report.*

[5] Including Wales.

[6] *Annual Statistical Report of Slovenia,* Ljubljana, Slovenia: Central Statistics Office, 1990.

[7] Counts are based on the 1989 census.

[8] *Education Statistics of the ROC,* Taipei: Ministry of Education, 1989.

[9] *Current Population Reports, Population Estimates and Projections,* Series p. 25, No. 1045, Washington, DC: U.S. Department of Commerce, n.d..

The last three columns of Figures A.2 and A.3 document the characteristics of the sampling frame and the achieved samples of each participant. The fifth column indicates the number of schools in the sampling frame and the sixth column, the estimated number of age-eligible students in those schools used to draw the school sample (i.e., the estimated measure of size). The last column shows the estimated number of age-eligible students represented by those who actually took the assessment (i.e., the sum of the student sampling weights).

Some inconsistencies can be seen in Figures A.2 and A.3 because data are drawn from different sources, cover different time frames, and in some cases reflect estimates. For example, estimated numbers of age-eligible students are often based on grade data rather than age data. On occasion, the estimated number of age-eligible students in the school frame or represented by the study is larger than the total number of age-eligible children in the country. Also, the estimated percentage of age-eligible children in the country included in the sampling frame is not always derived directly from the total number of age-eligible students in the school frame or represented by the study and the total number of age-eligible children in the country. The numbers presented represent the best available data for each characteristic of the sampling frames.

The numbers of schools and students assessed and the school and student cooperation rates for each participant at each age level are provided in FIGURES A.4 and A.5 that follow. Typically, if more than 5 percent of the originally sampled schools or school clusters refused to cooperate in the survey, alternate schools were selected. The total number of schools assessed (column 1) includes both originally selected and alternate schools that actually participated in the assessment. The total number of students assessed (column 2) includes all students assessed in mathematics in those schools.

Mathematics, Age 9
Numbers of Schools and Students Assessed and School and Student Cooperation Rates

	Number of Schools Assessed	Number of Students Assessed	Weighted School Response Rate	Student Completion Rate in Participating Schools	Combined Overall Response Rate
Canada[1]	797	9,365	97	95	92
England	89	1,071	56	94	53
Hungary	144	1,632	100	94	94
Ireland	126	1,261	94	97	91
Israel	116	1,612	100	96	96
Italy	70	1,142	65	94	61
Korea	114	1,630	100	98	98
Portugal	128	1,419	89	97	86
Scotland	90	1,151	62	93	58
Slovenia	113	1,609	100	94	94
Soviet Union	139	1,842	98[2]	92	84
Spain	110	1,624	89	95	85
Taiwan	110	1,814	100	99	99
United States	105	1,489	80	93	74

[1] Details of participation in individual Canadian populations are provided in the *IAEP Technical Report*.
[2] This is the school response rate within participating PSUs. The overall student response rates given in this table reflect nonresponse at all levels of sampling, including the sampling of PSUs.

Mathematics, Age 13
Numbers of Schools and Students Assessed and School and Student Cooperation Rates

	Number of Schools Assessed	Number of Students Assessed	Weighted School Response Rate	Student Completion Rate in Participating Schools	Combined Overall Response Rate
Brazil, São Paulo	108	1,484	95	93	88
Brazil, Fortaleza	118	1,482	97	93	89
Canada[1]	1,373	19,691	97	94	91
China	119	1,774	100[2]	99	96
England	83	890	52	91	47
France	103	1,768	93	97	90
Hungary	144	1,632	100	93	93
Ireland	110	1,654	96	94	90
Israel	110	1,583	98	95	93
Italy	90	1,478	82	95	78
Jordan	106	1,580	85	99	84
Korea	110	1,637	100	99	99
Mozambique	13	1,174	100	66	66
Portugal	89	1,510	82	94	77
Scotland	92	1,564	82	90	74
Slovenia	114	1,596	100	95	95
Soviet Union	138	1,816	97[2]	95	86
Spain	109	1,624	93	96	89
Switzerland	397	3,644	82	98	80
Taiwan	108	1,780	100	98	98
United States	96	1,407	77	92	71

[1] Details of participation in individual Canadian populations are provided in the *IAEP Technical Report*.
[2] This is the school response rate within participating PSUs. The overall student response rates given in this table reflect nonresponse at all levels of sampling, including the sampling of PSUs.

The school response rates in the third column reflect only the percentage of schools that were originally sampled and that participated in the assessment. The school response rate was calculated by using weights that take into account the number of students that would have been sampled if the school had participated in the study. Thus, the cooperation of large schools (in terms of expected numbers of students) received greater weight than the cooperation of smaller schools. The student completion rate (column 4) is the percentage of sampled students that were actually assessed in both the original and alternate schools. This rate was calculated without weights. The combined overall response rate (column 5) is the product of the weighted school response rate and student completion rate.

Populations with a combined nonresponse rate below .80 but at least .70 have been identified in all figures that show performance data with a warning that the results should be interpreted with caution because of possible nonresponse bias. Populations with a combined nonresponse rate below .70 have been identified in all figures that show performance data with a warning that results should be interpreted with extreme caution because of possible large nonresponse biases, and for that reason, these populations have been listed in a special group of populations with exclusions or low participation.

Sampling weights have been adjusted to account for school and student nonresponse. No other adjustments, such as post-stratification, have been made.[37]

Typically, most students age 9 are in their third and fourth years of schooling, and most students age 13 are in their seventh and eight years. However, because the entry age and promotion policies differ from country to country, the distributions of students by year in school vary among participants. While children in most countries begin their first year of schooling at age 6, children in England and Scotland start at age 5 and children in Brazil, parts of China, Mozambique, Slovenia, parts of the Soviet Union, and German Switzerland do not start until age 7. In Ireland, children are required to begin school at age 6 and in the distributions presented in FIGURES A.6 and A.7 this is considered to be year 1. However, almost all Irish children have had two additional years of infant school, which is available to all children and which includes academic work.

[37]Details of the computation of school and student weight are provided in the *IAEP Technical Report*.

Mathematics, Age 9
Percentage Distributions of Sampled Students by Year of Schooling**

	Year 2	Year 3	Year 4	Year 5	Year 6
Canada	0	17	81	1	0
England[1]	0	0	37	63	0
Hungary	0	51	49	0	0
Ireland[2]	2	57	40	0	0
Israel	0	9	91	0	0
Italy	0	0	99	1	0
Korea	0	28	72	0	0
Portugal	0	13	87	0	0
Scotland[1]	0	0	0	83	16
Slovenia	3	89	9	0	0
Soviet Union	7	68	24	0	0
Spain	0	10	90	0	0
Taiwan	0	30	70	0	0
United States	2	36	62	0	0

** Percentages may not total 100 due to rounding.
[1] Since children are age 5 when they begin their first academic year of school, the majority of 9-year-olds are in their fifth year of school.
[2] Children are required to begin school at age 6 and for these distributions this is considered to be year 1. However, almost all children have had two additional years of infant school, which is available to all children and which includes academic work.

Mathematics, Age 13
Percentage Distributions of Sampled Students by Year of Schooling**

	Year 5	Year 6	Year 7	Year 8	Year 9	Year 10
Brazil	29	29	34	8	0	0
Canada	0	1	18	80	1	0
China	0	0	71	26	3	0
England[1]	0	0	0	48	52	0
France	0	10	31	56	3	0
Hungary	0	3	38	58	0	0
Ireland[2]	0	1	62	37	0	0
Israel	0	0	10	89	0	0
Italy	0	0	9	90	0	0
Jordan	0	5	16	78	1	0
Korea	0	0	30	67	2	0
Mozambique	0	88	12	1	0	0
Portugal	3	6	35	56	1	0
Scotland[1]	0	0	0	1	85	14
Slovenia	0	6	81	13	0	0
Soviet Union	0	0	14	85	1	0
Spain	0	0	21	78	0	0
Switzerland	0	7	69	24	0	0
Taiwan	0	0	28	72	0	0
United States	0	4	35	60	1	0

** Percentages may not total 100 due to rounding.
[1] Since children are age 5 when they begin their first academic year of school, the majority of 13-year-olds are in their 9th year of school.
[2] Children are required to begin school at age 6 and for these distributions this is considered to be year 1. However, almost all children have had two additional years of infant school, which is available to all children and which includes academic work.

Each participating country and Canadian province appointed a National Coordinator to administer data collection for the IAEP project. These individuals were provided with a detailed *IAEP National Coordinator's Manual* and training at one of two regional meetings. While participants strove to implement all procedures as outlined, occasionally they encountered situations where deviations were necessary. The administration procedures used by each participating country and Canadian province are summarized in FIGURE A.8.

Local school personnel or external administrators conducted the assessments at the selected schools, using standardized procedures provided in the IAEP *School Coordinator's Manual* during the specified assessment period (see Figure A.8). The administration script read aloud to students and the time limits for each part of the test were the same in all countries.

In addition to providing administrators with the IAEP *School Coordinator's Manual*, IAEP recommended that each country train each administrator in the procedures for conducting the assessment. To facilitate the training process, IAEP developed a training package that included a script for the trainers, suggested overhead transparencies, and simulations on how to complete the forms and implement the procedures. Based on their own testing programs, participants determined which method of training would be most helpful and efficient. Some of the countries conducted regional training sessions or used telephone conferences and audiotapes to supplement the IAEP *School Coordinator's Manual* (see Figure A.8).

Countries were provided with a practice test that students could take a day or two prior to the assessment to help them prepare for the assessment. It was designed particularly for students who were unfamiliar with multiple-choice formats. Countries were not required to use the practice test if they felt it was unnecessary (see Figure A.8).

In order to ensure that the assessments had been conducted uniformly in all locations, each country was required to develop and follow a quality-control plan approved by ETS. The participants were encouraged to conduct unannounced site visits to a random number of participating schools on the day of the assessment to determine if the standardized procedures of the assessment were being followed. Observation of 20 percent on the assessments was recommended. Because of limited resources, some countries conducted fewer visits (see Figure A.8). Some countries felt that making unannounced site visits would jeopardize their relationship with schools and instead implemented informal monitoring systems.

The quality control visits were typically conducted by officials from the ministry, research center, or by external staff hired and trained in IAEP test administration procedures. An *IAEP Quality Control Observers Manual* was developed as a guide for observation visits. The main purpose of the visits was to document that the test administrator had maintained test security and correctly followed the administration script, time limits, and rules for answering student questions.

Overall Summary of
Test Administration by
Country and Canadian Province

	Scheduled Assessment Month	Who Gave Test	Test Administrator Trained	Practice Test Used	Percent of Site Visits	Percent of Accurate Scores***
Brazil, Fortaleza and São Paulo	Sept. '90	External Administrators	Yes	No	23	99.5
Canada, Alberta	March '91	School Personnel	No	No	20	99.7
British Columbia	March '91	School Personnel	No	No	Informal	99.5
Manitoba	March '91	School Personnel	Yes	No	18	99.6
New Brunswick, English	March '91	School Personnel	Yes	Optional	15	99.8
New Brunswick, French	March '91	School Personnel	Yes	Yes	39	Not Done
Newfoundland	March '91	School Personnel	No	No	21	99.0
Nova Scotia	March '91	School Personnel	No	No	21	99.9
Ontario	March '91	School Personnel	Yes	Yes (9) Optional (13)	19	98.1
Quebec	March '91	School Personnel	Yes	Yes	22	98.2
Saskatchewan	March '91	School Personnel	No	No	Informal	99.3
China	March '91	School Personnel	Yes	No	19	99.3
England	March. '91	School Personnel	No	No	Informal	99.6
France	March '91	School Personnel	Yes	Yes	21	99.4
Hungary	March '91	External Adminstrators	Yes	No	16	99.5
Ireland	March '91	School Personnel	No	No	Informal	99.6
Israel	March '91	School Personnel	Yes	No	19	100
Italy	March '91	School Personnel	Yes	No	21	98.0
Jordan	March '91	School Personnel	Yes	Yes	24	99.3
Korea	Sept. '90	School Personnel	Yes	Yes	20	99.5
Mozambique	Sept. '90	External Administrator	Yes	No	Informal	Not Done
Portugal	March '91	External Administrators	Yes	Yes (9) No (13)	20	99.8
Scotland	March '91	School Personnel	No	Optional (9) No (13)	Informal	99.2
Slovenia	March '91	External Administrators	Yes	Optional	10	99.8
Soviet Union	March '91 (9) April '91 (13)	School Personnel	Yes	Yes	52	99.3
Spain	March '91	External Administrators	Yes	Optional (9) No (13)	20	99.7
Switzerland	March '91	School Personnel	Yes	No	Informal	99.5
Taiwan	March '91	School Personnel	Yes	No	20	99.8
United States	March '91	School Personnel	No	No	16	99.8

*** This number represents the mean of the percents of accurate scores for mathematics constructed-response questions.
— Information is not available.

The project considered quality control of administration crucial to the validity and reliability of assessment results, and therefore, a second, independent group of observers was hired by ETS to make site visits within each of the countries. These observers, trained in the same procedures, in most cases, were fluent in the language of the assessment and familiar with the cultural idiosyncrasies of the populations being assessed. They visited testing sessions and interviewed project personnel on the management of the assessment in all participating countries except Brazil and Mozambique.

DATA PROCESSING Once the assessments had been completed, the booklets were returned to a central location within each country and checked for completeness. The constructed-response items for the mathematics assessment were hand-scored, using standardized scoring guides. Ten percent of these booklets were scored by a second scorer. The average of the percentage of accurate scores across all questions is given in Figure A.8. Afterwards, all responses were either key-entered or scanned into a database.

Each country was responsible for developing a preliminary data file that followed standard formats and contained student responses and other demographic information for each population assessed. Requirements for the data files, including 100 percent verification of key entry, were specified in the *IAEP Data Processing Manual*. Specially designed software was created for data entry and verification, and data processing personnel from each country received training in these procedures at one of five regional meetings. All participants were required to use the verification program, which checked for duplicate identification numbers and responses that fell outside the expected ranges, and to resolve inconsistencies in the data.

All database management and data analysis activities were conducted by a Canadian Data Analysis Group consisting of individuals from Educan, Inc., GRICS, the Quebec Ministry of Education, and the University of Montreal.

Completed data files were sent to the IAEP Data Processing Center where files were verified a second time and item analyses were conducted to identify other problems in the data files. In several cases, responses to a specific item from a specific population had to be removed from the master data file because of a printing or translation error. Each participant also sent 10 samples (selected at random) of each type of test booklet and questionnaire so that the data files could be re-checked against the original source documents. If the student response portion of the records that were checked contained one percent or more errors, participants were required to rekey the entire data file. This happened in one instance and the data file was rekeyed.

ITEM PERCENTS CORRECT The first stage of analysis involved the calculation of the percentage of correct answers and standard errors for individual questions. For each population, the weighted percentage of correct answers was calculated for each question. The results of students who omitted questions at the ends of sections because they did not reach them were excluded from the calculations for those questions. For each percent correct, an estimate of its standard error was calculated using the jackknife procedure. Percentages and standard errors were calculated for subgroups within each population, including gender and grade. Statistics for Canada were calculated using an appropriately weighted sample of responses drawn from the individual Canadian populations.

To be most useful, survey results should provide educators, policymakers, and the public at large with an easily understood summary of performance in a specific content area, while taking into account country-to-country differences in performance within sub-areas of the subject being assessed. For example, it is possible that a certain topic within a subject might be more difficult for some populations than for others. This country-by-topic interaction, due to a large extent to differences in curricular emphasis, might affect the relative performance standings of the various populations depending upon the relative importance assigned to each of the topics in the overall summary measure.

To meet these dual needs, IAEP conducted a series of analyses before deciding which questions could be combined into a summary measure of mathematics. These analyses began with a matrix with rows corresponding to the countries and with columns corresponding to the cells in the topic by process matrix (e.g., one cell consisted of questions measuring the Numbers and Operations topic and the Conceptual Understanding process). The entries in the table were the average percent correct for a given country for questions in the topic-by-process cell. These average percents correct were transformed into normal deviates and then converted into country-by-cell interactions by removing the overall country and topic-by-process main effects. The interaction matrix was then analyzed using the interactive K-Means cluster-analysis technique.[38] The aim of the analysis was to obtain aggregate sets of questions where the country-by-cell type interaction within an aggregate set was negligible. Solutions involving one, two, three, and sometimes more clusters were examined in order to define legitimate groups of items for summary analyses. These analyses confirmed the reasonableness of summarizing across all questions in mathematics at each age level except for one item at age 9 and one at age 13 that were identified in the differential item functioning (DIF) analyses described below.

While cluster analyses focus on differences in performance across groups of questions defined by topics and processes, differential item functioning (DIF) analyses identify differences in performance on a single item. These latter analyses are likely to pick up the effects of cultural and linguistic differences as well as curricular differences. A generalized Mantel-Haenszel statistic was used for these analyses.[39] A test question was identified as functioning differentially across populations if students of equal ability but from different populations had different probabilities of answering it correctly.

Differential item functioning analyses were conducted for each question for each country. For countries assessing in more than one language, items within language groups were considered separately. The questions were then ranked in terms of their across-population DIF statistics and the magnitude of their ordered DIF statistics was compared with reference values that would be expected to be obtained if there were no differential item functioning for any question. Questions with across-population DIF statistics that were significantly larger than the reference values were identified as outliers. These questions were deemed to be exhibiting differential item functioning and therefore inappropriate for inclusion in summary statistics.

---

[38] J.A. Hartigan and M.A. Wong, A K-Means Clustering Algorithm, *Applied Statistics*, Vol. 28, No. 1, 1979.

[39] Grant W. Somes, The Generalized Mantel-Haenszel Statistic, *The American Statistician*, Vol. 40, No. 2, 1986.

The differential item functioning analyses identified one question at age 9 and one question at age 13 that were outliers. These questions were removed from subsequent summary analyses. The question removed at age 9 was categorized as Algebra and Functions, Conceptual Understanding. The question removed at age 13 was categorized as Numbers and Operations, Procedural Knowledge.

SUMMARY MEASURES Weighted average percentages of correct responses were computed for each topic and process area and across all questions within mathematics for each population. They were computed by averaging across the individual weighted percents correct for the items included in each category. For each average, an estimate of its standard error was calculated using the jackknife procedure. Average percentages and standard errors were calculated for subgroups within each population including gender and grade. Statistics for Canada were calculated using an appropriately weighted sample of responses drawn from the individual Canadian populations.

TESTS OF SIGNIFICANCE A Bonferroni multiple comparison procedure was used to determine the statistical significance of differences in performance between participating countries. This procedure holds the probability of falsely declaring a significant difference to 5 percent across the entire set of possible pairwise comparisons between the comprehensive populations, populations with exclusions or low participation, and Canadian populations.

The procedure used to determine the statistical significance of differences in the performance between males and females was to divide the difference between the two averages by the square root of the sum of the two variances. Values of 2 or larger were cited as statistically significant.

The procedure used to determine the statistical significance of differences in performance of a population on a particular topic or process area and on the mathematics test as a whole looked at the difference between a population's deviation from the average for the topic or process and its deviation from the overall average. Values greater than 0 indicated performance in the category was relatively higher than performance overall and values less than 0 indicated performance was relatively lower than performance overall. If the absolute value of the difference in those deviations was equal to or greater than twice the standard error of that difference, it was cited as statistically significant.

The linear relationship between levels of a background variable and average performance was estimated by applying a set of orthogonal contrasts to the set of average performance by level of the background variable. The linear component was estimated by the sum of $b = \sum c_j x_j$, where the x_j are the average percent correct for students with level j on the background variable and the c_j are defined so that b corresponds to the slope of the unweighted regression of the average percents correct on the levels of the background variable. The statistical significance of b was evaluated by comparison with its standard error, computed as the square root of the sum $\sum c_j^2 SE_j^2$, where SE_j is the standard error of x_j. Values of b that were equal to or greater than twice the standard error were considered to be statistically significant.

Data Appendix

Mathematics: Age 13

	TOTAL	MALE	FEMALE		TOTAL	MALE	FEMALE
IAEP AVERAGE	58.3			**Canadian Populations**			
Populations				ALBERTA	64.0 (0.7)	64.5 (0.8)	63.4 (0.8)
				BRITISH COLUMBIA	66.2 (0.7)	66.8 (0.8)	65.4 (1.0)
BRAZIL, FORTALEZA	32.4 (0.6)	35.2 (0.9)	30.5 (0.6)	MANITOBA-ENGLISH	58.0 (0.8)	58.0 (0.9)	57.9 (1.0)
BRAZIL, SÃO PAULO	37.0 (0.8)	37.9 (0.9)	36.2 (0.9)	MANITOBA-FRENCH	63.1 (0.6)	64.5 (1.1)	61.9 (0.8)
CANADA	62.0 (0.6)	63.0 (0.7)	60.9 (0.6)	NEW BRUNSWICK-ENGLISH	57.7 (0.5)	58.3 (0.7)	57.1 (0.7)
CHINA	80.2 (1.0)	81.7 (1.0)	78.5 (1.1)	NEW BRUNSWICK-FRENCH	60.6 (0.4)	60.5 (0.6)	60.7 (0.6)
ENGLAND	60.6 (2.2)	60.8 (3.0)	60.4 (2.2)	NEWFOUNDLAND	58.9 (0.6)	57.8 (0.7)	59.9 (0.8)
FRANCE	64.2 (0.8)	65.5 (0.9)	62.8 (0.9)	NOVA SCOTIA	59.7 (0.6)	60.7 (0.9)	58.8 (0.8)
HUNGARY	68.4 (0.8)	68.5 (1.0)	68.3 (0.9)	ONTARIO-ENGLISH	58.3 (0.8)	59.3 (1.0)	57.4 (0.9)
IRELAND	60.5 (0.9)	62.6 (1.2)	58.4 (1.1)	ONTARIO-FRENCH	53.5 (0.6)	53.5 (0.8)	53.5 (0.8)
ISRAEL	63.1 (0.8)	64.4 (0.9)	61.8 (1.1)	QUEBEC-ENGLISH	65.7 (0.9)	65.7 (1.6)	65.7 (0.8)
ITALY	64.0 (0.9)	65.8 (1.1)	62.1 (0.9)	QUEBEC-FRENCH	68.7 (0.7)	69.8 (1.0)	67.5 (0.8)
JORDAN	40.4 (1.0)	41.4 (1.2)	39.1 (1.9)	SASKATCHEWAN-ENGLISH	62.0 (0.7)	63.2 (0.9)	60.7 (1.0)
KOREA	73.4 (0.6)	74.4 (0.9)	72.2 (1.0)	SASKATCHEWAN-FRENCH	67.5 (1.0)	68.8 (1.5)	66.3 (1.4)
MOZAMBIQUE	28.3 (0.3)	28.8 (0.5)	27.8 (0.3)				
PORTUGAL	48.3 (0.8)	48.9 (1.3)	47.9 (0.9)				
SCOTLAND	60.6 (0.9)	60.4 (1.0)	60.8 (1.1)				
SLOVENIA	57.1 (0.8)	58.1 (0.8)	56.1 (1.0)				
SOVIET UNION	70.2 (1.0)	70.0 (1.3)	70.3 (0.9)				
SPAIN	55.4 (0.8)	57.1 (1.1)	53.8 (0.8)				
SWITZERLAND	70.8 (1.3)	72.8 (1.5)	68.7 (1.1)				
TAIWAN	72.7 (0.7)	73.1 (0.9)	72.4 (0.9)				
UNITED STATES	55.3 (1.0)	55.8 (1.1)	54.8 (1.3)				

	1ST	5TH	10TH	90TH	95TH	99TH
Populations						
BRAZIL, FORTALEZA	10.9 (0.4)	14.7 (0.6)	17.3 (0.3)	56.8 (2.1)	65.3 (0.6)	80.8 (3.5)
BRAZIL, SÃO PAULO	10.3 (2.1)	16.7 (1.0)	18.7 (0.9)	62.7 (0.7)	70.7 (1.5)	82.7 (0.7)
CANADA	21.3 (0.6)	32.0 (0.0)	37.3 (0.0)	86.7 (0.0)	91.8 (4.3)	97.3 (1.3)
CHINA	37.0 (2.2)	49.3 (2.7)	57.3 (3.3)	96.0 (1.3)	98.7 (1.3)	100.0 (0.0)
ENGLAND	18.7 (1.9)	27.4 (3.3)	34.5 (3.7)	89.3 (0.5)	93.3 (1.3)	97.3 (1.0)
FRANCE	22.7 (3.0)	30.7 (0.8)	37.3 (1.0)	89.3 (0.0)	92.0 (5.3)	97.3 (1.3)
HUNGARY	21.3 (0.9)	32.4 (2.3)	38.7 (1.3)	93.3 (0.0)	96.0 (0.0)	98.7 (0.0)
IRELAND	17.8 (1.3)	26.8 (1.7)	33.3 (2.0)	86.7 (0.0)	90.7 (0.0)	96.0 (4.2)
ISRAEL	21.3 (1.0)	30.7 (1.0)	37.3 (0.2)	87.8 (2.6)	90.7 (0.0)	96.0 (3.9)
ITALY	23.0 (1.3)	32.4 (0.9)	36.5 (1.5)	88.0 (0.0)	91.8 (0.5)	96.0 (0.0)
JORDAN	13.3 (0.0)	17.6 (1.2)	21.3 (1.5)	65.3 (3.1)	75.7 (3.3)	89.3 (5.2)
KOREA	20.0 (0.0)	33.3 (1.5)	41.3 (1.5)	96.0 (0.0)	97.3 (1.9)	100.0 (0.0)
MOZAMBIQUE	11.5 (1.1)	16.2 (0.6)	18.7 (0.1)	44.6 (1.4)	50.0 (3.2)	60.0 (2.2)
PORTUGAL	17.3 (0.9)	23.9 (1.3)	28.0 (0.5)	74.7 (0.9)	80.6 (1.7)	89.7 (2.6)
SCOTLAND	21.3 (0.8)	29.0 (2.8)	34.7 (0.0)	86.7 (0.0)	90.7 (0.0)	96.0 (0.0)
SLOVENIA	21.3 (0.0)	27.1 (3.9)	32.0 (0.1)	82.7 (0.2)	88.0 (2.6)	94.7 (0.0)
SOVIET UNION	20.9 (2.4)	35.2 (1.4)	42.7 (0.8)	92.0 (0.0)	94.7 (0.0)	98.7 (0.0)
SPAIN	20.3 (1.6)	28.6 (0.5)	32.9 (2.0)	78.4 (0.8)	84.7 (1.3)	91.9 (2.0)
SWITZERLAND	30.7 (1.2)	42.7 (0.8)	50.7 (1.9)	93.3 (1.3)	94.7 (0.0)	98.7 (0.0)
TAIWAN	18.7 (1.4)	26.7 (0.0)	35.0 (3.0)	97.3 (1.3)	98.7 (0.0)	100.0 (0.0)
UNITED STATES	17.3 (3.8)	24.0 (0.6)	29.3 (0.0)	82.7 (1.3)	90.7 (0.1)	97.3 (0.0)
Canadian Populations						
ALBERTA	23.5 (2.6)	33.3 (0.0)	38.7 (3.5)	88.0 (0.3)	92.0 (1.8)	97.3 (0.0)
BRITISH COLUMBIA	25.3 (0.7)	35.6 (2.1)	41.3 (0.0)	90.7 (4.0)	94.7 (3.6)	97.3 (1.3)
MANITOBA-ENGLISH	20.0 (1.7)	28.0 (2.7)	33.3 (4.2)	82.7 (0.0)	86.7 (0.0)	96.0 (3.5)
MANITOBA-FRENCH	26.7 (2.7)	34.7 (2.4)	41.3 (0.0)	85.3 (0.0)	89.3 (0.0)	94.7 (0.0)
NEW BRUNSWICK-ENGLISH	20.0 (0.0)	27.5 (1.6)	33.3 (0.0)	82.7 (0.0)	89.3 (2.0)	96.0 (0.0)
NEW BRUNSWICK-FRENCH	20.3 (1.3)	30.2 (3.1)	36.0 (0.0)	85.1 (1.3)	89.3 (0.0)	93.3 (0.0)
NEWFOUNDLAND	18.7 (1.3)	29.3 (0.4)	34.7 (0.0)	84.0 (2.1)	88.0 (5.8)	96.0 (2.7)
NOVA SCOTIA	20.0 (0.0)	29.3 (1.2)	35.1 (1.5)	85.3 (0.0)	90.7 (0.0)	97.3 (0.0)
ONTARIO-ENGLISH	20.0 (1.2)	29.3 (0.0)	34.7 (0.0)	84.0 (2.0)	89.3 (1.3)	96.0 (1.3)
ONTARIO-FRENCH	18.7 (0.2)	25.3 (1.1)	32.0 (0.0)	76.0 (3.0)	82.7 (0.0)	92.0 (2.3)
QUEBEC-ENGLISH	23.0 (2.5)	33.8 (3.9)	41.3 (1.3)	90.7 (0.0)	94.7 (2.4)	98.7 (0.0)
QUEBEC-FRENCH	29.3 (1.4)	39.7 (1.8)	45.3 (2.8)	89.3 (0.0)	93.3 (0.0)	96.4 (2.7)
SASKATCHEWAN-ENGLISH	21.3 (1.3)	29.7 (4.5)	37.3 (5.8)	86.7 (3.8)	90.7 (0.0)	96.0 (0.0)
SASKATCHEWAN-FRENCH	32.0 (1.3)	36.0 (2.9)	46.5 (3.7)	87.8 (3.9)	90.7 (2.5)	96.0 (1.3)

Mathematics: Age 13

	NUMBERS AND OPERATIONS	MEASURE-MENT	GEOMETRY	DATA ANALY-SIS, STATIS-TICS, AND PROBABILITY	ALGEBRA AND FUNCTIONS	CONCEPTUAL UNDER-STANDING	PROCEDURAL KNOWLEDGE	PROBLEM SOLVING
IAEP TOPIC AVERAGE	**61.0**	**46.9**	**62.2**	**69.1**	**54.2**	**60.6**	**58.4**	**55.9**
Populations								
BRAZIL, FORTALEZA	35.8 (0.7)	20.5 (0.5)	28.6 (0.8)	43.8 (0.8)	32.3 (0.9)	35.3 (0.7)	30.8 (0.8)	31.0 (0.5)
BRAZIL, SÃO PAULO	40.9 (0.8)	24.1 (0.5)	34.3 (1.5)	49.7 (1.0)	35.6 (1.1)	38.5 (0.9)	36.5 (1.1)	36.0 (0.6)
CANADA	65.6 (0.6)	49.9 (0.6)	68.1 (0.7)	76.4 (0.6)	52.7 (0.7)	65.1 (0.6)	61.9 (0.7)	58.9 (0.5)
CHINA	84.9 (0.9)	71.3 (1.5)	80.2 (1.1)	75.4 (1.2)	82.4 (0.9)	81.6 (1.0)	83.0 (0.9)	75.6 (1.2)
ENGLAND	58.5 (2.0)	51.2 (2.5)	70.3 (2.4)	79.5 (1.8)	54.0 (2.8)	62.0 (2.1)	59.0 (2.6)	60.8 (2.0)
FRANCE	65.0 (0.7)	52.7 (1.0)	73.1 (0.8)	79.3 (0.7)	57.0 (1.0)	67.4 (0.7)	65.7 (0.9)	59.3 (0.8)
HUNGARY	69.4 (0.7)	55.1 (1.0)	73.3 (0.8)	75.9 (0.8)	69.8 (0.9)	69.8 (0.7)	70.8 (0.8)	64.2 (0.8)
IRELAND	65.1 (0.8)	49.4 (1.0)	59.9 (1.1)	71.8 (1.0)	55.6 (1.1)	61.5 (0.8)	62.0 (1.2)	57.9 (0.8)
ISRAEL	64.8 (0.7)	47.2 (1.1)	65.8 (1.0)	74.8 (0.8)	64.7 (1.0)	63.8 (0.8)	65.3 (0.9)	59.8 (0.9)
ITALY	63.8 (0.8)	62.8 (1.1)	75.3 (1.0)	71.7 (0.8)	52.6 (1.2)	66.6 (0.8)	62.1 (1.1)	63.3 (0.9)
JORDAN	42.8 (1.0)	32.0 (1.0)	43.5 (1.1)	45.7 (1.0)	38.1 (1.3)	44.9 (0.9)	38.5 (1.2)	37.9 (1.0)
KOREA	77.4 (0.6)	59.5 (0.9)	77.4 (0.6)	81.2 (0.7)	70.8 (0.8)	78.3 (0.5)	73.4 (0.7)	68.5 (0.7)
MOZAMBIQUE	33.8 (0.4)	20.1 (0.3)	29.2 (0.5)	35.4 (0.6)	20.5 (0.5)	34.0 (0.4)	22.9 (0.4)	28.2 (0.4)
PORTUGAL	52.1 (0.8)	31.9 (0.7)	49.0 (1.3)	68.6 (1.0)	43.1 (1.1)	51.5 (0.9)	47.1 (1.0)	46.4 (0.7)
SCOTLAND	59.7 (0.8)	51.0 (1.2)	69.6 (0.9)	79.1 (0.8)	52.8 (1.2)	61.8 (0.9)	59.2 (1.0)	60.9 (0.9)
SLOVENIA	62.2 (0.7)	43.1 (0.9)	63.1 (1.0)	63.6 (0.8)	51.8 (1.0)	58.5 (0.7)	59.0 (0.9)	53.7 (0.8)
SOVIET UNION	69.2 (1.0)	59.7 (1.1)	77.6 (1.0)	76.1 (1.3)	71.9 (1.1)	70.3 (1.0)	73.2 (1.2)	66.7 (1.0)
SPAIN	60.1 (0.6)	37.9 (0.8)	60.0 (1.2)	67.7 (0.8)	52.2 (1.2)	58.4 (0.7)	55.8 (0.9)	51.9 (0.8)
SWITZERLAND	73.6 (1.0)	62.0 (1.5)	76.6 (1.3)	81.8 (1.1)	62.7 (1.9)	71.7 (1.1)	69.0 (1.4)	71.9 (1.3)
TAIWAN	74.7 (0.6)	63.7 (0.9)	76.6 (0.8)	81.2 (0.6)	69.2 (0.9)	74.7 (0.7)	74.7 (0.7)	68.6 (0.8)
UNITED STATES	61.0 (1.0)	39.5 (1.0)	54.3 (1.0)	72.2 (1.0)	49.2 (1.6)	57.4 (0.9)	56.0 (1.3)	52.3 (1.0)
Canadian Populations								
ALBERTA	68.6 (0.7)	54.3 (0.9)	67.2 (0.8)	80.0 (0.7)	52.1 (0.9)	68.3 (0.7)	62.6 (0.8)	61.0 (0.7)
BRITISH COLUMBIA	69.3 (0.7)	54.1 (0.9)	69.6 (0.9)	79.9 (0.7)	60.2 (0.8)	68.5 (0.7)	68.0 (0.8)	61.8 (0.7)
MANITOBA-ENGLISH	62.5 (0.7)	45.6 (0.9)	58.4 (0.9)	73.6 (0.9)	50.8 (1.0)	60.5 (0.8)	58.8 (0.9)	54.4 (0.7)
MANITOBA-FRENCH	67.1 (0.7)	48.5 (0.7)	66.6 (0.8)	75.0 (0.8)	58.5 (0.7)	64.6 (0.7)	66.0 (0.7)	58.2 (0.6)
NEW BRUNSWICK-ENGLISH	62.4 (0.5)	51.3 (0.6)	62.4 (0.6)	71.0 (0.6)	43.2 (0.6)	61.4 (0.5)	55.4 (0.6)	56.4 (0.5)
NEW BRUNSWICK-FRENCH	65.4 (0.4)	46.5 (0.5)	64.5 (0.5)	72.3 (0.5)	54.3 (0.4)	63.7 (0.4)	62.6 (0.4)	55.3 (0.4)
NEWFOUNDLAND	61.9 (0.6)	45.1 (0.7)	65.1 (0.9)	72.4 (0.7)	52.7 (0.6)	61.8 (0.7)	60.3 (0.7)	54.3 (0.6)
NOVA SCOTIA	62.9 (0.6)	47.3 (0.8)	63.7 (0.7)	73.9 (0.7)	53.5 (0.8)	61.8 (0.6)	60.2 (0.6)	57.1 (0.6)
ONTARIO-ENGLISH	61.8 (0.8)	46.2 (0.9)	63.4 (1.0)	73.6 (0.8)	49.5 (1.0)	60.8 (0.8)	58.5 (0.9)	55.5 (0.8)
ONTARIO-FRENCH	58.0 (0.6)	38.8 (0.7)	59.0 (1.0)	69.0 (0.7)	44.7 (0.9)	56.6 (0.7)	54.1 (0.8)	49.6 (0.6)
QUEBEC-ENGLISH	68.7 (0.9)	53.5 (1.1)	70.6 (1.0)	78.1 (1.0)	59.6 (1.1)	68.3 (0.9)	66.6 (1.0)	61.9 (1.0)
QUEBEC-FRENCH	72.3 (0.6)	56.4 (1.0)	78.1 (0.8)	81.1 (0.6)	58.4 (1.0)	72.6 (0.7)	68.0 (0.8)	65.3 (0.8)
SASKATCHEWAN-ENGLISH	66.1 (0.6)	49.6 (0.9)	62.9 (1.2)	78.3 (0.7)	54.6 (0.8)	64.0 (0.7)	64.4 (0.8)	57.2 (0.7)
SASKATCHEWAN-FRENCH	73.9 (1.0)	53.8 (1.3)	69.2 (1.3)	76.0 (1.2)	61.6 (1.4)	70.1 (1.2)	69.3 (1.0)	62.9 (1.1)

Mathematics: Age 13

Amounts of Weekly Mathematics Homework

Populations		0-1 HR	2-3 HRS	4 HRS/MORE
BRAZIL, FORTALEZA	%	43 (1.4)	39 (1.2)	18 (1.4)
	P	31 (0.6)	34 (0.8)	40 (1.5)
BRAZIL, SÃO PAULO	%	55 (1.7)	30 (1.2)	16 (1.2)
	P	37 (1.1)	38 (1.0)	43 (1.3)
CANADA	%	58 (1.1)	27 (0.9)	15 (0.8)
	P	61 (0.6)	64 (0.8)	62 (0.9)
CHINA	%	28 (1.8)	35 (1.6)	37 (1.8)
	P	78 (1.3)	80 (1.3)	84 (0.9)
ENGLAND	%	65 (3.4)	30 (3.2)	6 (0.8)
	P	59 (2.3)	65 (2.5)	61 (3.5)
FRANCE	%	45 (1.5)	38 (1.4)	17 (1.3)
	P	59 (0.9)	69 (1.0)	69 (1.0)
HUNGARY	%	68 (1.3)	21 (1.2)	11 (0.7)
	P	67 (0.9)	72 (1.1)	75 (1.4)
IRELAND	%	48 (1.6)	35 (1.4)	17 (1.3)
	P	57 (1.1)	66 (1.2)	63 (1.2)
ISRAEL	%	41 (1.4)	42 (1.3)	17 (1.1)
	P	61 (0.9)	64 (1.1)	67 (1.1)
ITALY	%	43 (1.7)	30 (1.6)	27 (1.4)
	P	65 (0.9)	62 (1.7)	66 (1.2)
JORDAN	%	57 (1.5)	29 (1.2)	14 (1.0)
	P	41 (1.1)	38 (0.9)	47 (2.0)
KOREA	%	29 (1.2)	38 (1.1)	33 (1.1)
	P	71 (1.3)	74 (0.8)	75 (0.9)
MOZAMBIQUE	%	63 (1.6)	27 (1.4)	11 (1.2)
	P	32 (0.5)	30 (0.7)	29 (1.3)
PORTUGAL	%	72 (1.4)	19 (1.3)	9 (0.8)
	P	48 (0.8)	53 (1.4)	53 (1.8)
SCOTLAND	%	75 (1.6)	21 (1.4)	4 (0.6)
	P	59 (0.9)	65 (1.5)	61 (2.2)
SLOVENIA	%	54 (1.5)	32 (1.4)	15 (0.9)
	P	57 (0.7)	59 (1.3)	57 (1.4)
SOVIET UNION	%	39 (1.9)	28 (1.0)	33 (1.5)
	P	66 (1.3)	72 (1.2)	73 (1.4)
SPAIN	%	52 (1.9)	26 (1.4)	22 (1.3)
	P	55 (1.0)	56 (1.0)	61 (1.1)
SWITZERLAND	%	51 (1.7)	34 (1.3)	15 (1.2)
	P	71 (1.5)	73 (1.2)	69 (1.6)
TAIWAN	%	47 (1.3)	29 (1.2)	24 (1.2)
	P	63 (0.9)	76 (1.0)	88 (0.8)
UNITED STATES	%	63 (2.1)	22 (1.5)	15 (1.3)
	P	52 (0.9)	60 (1.9)	63 (1.6)

Canadian Populations

Populations		0-1 HR	2-3 HRS	4 HRS/MORE
ALBERTA	%	58 (1.6)	27 (1.3)	15 (1.2)
	P	64 (0.8)	66 (1.1)	63 (1.5)
BRITISH COLUMBIA	%	59 (1.5)	30 (1.4)	12 (0.8)
	P	65 (0.8)	69 (1.0)	66 (1.3)
MANITOBA-ENGLISH	%	70 (1.1)	20 (1.0)	10 (0.8)
	P	58 (0.9)	59 (1.1)	55 (1.6)
MANITOBA-FRENCH	%	52 (1.6)	31 (1.6)	17 (1.5)
	P	63 (0.8)	66 (1.0)	59 (1.2)
NEW BRUNSWICK-ENGLISH	%	67 (1.1)	23 (1.0)	10 (0.9)
	P	57 (0.6)	59 (1.0)	59 (1.3)
NEW BRUNSWICK-FRENCH	%	57 (1.3)	26 (1.0)	17 (0.9)
	P	60 (0.6)	64 (0.9)	61 (1.0)
NEWFOUNDLAND	%	53 (1.4)	29 (1.0)	19 (1.1)
	P	59 (0.7)	60 (1.0)	59 (1.0)
NOVA SCOTIA	%	59 (1.2)	27 (0.9)	14 (0.9)
	P	58 (0.6)	63 (0.9)	62 (1.2)
ONTARIO-ENGLISH	%	58 (1.7)	27 (1.3)	16 (1.3)
	P	58 (0.8)	59 (1.4)	59 (1.5)
ONTARIO-FRENCH	%	63 (1.7)	24 (1.4)	14 (1.2)
	P	54 (0.7)	56 (1.0)	55 (1.2)
QUEBEC-ENGLISH	%	55 (1.9)	30 (1.6)	15 (1.1)
	P	64 (1.2)	69 (1.4)	67 (1.4)
QUEBEC-FRENCH	%	57 (1.4)	28 (1.3)	14 (0.8)
	P	68 (0.8)	71 (0.9)	68 (1.1)
SASKATCHEWAN-ENGLISH	%	65 (1.5)	24 (1.3)	11 (1.0)
	P	62 (0.8)	63 (1.1)	59 (1.2)
SASKATCHEWAN-FRENCH	%	52 (3.4)	32 (2.8)	16 (2.6)
	P	69 (1.5)	67 (1.5)	65 (2.2)

Amounts of Daily Homework

Populations		NO HMWK	1 HR/LESS	2 HRS/MORE
BRAZIL, FORTALEZA	%	7 (0.7)	45 (1.7)	48 (1.8)
	P	28 (1.1)	32 (0.6)	36 (0.9)
BRAZIL, SÃO PAULO	%	6 (1.0)	49 (1.8)	45 (1.9)
	P	29 (1.3)	37 (1.2)	41 (0.8)
CANADA	%	8 (0.6)	65 (0.9)	27 (1.0)
	P	63 (1.3)	63 (0.6)	59 (0.9)
CHINA	%	3 (0.7)	52 (1.8)	44 (1.8)
	P	78 (2.9)	80 (1.2)	80 (1.0)
ENGLAND	%	2 (0.5)	64 (2.7)	33 (2.8)
	P	50 (3.7)	60 (2.1)	63 (2.8)
FRANCE	%	0 (0.2)	44 (1.6)	55 (1.6)
	P	52 (5.2)	62 (1.1)	66 (0.7)
HUNGARY	%	0 (0.1)	42 (1.3)	58 (1.3)
	P	31 (1.9)	66 (1.1)	70 (0.9)
IRELAND	%	1 (0.5)	35 (1.8)	63 (1.9)
	P	33 (8.3)	57 (1.3)	64 (0.9)
ISRAEL	%	1 (0.2)	49 (1.9)	50 (1.9)
	P	52 (***)	65 (0.8)	62 (0.9)
ITALY	%	0 (0.1)	19 (1.2)	79 (1.3)
	P	43 (3.8)	63 (1.7)	65 (0.9)
JORDAN	%	3 (0.5)	40 (1.9)	56 (2.0)
	P	34 (2.2)	40 (1.0)	42 (1.3)
KOREA	%	3 (0.5)	56 (1.6)	41 (1.7)
	P	69 (4.0)	73 (0.7)	75 (0.9)
MOZAMBIQUE	%	2 (0.5)	55 (1.8)	42 (1.8)
	P	31 (2.3)	32 (0.4)	30 (0.4)
PORTUGAL	%	5 (1.3)	65 (1.7)	30 (1.6)
	P	44 (2.4)	51 (1.0)	47 (1.3)
SCOTLAND	%	16 (1.4)	70 (1.2)	14 (1.1)
	P	57 (1.6)	62 (0.9)	62 (1.7)
SLOVENIA	%	1 (0.2)	70 (1.6)	28 (1.7)
	P	57 (8.0)	59 (0.8)	53 (1.1)
SOVIET UNION	%	0 (0.2)	47 (1.6)	52 (1.6)
	P	55 (6.7)	69 (1.5)	71 (1.1)
SPAIN	%	1 (0.4)	33 (1.5)	64 (1.5)
	P	47 (4.5)	56 (1.0)	57 (0.8)
SWITZERLAND	%	1 (0.2)	79 (1.3)	20 (1.3)
	P	62 (5.1)	71 (1.3)	71 (1.3)
TAIWAN	%	4 (0.6)	55 (1.1)	41 (1.3)
	P	54 (2.9)	68 (0.9)	81 (1.0)
UNITED STATES	%	10 (1.2)	61 (1.7)	29 (1.8)
	P	53 (1.9)	56 (1.3)	56 (1.1)

Canadian Populations

Populations		NO HMWK	1 HR/LESS	2 HRS/MORE
ALBERTA	%	11 (1.1)	68 (1.5)	20 (1.3)
	P	64 (2.1)	65 (0.8)	62 (1.3)
BRITISH COLUMBIA	%	8 (0.8)	66 (1.4)	25 (1.5)
	P	66 (2.1)	66 (0.8)	66 (1.1)
MANITOBA-ENGLISH	%	18 (1.2)	63 (1.7)	18 (1.4)
	P	59 (1.7)	59 (0.8)	53 (1.4)
MANITOBA-FRENCH	%	11 (0.9)	69 (1.4)	19 (1.3)
	P	68 (2.2)	64 (0.7)	59 (1.4)
NEW BRUNSWICK-ENGLISH	%	8 (0.7)	75 (1.1)	16 (0.9)
	P	56 (1.6)	59 (0.5)	55 (1.2)
NEW BRUNSWICK-FRENCH	%	9 (0.7)	74 (1.3)	17 (1.1)
	P	65 (1.4)	62 (0.4)	55 (0.9)
NEWFOUNDLAND	%	6 (0.8)	68 (1.5)	26 (1.5)
	P	59 (2.1)	60 (0.6)	56 (1.1)
NOVA SCOTIA	%	7 (0.8)	69 (1.2)	23 (1.2)
	P	60 (2.0)	61 (0.6)	56 (1.2)
ONTARIO-ENGLISH	%	9 (1.0)	63 (1.4)	28 (1.6)
	P	62 (1.7)	60 (0.8)	54 (1.2)
ONTARIO-FRENCH	%	9 (0.8)	68 (1.3)	23 (1.3)
	P	56 (1.7)	54 (0.6)	52 (1.2)
QUEBEC-ENGLISH	%	5 (1.1)	61 (2.0)	33 (1.9)
	P	69 (1.6)	66 (1.3)	65 (1.0)
QUEBEC-FRENCH	%	4 (0.6)	67 (1.8)	29 (1.9)
	P	71 (2.2)	69 (0.8)	69 (1.2)
SASKATCHEWAN-ENGLISH	%	21 (1.4)	66 (1.4)	13 (0.9)
	P	66 (1.2)	62 (0.8)	57 (1.5)
SASKATCHEWAN-FRENCH	%	13 (2.5)	72 (2.9)	15 (2.1)
	P	69 (3.7)	68 (1.0)	63 (3.2)

% = Percentages of Students
P = Average Percent Correct

Mathematics: Age 13

Populations		Amounts of Daily Television Viewing		
		0-1 HR	2-4 HRS	5 HRS/MORE
BRAZIL, FORTALEZA	%	30 (1.4)	49 (1.4)	21 (1.5)
	P	31 (0.7)	36 (0.8)	32 (0.9)
BRAZIL, SÃO PAULO	%	27 (0.9)	54 (1.0)	19 (1.2)
	P	34 (1.0)	40 (0.9)	39 (1.4)
CANADA	%	18 (0.9)	68 (1.0)	14 (0.7)
	P	65 (1.0)	63 (0.6)	55 (1.0)
CHINA	%	65 (1.6)	29 (1.5)	7 (0.5)
	P	80 (1.1)	80 (1.4)	77 (1.6)
ENGLAND	%	17 (4.6)	68 (3.9)	14 (2.2)
	P	66 (3.0)	61 (2.3)	51 (2.5)
FRANCE	%	51 (1.5)	44 (1.3)	5 (0.7)
	P	66 (1.0)	64 (0.9)	57 (1.7)
HUNGARY	%	11 (0.8)	75 (1.2)	13 (1.0)
	P	70 (1.9)	69 (0.7)	61 (1.7)
IRELAND	%	29 (1.5)	63 (1.4)	9 (0.9)
	P	64 (1.1)	61 (1.0)	50 (1.8)
ISRAEL	%	11 (1.1)	69 (1.3)	20 (1.2)
	P	60 (1.9)	65 (0.8)	60 (1.3)
ITALY	%	26 (1.6)	69 (1.4)	5 (0.7)
	P	60 (1.7)	66 (0.7)	59 (2.7)
JORDAN	%	35 (1.2)	58 (1.2)	7 (0.8)
	P	39 (1.0)	42 (1.3)	40 (1.8)
KOREA	%	24 (1.3)	65 (1.3)	11 (0.9)
	P	81 (1.0)	72 (0.7)	63 (1.4)
MOZAMBIQUE	%	36 (1.5)	44 (1.6)	20 (1.2)
	P	31 (0.6)	31 (0.4)	30 (0.6)
PORTUGAL	%	22 (1.5)	66 (1.6)	11 (1.0)
	P	43 (1.5)	51 (0.8)	50 (1.4)
SCOTLAND	%	10 (1.0)	66 (1.3)	24 (1.3)
	P	65 (2.6)	62 (0.9)	54 (0.8)
SLOVENIA	%	32 (1.6)	63 (1.6)	4 (0.5)
	P	58 (1.0)	57 (0.9)	54 (2.1)
SOVIET UNION	%	12 (1.1)	71 (1.9)	17 (1.0)
	P	70 (1.8)	71 (1.0)	67 (0.8)
SPAIN	%	26 (1.2)	63 (1.3)	10 (0.8)
	P	58 (1.2)	57 (0.9)	49 (1.3)
SWITZERLAND	%	41 (1.3)	52 (1.3)	7 (0.8)
	P	72 (1.1)	70 (1.5)	72 (2.3)
TAIWAN	%	32 (1.2)	57 (1.4)	10 (0.7)
	P	82 (1.0)	70 (0.9)	59 (1.8)
UNITED STATES	%	16 (1.6)	63 (1.6)	20 (1.7)
	P	60 (2.2)	57 (0.9)	47 (1.8)

Canadian Populations		Amounts of Daily Television Viewing		
		0-1 HR	2-4 HRS	5 HRS/MORE
ALBERTA	%	20 (1.5)	68 (1.4)	12 (1.0)
	P	68 (1.3)	64 (0.7)	56 (1.4)
BRITISH COLUMBIA	%	23 (1.5)	64 (1.5)	13 (1.0)
	P	69 (1.3)	67 (0.7)	59 (1.5)
MANITOBA-ENGLISH	%	15 (1.1)	68 (1.2)	18 (1.2)
	P	60 (1.7)	59 (0.7)	52 (1.4)
MANITOBA-FRENCH	%	19 (1.6)	66 (1.9)	15 (1.3)
	P	67 (1.3)	64 (0.9)	57 (1.7)
NEW BRUNSWICK-ENGLISH	%	13 (0.8)	68 (1.1)	19 (1.1)
	P	60 (1.3)	59 (0.6)	52 (0.9)
NEW BRUNSWICK-FRENCH	%	14 (1.0)	70 (1.1)	16 (1.0)
	P	61 (1.4)	62 (0.5)	54 (0.9)
NEWFOUNDLAND	%	11 (0.8)	66 (1.2)	23 (1.0)
	P	57 (1.5)	61 (0.6)	55 (1.0)
NOVA SCOTIA	%	12 (0.9)	68 (1.7)	21 (1.5)
	P	61 (1.6)	62 (0.8)	54 (1.8)
ONTARIO-ENGLISH	%	17 (1.2)	67 (1.4)	16 (1.2)
	P	61 (1.7)	59 (0.8)	51 (1.2)
ONTARIO-FRENCH	%	15 (1.0)	68 (1.4)	17 (1.1)
	P	58 (1.4)	54 (0.6)	50 (1.2)
QUEBEC-ENGLISH	%	22 (1.5)	64 (1.3)	14 (0.9)
	P	68 (1.7)	66 (1.1)	60 (1.5)
QUEBEC-FRENCH	%	18 (1.3)	71 (1.4)	11 (1.0)
	P	71 (1.2)	69 (0.7)	64 (1.7)
SASKATCHEWAN-ENGLISH	%	14 (1.0)	73 (0.9)	13 (0.9)
	P	65 (1.6)	63 (0.8)	55 (1.4)
SASKATCHEWAN-FRENCH	%	22 (2.6)	69 (3.1)	9 (1.8)
	P	73 (2.2)	68 (1.2)	59 (4.3)

% = Percentages of Students
P = Average Percent Correct

Mathematics: Age 13

Topic: Numbers and Operations

	IAEP Item Average
Identify a whole number given some of its properties	86
Identify what information is missing from a problem	81
Translate a fraction with denominator 10 into decimal form	79
Subtract (with regrouping) a decimal from a decimal	79
Choose a number that makes an inequality true	78
Solve a problem about temperature in which the numbers go below zero	77
Relate a subtraction fact to an addition fact	76
Find two digits that are missing from an addition problem	75
Identify the operation needed to solve a one-step word problem	72
On a map, find the length of the shortest route between two cities	70
Supply the number being subtracted in a subtraction problem	68
Identify a property of odd and even numbers	67
Solve a two-step problem involving age and year of birth	67
Solve a word problem involving simple ratios	65
Translate a fraction into a decimal	57
Relate odd and even to consecutive integers	57
Interpret a whole number that is given as the sum of multiples of powers of ten	56
Solve a problem by finding a percent of a number	55
Choose the mixed number that corresponds to a point on a number line	54
Solve a problem by using division and treating the remainder appropriately	50
Multiply a decimal by a decimal	47
Express a decimal as a percent	46
Solve a three-step problem by using several operations on whole numbers	45
Reinterpret multiplication by a decimal as division	42
Pick out the smallest decimal from a set of five decimals	36
Find the smallest common multiple of two integers	34
Solve a problem requiring division by a mixed number	34

Topic: Measurement

	IAEP Item Average
Determine a length on a map using a map scale	60
Pick out possible dimensions of a rectangle of a given area	60
Find the length of one side of a square, given its area	58
Relate length of a stick to the number of stick-lengths in some given length	53
Find the volume of a box	52
Solve a word problem involving perimeter of a rectangle	50
Solve a word problem using division and conversion between meters and centimeters	46
Pick a possible length and width for a rectangle of a given distance around	44
Solve a two-step problem involving area and volume	43
Compare the areas and perimeters of two figures	43

Topic: Measurement (continued)

	IAEP Item Average
Find the perimeter on an irregular figure	41
Find area of a region bounded by straight lines and part of a circle	38
Find the total surface area of a cube	33

Topic: Geometry

	IAEP Item Average
Pick out a possible scale drawing, based on a description	79
Identify a line of symmetry	75
Recognize the diameter of a circle	74
Identify a circle from its basic properties	72
Solve a problem involving angle measure	66
Solve a problem involving perimeter	60
Relate a two-dimensional pattern to the shape obtained by folding the pattern	58
Find how many of a shape are needed to cover a larger figure	57
Solve a problem involving angle measure	56
Solve a problem involving angle measure	53
Solve a problem involving acute angles	41

Topic: Data Analysis, Statistics, and Probability

	IAEP Item Average
Interpret data from a circle graph	87
Using clues about cards, figure out which card was chosen	82
Interpret data from a bar graph	80
Interpret data from a line graph	72
Use data from a pictograph	70
Solve a simple probability problem	65
Interpret data from a line graph	57
Compute an average	56
Interpret data from a line graph	53

Topic: Algebra and Functions

	IAEP Item Average
Solve a linear equation	80
Solve a word problem using ratios and multiplication	72
Solve a linear equation	67
Solve a word problem about positions of people on a line	66
Evaluate an algebraic expression for certain values of the variables	66
Solve a linear equation	61
Solve a word problem involving a balance scale	56
Translate from a verbal description into an algebraic equation	54
Simplify an algebraic expression	48
Evaluate an algebraic expression for a certain value of the variable	48
Evaluate an algebraic expression for a certain value of the variable	48
Write an expression using one variable	45
Relate a table of values to an equation	44
Solve a two-step number problem	42
Count the cubes used to make a tower (shown in a picture)	27

Mathematics: Age 9

	TOTAL	MALE	FEMALE
IAEP AVERAGE	63.3		
Populations			
CANADA	59.9 (0.5)	59.9 (0.7)	60.0 (0.6)
ENGLAND	59.5 (1.9)	58.5 (1.5)	60.3 (2.9)
HUNGARY	68.2 (0.6)	68.2 (0.8)	68.2 (0.8)
IRELAND	60.0 (0.8)	59.9 (0.9)	60.1 (1.1)
ISRAEL	64.4 (0.7)	66.0 (0.8)	62.7 (0.9)
ITALY	67.8 (0.9)	69.5 (1.0)	65.9 (1.1)
KOREA	74.8 (0.6)	77.2 (0.7)	72.4 (0.8)
PORTUGAL	55.5 (0.9)	56.8 (1.1)	54.2 (1.1)
SCOTLAND	65.7 (0.9)	65.8 (1.1)	65.6 (1.1)
SLOVENIA	55.8 (0.6)	55.8 (0.7)	55.9 (0.7)
SOVIET UNION	65.9 (1.3)	66.4 (1.2)	65.4 (1.4)
SPAIN	61.9 (1.0)	61.9 (1.3)	61.8 (1.1)
TAIWAN	68.1 (0.8)	68.4 (0.8)	67.8 (0.9)
UNITED STATES	58.4 (1.0)	58.7 (1.1)	58.0 (1.2)
Canadian Populations			
BRITISH COLUMBIA	61.9 (0.7)	61.8 (0.9)	62.0 (0.9)
NEW BRUNSWICK-ENGLISH	59.8 (0.5)	60.3 (0.7)	59.3 (0.6)
ONTARIO-ENGLISH	56.8 (0.7)	56.3 (0.9)	57.2 (0.9)
ONTARIO-FRENCH	54.5 (0.6)	54.7 (0.7)	54.3 (0.6)
QUEBEC-ENGLISH	62.5 (0.8)	62.9 (0.9)	62.0 (1.0)
QUEBEC-FRENCH	64.5 (0.7)	65.1 (0.8)	64.0 (0.8)

Mathematics: Ages 9 & 13

	AGE 9	AGE 13
Populations		
CANADA	45.1 (0.5)	76.1 (0.5)
ENGLAND	43.9 (1.9)	73.7 (1.9)
HUNGARY	54.1 (0.8)	79.8 (0.6)
IRELAND	43.6 (0.9)	74.1 (0.8)
ISRAEL	52.5 (0.9)	78.9 (0.7)
ITALY	54.8 (1.1)	77.2 (0.9)
KOREA	60.0 (0.7)	82.2 (0.7)
PORTUGAL	41.1 (1.0)	68.3 (1.0)
SCOTLAND	47.7 (0.9)	74.2 (0.8)
SLOVENIA	40.6 (0.7)	72.8 (0.7)
SOVIET UNION	53.8 (1.5)	80.8 (0.8)
SPAIN	49.6 (1.0)	74.4 (0.7)
TAIWAN	50.6 (0.8)	78.2 (0.6)
UNITED STATES	45.6 (1.1)	71.0 (1.1)
Canadian Populations		
BRITISH COLUMBIA	48.0 (0.7)	78.2 (0.7)
NEW BRUNSWICK-ENGLISH	45.5 (0.6)	70.8 (0.6)
ONTARIO-ENGLISH	42.2 (0.7)	72.4 (0.8)
ONTARIO-FRENCH	39.9 (0.7)	69.5 (0.6)
QUEBEC-ENGLISH	48.3 (0.9)	78.3 (0.9)
QUEBEC-FRENCH	49.3 (0.7)	83.3 (0.6)

Mathematics: Age 9

	1ST	5TH	10TH	90TH	95TH	99TH
Populations						
CANADA	19.6 (1.6)	28.3 (2.5)	35.7 (1.5)	83.6 (0.0)	88.5 (0.0)	93.4 (2.8)
ENGLAND	17.2 (2.1)	26.7 (1.6)	32.8 (0.5)	86.9 (2.5)	91.8 (3.3)	96.7 (0.0)
HUNGARY	20.4 (2.3)	33.3 (1.5)	40.7 (1.2)	90.2 (2.5)	93.4 (0.0)	98.4 (0.0)
IRELAND	16.0 (3.3)	24.6 (0.4)	31.2 (1.5)	85.0 (3.9)	90.2 (0.0)	95.1 (0.0)
ISRAEL	21.3 (0.4)	30.4 (2.8)	38.6 (3.1)	86.9 (2.1)	91.8 (0.0)	96.7 (0.0)
ITALY	23.0 (2.0)	34.4 (1.6)	42.6 (0.3)	90.2 (1.7)	93.4 (4.9)	98.4 (0.0)
KOREA	26.2 (0.9)	41.0 (3.7)	50.8 (4.6)	93.4 (0.0)	95.1 (0.0)	98.4 (0.0)
PORTUGAL	16.7 (1.9)	26.2 (0.5)	31.6 (0.8)	81.7 (2.6)	86.9 (0.0)	93.4 (1.6)
SCOTLAND	23.0 (0.1)	32.8 (0.0)	39.3 (2.8)	89.8 (4.6)	93.3 (2.7)	96.7 (4.6)
SLOVENIA	18.9 (0.8)	27.7 (1.8)	34.0 (0.8)	79.3 (0.3)	84.5 (0.0)	93.1 (0.0)
SOVIET UNION	20.0 (0.6)	30.8 (1.0)	37.7 (0.7)	90.2 (0.7)	93.4 (2.3)	98.4 (0.0)
SPAIN	18.8 (0.6)	26.8 (1.8)	32.8 (2.0)	86.9 (0.0)	90.2 (2.4)	96.7 (0.0)
TAIWAN	19.2 (1.6)	32.1 (4.6)	41.0 (1.8)	91.8 (1.7)	95.1 (0.0)	98.4 (0.0)
UNITED STATES	18.0 (1.1)	24.6 (0.0)	29.5 (2.1)	83.6 (0.0)	90.2 (2.3)	96.7 (1.6)
Canadian Populations						
BRITISH COLUMBIA	18.2 (3.5)	29.5 (0.0)	36.1 (3.6)	85.3 (0.0)	90.2 (5.5)	96.7 (0.0)
NEW BRUNSWICK-ENGLISH	17.5 (1.3)	26.7 (2.3)	33.9 (3.1)	83.6 (0.0)	88.5 (0.2)	95.1 (0.0)
ONTARIO-ENGLISH	18.0 (0.0)	24.6 (2.4)	31.2 (1.5)	81.1 (4.6)	85.7 (3.1)	93.4 (0.0)
ONTARIO-FRENCH	18.0 (2.7)	26.3 (0.4)	31.2 (0.0)	77.1 (1.0)	82.0 (0.0)	90.2 (5.3)
QUEBEC-ENGLISH	18.0 (0.0)	29.5 (0.4)	36.1 (1.7)	86.9 (0.9)	90.2 (0.0)	96.7 (0.0)
QUEBEC-FRENCH	23.0 (0.0)	32.8 (0.6)	40.7 (4.5)	85.3 (0.0)	88.5 (1.3)	95.1 (0.0)

Mathematics: Age 9

	NUMBERS AND OPERATIONS	MEASURE-MENT	GEOMETRY	DATA ANALY-SIS, STATIS-TICS, AND PROBABILITY	ALGEBRA AND FUNCTIONS	CONCEPTUAL UNDER-STANDING	PROCEDURAL KNOWLEGE	PROBLEM SOLVING
IAEP TOPIC AVERAGE	61.2	67.2	63.9	67.6	61.8	63.2	66.7	58.5
Populations								
CANADA	55.0 (0.6)	65.4 (0.5)	64.7 (0.6)	72.3 (0.5)	56.4 (0.6)	60.4 (0.5)	61.1 (0.6)	57.4 (0.5)
ENGLAND	53.6 (2.1)	67.2 (1.6)	67.0 (1.5)	70.4 (1.7)	56.9 (2.1)	60.7 (1.7)	59.2 (2.0)	57.9 (1.9)
HUNGARY	67.5 (0.7)	71.6 (0.7)	68.6 (0.7)	63.4 (0.8)	72.4 (0.8)	68.2 (0.6)	70.8 (0.7)	64.4 (0.7)
IRELAND	58.0 (0.9)	64.2 (0.8)	57.9 (0.9)	65.2 (0.8)	59.4 (1.0)	59.3 (0.8)	63.9 (0.8)	55.5 (0.9)
ISRAEL	63.6 (0.8)	69.9 (0.7)	58.8 (0.9)	63.9 (1.0)	66.8 (0.7)	62.6 (0.8)	68.3 (0.8)	61.6 (0.8)
ITALY	67.3 (0.9)	73.3 (0.9)	64.6 (1.1)	71.1 (0.9)	60.8 (1.3)	67.8 (0.9)	72.5 (0.9)	60.6 (1.1)
KOREA	74.6 (0.6)	73.0 (0.8)	75.4 (0.7)	79.3 (0.6)	72.1 (0.7)	75.0 (0.6)	78.7 (0.6)	68.8 (0.6)
PORTUGAL	54.4 (1.1)	58.3 (0.7)	55.6 (1.2)	57.1 (1.0)	54.6 (1.0)	55.7 (0.9)	59.5 (1.1)	49.2 (1.0)
SCOTLAND	62.1 (1.0)	71.3 (0.9)	68.5 (0.8)	73.9 (0.8)	63.1 (1.2)	66.3 (0.8)	67.9 (1.0)	61.8 (0.8)
SLOVENIA	52.7 (0.6)	62.4 (0.6)	63.1 (0.8)	54.2 (0.8)	57.8 (0.6)	56.3 (0.6)	57.6 (0.6)	52.3 (0.7)
SOVIET UNION	65.7 (1.3)	71.3 (1.0)	64.4 (1.3)	60.1 (1.5)	67.8 (1.3)	63.0 (1.3)	72.0 (1.2)	61.7 (1.4)
SPAIN	61.3 (1.1)	60.8 (0.8)	60.1 (1.1)	69.3 (1.1)	58.3 (1.1)	60.8 (1.0)	66.1 (1.0)	57.3 (1.1)
TAIWAN	67.1 (0.8)	69.3 (0.8)	69.2 (0.8)	72.8 (0.8)	64.2 (0.8)	68.5 (0.8)	76.1 (0.8)	55.7 (0.8)
UNITED STATES	54.3 (1.1)	63.2 (1.0)	56.9 (1.0)	72.8 (1.1)	55.3 (1.0)	59.7 (1.0)	59.5 (1.1)	54.5 (1.0)
Canadian Populations								
BRITISH COLUMBIA	58.7 (0.8)	67.4 (0.7)	62.4 (1.0)	72.3 (0.8)	56.5 (0.7)	62.1 (0.7)	63.7 (0.8)	59.1 (0.7)
NEW BRUNSWICK-ENGLISH	56.1 (0.6)	66.0 (0.5)	63.1 (0.5)	69.3 (0.6)	54.6 (0.5)	61.2 (0.4)	61.1 (0.6)	55.7 (0.6)
ONTARIO-ENGLISH	52.0 (0.8)	63.3 (0.7)	60.0 (0.9)	69.5 (0.7)	52.2 (0.7)	57.6 (0.7)	57.6 (0.8)	54.3 (0.7)
ONTARIO-FRENCH	48.2 (0.6)	60.0 (0.7)	61.7 (0.7)	67.6 (0.7)	55.1 (0.6)	55.9 (0.6)	54.4 (0.6)	52.4 (0.7)
QUEBEC-ENGLISH	58.5 (0.9)	69.1 (0.7)	64.1 (0.9)	73.2 (0.7)	57.5 (0.8)	63.5 (0.8)	63.9 (0.8)	58.7 (0.8)
QUEBEC-FRENCH	59.1 (0.8)	68.1 (0.7)	72.8 (0.7)	76.8 (0.7)	63.6 (0.8)	64.6 (0.6)	66.2 (0.9)	62.0 (0.8)

Populations		Amounts of Weekly Mathematics Homework 0-1 HR	2-3 HRS	4 HRS/MORE	Populations		Amounts of Daily Homework NO HMWK	1 HR/LESS	2 HRS/MORE
CANADA	%	72 (0.9)	19 (0.8)	10 (0.6)	CANADA	%	29 (1.2)	58 (1.1)	13 (0.6)
	P	61 (0.5)	59 (0.8)	61 (1.5)		P	61 (0.8)	61 (0.5)	53 (1.3)
ENGLAND	%	84 (2.3)	12 (1.9)	5 (0.9)	ENGLAND	%	54 (4.6)	37 (4.4)	9 (1.2)
	P	60 (1.7)	61 (4.1)	55 (4.2)		P	58 (1.4)	63 (3.8)	53 (3.2)
HUNGARY	%	49 (1.8)	27 (1.4)	23 (1.6)	HUNGARY	%	2 (0.5)	72 (1.4)	25 (1.4)
	P	67 (0.9)	66 (1.2)	74 (1.3)		P	65 (4.2)	69 (0.7)	66 (1.1)
IRELAND	%	63 (2.1)	22 (1.5)	15 (1.6)	IRELAND	%	2 (0.4)	80 (1.7)	18 (1.5)
	P	59 (0.9)	64 (1.7)	61 (1.8)		P	39 (3.7)	62 (0.9)	56 (1.4)
ISRAEL	%	55 (1.4)	26 (1.2)	19 (1.0)	ISRAEL	%	4 (0.7)	60 (1.6)	35 (1.5)
	P	63 (0.7)	62 (1.2)	70 (1.4)		P	55 (2.5)	65 (0.9)	64 (1.0)
ITALY	%	62 (2.2)	23 (1.8)	15 (1.6)	ITALY	%	6 (0.9)	76 (1.7)	17 (1.5)
	P	67 (0.8)	66 (1.4)	73 (2.0)		P	75 (2.0)	67 (1.0)	68 (1.8)
KOREA	%	51 (1.6)	32 (1.2)	17 (1.0)	KOREA	%	2 (0.4)	77 (1.1)	22 (1.1)
	P	75 (0.6)	74 (0.9)	77 (1.2)		P	68 (4.1)	75 (0.6)	75 (1.1)
PORTUGAL	%	59 (1.6)	23 (1.6)	18 (1.4)	PORTUGAL	%	2 (0.6)	78 (1.8)	20 (1.7)
	P	53 (1.0)	55 (1.4)	63 (2.1)		P	48 (5.6)	57 (1.1)	51 (1.6)
SCOTLAND	%	84 (1.4)	12 (1.3)	4 (0.7)	SCOTLAND	%	18 (2.8)	78 (3.0)	4 (0.6)
	P	66 (0.9)	68 (1.8)	66 (3.7)		P	65 (2.3)	67 (0.9)	52 (4.7)
SLOVENIA	%	61 (1.7)	24 (1.4)	16 (1.1)	SLOVENIA	%	4 (0.7)	81 (1.2)	15 (1.1)
	P	56 (0.7)	56 (1.0)	59 (1.5)		P	53 (2.6)	57 (0.6)	53 (1.3)
SOVIET UNION	%	52 (2.9)	23 (1.4)	25 (2.3)	SOVIET UNION	%	2 (0.3)	68 (1.4)	31 (1.3)
	P	63 (1.3)	67 (2.0)	72 (1.0)		P	55 (6.2)	66 (1.4)	66 (1.2)
SPAIN	%	46 (2.0)	29 (1.5)	25 (1.6)	SPAIN	%	15 (1.6)	55 (1.9)	29 (1.8)
	P	59 (1.0)	61 (1.2)	69 (1.5)		P	61 (2.0)	62 (1.0)	63 (1.2)
TAIWAN	%	50 (1.6)	35 (1.2)	15 (1.3)	TAIWAN	%	2 (0.5)	67 (1.3)	31 (1.2)
	P	68 (0.7)	67 (1.1)	70 (1.8)		P	45 (5.7)	70 (0.7)	67 (1.1)
UNITED STATES	%	65 (1.7)	20 (1.1)	14 (1.1)	UNITED STATES	%	20 (1.8)	59 (2.0)	20 (1.2)
	P	59 (1.1)	58 (1.6)	58 (2.5)		P	59 (1.4)	59 (1.1)	56 (1.4)
Canadian Populations					*Canadian Populations*				
BRITISH COLUMBIA	%	69 (1.6)	19 (1.4)	12 (1.0)	BRITISH COLUMBIA	%	32 (2.0)	54 (2.0)	13 (1.0)
	P	62 (0.8)	60 (1.2)	64 (1.7)		P	62 (1.1)	63 (0.8)	56 (1.3)
NEW BRUNSWICK-ENGLISH	%	73 (1.2)	17 (1.1)	10 (0.7)	NEW BRUNSWICK-ENGLISH	%	7 (0.6)	79 (0.9)	14 (0.9)
	P	61 (0.6)	58 (1.1)	57 (1.6)		P	63 (1.8)	61 (0.6)	50 (1.3)
ONTARIO-ENGLISH	%	74 (1.5)	18 (1.2)	7 (0.8	ONTARIO-ENGLISH	%	45 (2.1)	42 (1.8)	13 (1.0)
	P	58 (0.7)	55 (1.2)	53 (2.4)		P	61 (0.9)	56 (0.9)	48 (1.4)
ONTARIO-FRENCH	%	70 (1.5)	19 (1.3)	11 (0.8)	ONTARIO-FRENCH	%	15 (1.2)	73 (1.6)	11 (0.9)
	P	55 (0.6)	54 (1.3)	59 (1.8)		P	58 (1.3)	55 (0.6)	47 (1.5)
QUEBEC-ENGLISH	%	66 (1.5)	21 (1.3)	14 (1.1)	QUEBEC-ENGLISH	%	8 (1.4)	71 (1.9)	20 (1.2)
	P	61 (0.8)	64 (1.3)	67 (1.8)		P	62 (1.8)	63 (0.8)	62 (1.4)
QUEBEC-FRENCH	%	68 (1.3)	20 (0.9)	13 (1.0)	QUEBEC-FRENCH	%	3 (0.5)	84 (1.0)	13 (1.0)
	P	65 (0.7)	64 (1.2)	68 (1.3)		P	58 (2.9)	66 (0.7)	62 (1.8)

% = Percentages of Students
P = Average Percent Correct

Mathematics: Age 9

Populations		Amounts of Daily Television Viewing		
		0-1 HR	**2-4 HRS**	**5 HRS/MORE**
CANADA	%	28 (0.8)	50 (1.0)	22 (0.8)
	P	60 (0.8)	63 (0.6)	54 (0.8)
ENGLAND	%	26 (2.9)	51 (2.5)	23 (2.0)
	P	60 (4.8)	62 (1.7)	54 (1.5)
HUNGARY	%	27 (1.3)	58 (1.3)	16 (1.2)
	P	67 (1.2)	70 (0.8)	61 (1.4)
IRELAND	%	24 (1.5)	53 (1.8)	23 (1.5)
	P	59 (1.4)	62 (1.0)	56 (1.4)
ISRAEL	%	23 (1.1)	53 (1.4)	24 (1.1)
	P	58 (0.9)	68 (0.9)	63 (1.3)
ITALY	%	46 (1.2)	45 (1.1)	9 (0.8)
	P	67 (1.3)	69 (0.7)	63 (2.1)
KOREA	%	26 (1.1)	65 (1.2)	9 (0.7)
	P	74 (1.0)	76 (0.7)	69 (1.6)
PORTUGAL	%	34 (1.6)	46 (1.7)	20 (1.5)
	P	52 (1.7)	59 (1.1)	54 (1.5)
SCOTLAND	%	23 (1.9)	54 (2.0)	23 (1.5)
	P	62 (1.9)	68 (0.9)	64 (1.7)
SLOVENIA	%	41 (1.6)	51 (1.7)	8 (0.6)
	P	56 (0.7)	57 (0.7)	51 (1.6)

% = Percentages of Students
P = Average Percent Correct

		Amounts of Daily Television Viewing		
		0-1 HR	**2-4 HRS**	**5 HRS/MORE**
SOVIET UNION	%	26 (1.5)	56 (1.4)	18 (0.7)
	P	64 (1.4)	68 (1.5)	62 (1.3)
SPAIN	%	33 (1.7)	50 (1.5)	17 (1.4)
	P	60 (1.4)	64 (1.0)	58 (1.5)
TAIWAN	%	43 (1.5)	48 (1.4)	8 (0.8)
	P	68 (1.0)	70 (0.8)	57 (1.6)
UNITED STATES	%	25 (1.2)	49 (1.4)	26 (1.6)
	P	57 (1.7)	62 (1.1)	54 (1.2)
Canadian Populations				
BRITISH COLUMBIA	%	28 (1.5)	51 (1.4)	21 (1.2)
	P	61 (1.0)	65 (0.8)	57 (1.1)
NEW BRUNSWICK-ENGLISH	%	23 (1.1)	51 (1.4)	27 (1.0)
	P	56 (1.1)	62 (0.6)	59 (0.9)
ONTARIO-ENGLISH	%	24 (1.1)	49 (1.4)	27 (1.3)
	P	55 (1.1)	60 (0.8)	53 (1.0)
ONTARIO-FRENCH	%	26 (1.0)	55 (1.3)	19 (1.2)
	P	55 (1.1)	56 (0.7)	52 (1.1)
QUEBEC-ENGLISH	%	30 (1.5)	51 (1.3)	19 (1.2)
	P	63 (1.3)	64 (0.8)	59 (1.1)
QUEBEC-FRENCH	%	36 (1.3)	52 (1.3)	12 (0.9)
	P	64 (1.0)	67 (0.8)	58 (1.6)

Mathematics: Age 9

Topic: Numbers and Operations

	IAEP Item Average
Solve a one-step problem using subtraction	87
Multiply a one-digit number by another one-digit number	84
Solve a one-step problem using division	80
Find one-half of a two-digit even number	80
Pick arithmetic operation appropriate for a simple word problem	78
Solve a word problem using addition and subtraction	77
Find a missing digit in a subtraction problem	72
Identify a whole number given some of its properties	71
Choose pictures that illustrate the meaning of a fraction	70
Solve a two-step problem using addition and subtraction	69
Solve a word problem using factors	69
Subtract, with regrouping, three-digit numbers	67
Solve a one-step problem using subtraction	66
Solve a word problem using multiplication	63
Identify the information missing from a problem	63
Count objects that are grouped in 100s and 10s	63
Pick the operation to solve a word problem that has extraneous information	59
Determine how a change in one digit affects the size of a number	59
Find a number that satisfies a certain inequality	59
Solve a two-step problem using multiplication	58
Solve a word problem using ratios and addition	58
Find one-third of a two-digit number, (whole number answer)	55
Supply the number being subtracted in a subtraction problem	55
Count the odd numbers in a given range of integers	54
Relate a subtraction fact to an addition fact	52
Identify a property of odd and even numbers	48
Solve a two-step problem involving age and year of birth	45
Translate a fraction with denominator 10 into decimal form	41
Relate odd and even to consecutive integers	39
On a map, find the length of the shortest route between two cities	39
Out of four digits, make a number satisfying certain conditions	37

Topic: Measurement

	IAEP Item Average
Complete a pattern involving squares	87
Figure out how to balance two groups of marbles	84

Topic: Measurement (continued)

	IAEP Item Average
Among figures divided into unit blocks, pick the one with greatest area	82
Solve a problem involving hours and minutes	75
Read a below-zero temperature shown on a thermometer	71
Relate volume of an object to how many of that object will fit into a box	65
Given the distance around a square, find the length of one side	55
Find the distance around a given rectangle	46
Measure a segment when zero-point of ruler is not at end of segment	42

Topic: Geometry

	IAEP Item Average
Identify a rectangle (from a picture)	92
Identify which figures have line symmetry	90
Visualize a rectangular solid	70
Count the faces of a solid figure	52
Identify a circle from its basic properties	44
Complete a pattern involving triangles	37

Topic: Data Analysis, Statistics, and Probability

	IAEP Item Average
Read a circle graph	86
Read a bar graph	86
Read a bar graph	81
Interpret data from a bar graph	71
Complete a bar graph	63
Using clues about cards, figure out which card was chosen	59
Interpret data from a circle graph	49
Solve a simple probability problem	42

Topic: Algebra and Functions

	IAEP Item Average
Given a pattern of numbers, find the next number	85
Complete a number sentence involving subtraction	74
Given a pattern of numbers, find the missing number	65
Complete a number sentence involving addition	64
Solve a word problem about positions of people on a line	45
Solve a word problem using ratios and multiplication	41

Canadian Data

Canadian Populations	MATH IS FOR BOYS AND GIRLS	MATH IS MOSTLY MEMORIZING	SOLVING PROBS IS IMPORTANT	LISTEN TO TEACHER EVERY DAY	DO MATH EXERCISES EVERY DAY	WORK IN GROUPS 1/WEEK	TAKE TESTS 1/WEEK	4 HRS/MORE MATH HMWK EACH WEEK
ALBERTA	96 (0.6)	57 (1.8)	83 (1.0)	62 (1.7)	50 (1.7)	41 (1.9)	38 (2.7)	15 (1.2)
BRITISH COLUMBIA	95 (0.7)	59 (1.2)	84 (1.1)	37 (1.7)	34 (1.6)	44 (1.6)	54 (1.9)	12 (0.8)
MANITOBA-ENGLISH	95 (0.6)	56 (1.1)	81 (1.1)	60 (1.5)	49 (1.8)	42 (1.6)	37 (2.1)	10 (0.8)
MANITOBA-FRENCH	95 (0.9)	61 (2.0)	88 (1.0)	16 (1.6)	31 (1.8)	41 (1.6)	59 (1.7)	17 (1.5)
NEW BRUNSWICK-ENGLISH	96 (0.5)	51 (1.1)	83 (1.0)	63 (1.1)	54 (1.2)	44 (1.3)	41 (1.2)	10 (0.9)
NEW BRUNSWICK-FRENCH	95 (0.5)	75 (1.0)	91 (0.6)	26 (1.1)	47 (1.2)	24 (0.9)	48 (1.1)	17 (0.9)
NEWFOUNDLAND	96 (0.6)	58 (1.3)	86 (1.0)	76 (1.2)	60 (1.4)	47 (1.6)	23 (1.4)	19 (1.1)
NOVA SCOTIA	97 (0.5)	45 (1.2)	82 (1.3)	70 (1.7)	55 (1.6)	44 (1.6)	32 (1.5)	14 (0.9)
ONTARIO-ENGLISH	97 (0.5)	59 (1.4)	84 (1.0)	67 (1.6)	55 (1.5)	48 (2.0)	32 (1.6)	16 (1.3)
ONTARIO-FRENCH	94 (0.7)	70 (1.2)	91 (0.8)	22 (1.4)	32 (1.4)	38 (1.4)	54 (1.5)	14 (1.2)
QUEBEC-ENGLISH	97 (0.3)	56 (1.7)	89 (0.8)	19 (1.4)	40 (1.8)	43 (1.8)	49 (2.0)	14 (0.8)
QUEBEC-FRENCH	95 (1.2)	44 (1.7)	83 (1.3)	73 (1.6)	62 (1.6)	21 (1.9)	99 (0.3)	15 (1.1)
SASKATCHEWAN-ENGLISH	96 (0.5)	57 (1.4)	87 (1.0)	55 (2.2)	44 (2.0)	43 (1.6)	20 (1.5)	11 (1.0)
SASKATCHEWAN-FRENCH	97 (1.2)	60 (4.0)	86 (2.4)	14 (2.3)	38 (3.2)	38 (3.1)	40 (3.3)	16 (2.6)

Canadian Populations	WORK WITH MATH TOOLS 1/WEEK	HAVE A CALCULATOR	EVER USE CALCULATOR	EVER USE COMPUTER	SAME LANGUAGE HOME/SCH	4/MORE BROTHERS OR SISTERS	LESS 25 BOOKS IN HOME	PARENTS WANT DO WELL
ALBERTA	13 (1.0)	92 (1.2)	85 (1.8)	52 (1.8)	91 (1.0)	10 (0.9)	10 (1.0)	97 (0.5)
BRITISH COLUMBIA	11 (1.1)	92 (0.8)	83 (1.8)	51 (1.9)	89 (1.1)	9 (0.9)	10 (1.0)	95 (0.6)
MANITOBA-ENGLISH	13 (1.1)	84 (1.3)	53 (2.4)	42 (1.7)	90 (1.0)	11 (1.0)	12 (1.1)	95 (0.6)
MANITOBA-FRENCH	10 (1.1)	88 (1.2)	55 (1.5)	35 (2.0)	17 (1.0)	9 (1.1)	14 (1.3)	89 (1.4)
NEW BRUNSWICK-ENGLISH	19 (0.9)	89 (0.9)	87 (0.8)	29 (1.2)	95 (0.5)	10 (0.8)	13 (0.7)	95 (0.5)
NEW BRUNSWICK-FRENCH	12 (0.6)	87 (0.7)	72 (0.8)	11 (0.7)	90 (0.7)	7 (0.6)	31 (1.1)	96 (0.4)
NEWFOUNDLAND	25 (1.5)	93 (0.6)	89 (1.2)	35 (1.9)	98 (0.3)	12 (0.8)	17 (1.1)	97 (0.4)
NOVA SCOTIA	18 (1.1)	86 (1.0)	60 (2.1)	41 (2.3)	98 (0.4)	10 (0.9)	12 (1.4)	97 (0.4)
ONTARIO-ENGLISH	16 (1.2)	91 (0.8)	74 (2.2)	53 (1.9)	87 (1.6)	9 (0.8)	11 (0.9)	97 (0.5)
ONTARIO-FRENCH	16 (1.2)	90 (0.9)	75 (1.8)	46 (1.7)	55 (2.1)	6 (0.7)	26 (1.2)	95 (0.6)
QUEBEC-ENGLISH	20 (1.5)	92 (0.9)	73 (2.4)	16 (1.3)	92 (0.9)	5 (0.6)	19 (1.6)	95 (0.6)
QUEBEC-FRENCH	10 (1.0)	92 (1.3)	76 (2.0)	43 (1.9)	76 (2.1)	10 (1.5)	10 (1.2)	97 (0.5)
SASKATCHEWAN-ENGLISH	15 (1.2)	86 (1.2)	67 (2.5)	49 (1.7)	95 (0.6)	10 (0.7)	13 (1.1)	95 (0.5)
SASKATCHEWAN-FRENCH	13 (2.1)	83 (2.1)	73 (2.6)	40 (3.0)	12 (1.9)	9 (1.9)	14 (2.3)	89 (2.1)

Canadian Populations	SOMEONE TALKS ABOUT MATH	SOMEONE HELPS WITH MATH	READ FOR FUN EVERY DAY	2 HRS/MORE ALL HMWK EVERY DAY	5 HRS/MORE TELEVISION EVERY DAY	POSITIVE MATH ATTITUDES
ALBERTA	63 (1.2)	74 (1.1)	40 (1.4)	20 (1.3)	12 (1.0)	91 (0.9)
BRITISH COLUMBIA	61 (1.4)	70 (1.4)	40 (1.5)	25 (1.5)	13 (1.0)	89 (0.9)
MANITOBA-ENGLISH	54 (1.3)	65 (1.1)	35 (1.3)	18 (1.4)	18 (1.2)	88 (0.8)
MANITOBA-FRENCH	56 (2.4)	60 (2.0)	42 (1.8)	19 (1.3)	15 (1.3)	90 (1.1)
NEW BRUNSWICK-ENGLISH	57 (1.3)	66 (1.1)	37 (1.4)	16 (0.9)	19 (1.1)	88 (0.8)
NEW BRUNSWICK-FRENCH	67 (1.3)	65 (1.1)	31 (1.1)	17 (1.1)	16 (1.0)	93 (0.6)
NEWFOUNDLAND	67 (1.4)	73 (1.1)	37 (1.3)	26 (1.5)	23 (1.0)	94 (0.6)
NOVA SCOTIA	63 (1.1)	69 (1.9)	35 (1.9)	23 (1.2)	21 (1.5)	93 (0.7)
ONTARIO-ENGLISH	63 (1.5)	72 (1.4)	40 (1.4)	28 (1.6)	16 (1.2)	94 (0.7)
ONTARIO-FRENCH	68 (1.4)	67 (1.7)	35 (1.4)	23 (1.3)	17 (1.1)	96 (0.5)
QUEBEC-ENGLISH	67 (1.3)	63 (1.5)	33 (1.2)	29 (1.9)	11 (1.0)	95 (0.7)
QUEBEC-FRENCH	69 (1.3)	62 (1.5)	37 (1.3)	33 (1.9)	14 (0.9)	92 (0.8)
SASKATCHEWAN-ENGLISH	58 (1.6)	72 (1.4)	40 (1.4)	13 (0.9)	13 (0.9)	91 (0.8)
SASKATCHEWAN-FRENCH	55 (3.1)	66 (3.2)	45 (3.1)	15 (2.1)	9 (1.8)	93 (1.7)

Canadian Populations	5 HRS/MORE TELEVISION EVERY DAY	READ FOR FUN EVERY DAY	2 HRS/MORE ALL HMWK EVERY DAY	MATH IS FOR BOYS AND GIRLS	DO MATH EXERCISES OFTEN	WORK WITH MATH TOOLS OFTEN
BRITISH COLUMBIA	21 (1.2)	50 (1.7)	13 (1.0)	88 (0.9)	50 (1.5)	13 (1.1)
NEW BRUNSWICK-ENGLISH	27 (1.0)	48 (1.1)	14 (0.9)	87 (0.8)	55 (1.1)	15 (1.0)
ONTARIO-ENGLISH	27 (1.3)	45 (1.3)	13 (1.0)	85 (1.0)	52 (1.4)	14 (0.9)
ONTARIO-FRENCH	19 (1.2)	46 (1.7)	11 (0.9)	67 (1.3)	44 (1.4)	10 (1.0)
QUEBEC-ENGLISH	19 (1.2)	48 (1.5)	20 (1.2)	87 (1.0)	61 (1.5)	12 (0.9)
QUEBEC-FRENCH	12 (0.9)	52 (1.3)	13 (1.0)	83 (1.0)	42 (1.3)	11 (1.0)

Canadian Data

Canadian Populations	EMPHASIZE NUMBERS	EMPHASIZE FRACTIONS	EMPHASIZE DECIMALS	EMPHASIZE RATIOS	EMPHASIZE PERCENT	EMPHASIZE MEASUREMENT	EMPHASIZE GEOMETRY	EMPHASIZE TABLES
ALBERTA	72 (5.3)	66 (7.1)	66 (5.4)	69 (5.6)	58 (5.9)	64 (5.4)	34 (4.9)	19 (6.1)
BRITISH COLUMBIA	67 (5.7)	57 (6.7)	61 (5.9)	43 (6.5)	45 (6.6)	44 (5.9)	38 (6.2)	12 (3.8)
MANITOBA-ENGLISH	68 (4.6)	58 (4.7)	73 (4.5)	36 (6.5)	48 (6.2)	47 (4.5)	34 (6.5)	20 (4.5)
MANITOBA-FRENCH	84 (0.0)	73 (0.0)	84 (0.0)	56 (0.0)	58 (0.0)	67 (0.0)	49 (0.0)	27 (0.0)
NEW BRUNSWICK-ENGLISH	62 (6.8)	36 (5.2)	48 (5.5)	40 (5.6)	48 (5.6)	58 (7.0)	31 (4.6)	9 (3.2)
NEW BRUNSWICK-FRENCH	92 (3.8)	44 (7.1)	44 (8.0)	49 (7.7)	41 (7.4)	49 (6.6)	48 (7.9)	3 (0.3)
NEWFOUNDLAND	55 (4.2)	36 (6.2)	44 (4.5)	32 (4.6)	42 (5.4)	43 (5.8)	41 (6.1)	11 (3.6)
NOVA SCOTIA	64 (5.3)	58 (6.7)	64 (7.2)	58 (8.5)	64 (5.2)	60 (6.6)	36 (7.2)	24 (5.3)
ONTARIO-ENGLISH	79 (5.0)	47 (7.2)	66 (5.8)	42 (7.6)	61 (6.1)	53 (5.9)	40 (5.3)	18 (4.4)
ONTARIO-FRENCH	89 (2.8)	79 (4.8)	92 (2.7)	55 (6.4)	72 (5.5)	72 (7.5)	70 (4.6)	38 (7.5)
QUEBEC-ENGLISH	37 (5.9)	43 (9.3)	43 (***)	36 (6.3)	39 (4.8)	45 (4.3)	44 (7.3)	24 (7.0)
QUEBEC-FRENCH	54 (7.1)	44 (6.5)	41 (6.7)	61 (7.6)	58 (6.6)	45 (6.3)	53 (7.2)	16 (4.9)
SASKATCHEWAN-ENGLISH	75 (3.4)	62 (4.9)	70 (4.3)	56 (4.7)	58 (4.5)	53 (4.4)	31 (4.6)	14 (3.1)
SASKATCHEWAN-FRENCH	66 (0.0)	72 (0.0)	79 (0.0)	79 (0.0)	79 (0.0)	55 (0.0)	38 (0.0)	17 (0.0)

Canadian Populations	EMPHASIZE PROBABILITY	EMPHASIZE STATISTICS	EMPHASIZE ALGEBRA	MATH MIN/WK	NUMBER OF COMPUTERS	TEACH ONLY MATH	ALL HAVE P-SEC MATH	MATH CLASS BY ABILITY
ALBERTA	3 (2.0)	9 (5.6)	31 (5.8)	214 (3.3)	26 (1.7)	53 (6.8)	58 (6.3)	2 (1.8)
BRITISH COLUMBIA	2 (1.3)	4 (1.5)	45 (7.8)	199 (6.7)	37 (2.8)	58 (6.5)	58 (7.5)	26 (6.1)
MANITOBA-ENGLISH	3 (1.5)	5 (2.3)	44 (5.6)	216 (4.3)	15 (1.0)	39 (6.0)	46 (4.3)	5 (2.2)
MANITOBA-FRENCH	9 (0.0)	11 (0.0)	64 (0.0)	238 (0.0)	18 (0.0)	36 (0.0)	51 (0.0)	0 (0.0)
NEW BRUNSWICK-ENGLISH	0 (0.0)	6 (2.7)	18 (4.0)	256 (3.8)	13 (0.8)	41 (5.6)	32 (5.5)	3 (1.8)
NEW BRUNSWICK-FRENCH	2 (1.6)	3 (2.3)	69 (6.1)	304 (4.3)	8 (0.9)	49 (8.0)	58 (7.0)	19 (6.5)
NEWFOUNDLAND	0 (0.0)	4 (1.6)	18 (5.1)	318 (7.4)	7 (1.0)	29 (5.4)	65 (7.1)	6 (2.8)
NOVA SCOTIA	4 (1.8)	14 (5.0)	28 (7.0)	260 (5.3)	12 (0.9)	78 (4.8)	60 (6.4)	10 (3.0)
ONTARIO-ENGLISH	3 (2.0)	7 (2.8)	39 (6.6)	211 (2.8)	15 (2.0)	7 (2.4)	31 (6.6)	6 (2.3)
ONTARIO-FRENCH	10 (3.5)	20 (9.2)	64 (5.5)	217 (4.3)	14 (1.4)	10 (2.5)	17 (4.1)	8 (2.6)
QUEBEC-ENGLISH	8 (2.1)	10 (6.6)	42 (4.8)	273 (11.9)	15 (1.6)	64 (3.9)	57 (6.0)	32 (7.1)
QUEBEC-FRENCH	14 (4.6)	16 (5.6)	90 (3.8)	270 (7.0)	18 (1.5)	98 (2.4)	58 (6.3)	34 (6.4)
SASKATCHEWAN-ENGLISH	4 (1.7)	5 (1.7)	15 (3.1)	221 (4.6)	14 (0.8)	19 (4.4)	62 (4.9)	9 (3.2)
SASKATCHEWAN-FRENCH	14 (0.0)	14 (0.0)	34 (0.0)	226 (0.0)	10 (0.0)	7 (0.0)	39 (0.0)	14 (0.0)

Canadian Populations	SCHOOL DAY/YEAR	INSTRUCTION MIN/DAY	AVERAGE CLASS SIZE	1/MORE PROBLEMS
ALBERTA	190 (0.3)	315 (2.8)	23 (0.7)	5 (1.8)
BRITISH COLUMBIA	190 (1.2)	304 (4.1)	25 (1.5)	19 (6.8)
MANITOBA-ENGLISH	192 (0.4)	312 (1.7)	21 (0.7)	10 (3.3)
MANITOBA-FRENCH	194 (0.0)	313 (0.0)	20 (0.0)	13 (0.0)
NEW BRUNSWICK-ENGLISH	185 (1.3)	296 (2.3)	23 (0.4)	11 (3.0)
NEW BRUNSWICK-FRENCH	188 (0.8)	303 (2.3)	24 (0.4)	27 (5.5)
NEWFOUNDLAND	187 (0.3)	289 (1.7)	24 (0.9)	35 (5.5)
NOVA SCOTIA	187 (0.5)	293 (1.7)	24 (1.1)	18 (3.3)
ONTARIO-ENGLISH	187 (0.3)	304 (1.4)	27 (0.5)	11 (2.8)
ONTARIO-FRENCH	187 (0.5)	300 (2.4)	22 (0.6)	20 (3.7)
QUEBEC-ENGLISH	181 (0.5)	302 (7.2)	26 (5.0)	14 (7.9)
QUEBEC-FRENCH	181 (0.2)	303 (2.0)	28 (1.0)	11 (3.5)
SASKATCHEWAN-ENGLISH	194 (0.5)	297 (1.5)	21 (0.6)	11 (3.2)
SASKATCHEWAN-FRENCH	195 (0.0)	309 (0.0)	20 (0.0)	21 (0.0)

Canadian Populations	MATH GROUPS BY ABILITY
BRITISH COLUMBIA	31 (4.6)
NEW BRUNSWICK-ENGLISH	13 (2.9)
ONTARIO-ENGLISH	51 (5.6)
ONTARIO-FRENCH	14 (3.3)
QUEBEC-ENGLISH	13 (3.7)
QUEBEC-FRENCH	1 (1.0)

PARTICIPANTS

BRAZIL

Rubens Murillo Marques, Carlos Chagas Foundation
Heraldo Marelim Vianna, Carlos Chagas Foundation

CANADA

ALBERTA

Dennis Belyk, Alberta Education
Chantey MacKay, Alberta Education

BRITISH COLUMBIA

Bill Postl, Ministry of Education and Ministry Responsible for
    Multiculturalism and Human Rights
Daina Watson, Ministry of Educationn and Ministry Responsible for
    Multiculturalism and Human Rights

MANITOBA

Kim Browning, Department of Education
Norman Mayer, Department of Education

NEW BRUNSWICK, ENGLISH

Frank Morehouse, Department of Education
Anne Vickers, Department of Education

NEW BRUNSWICK, FRENCH

Robert Chouinard, Ministry of Education

NEW FOUNDLAND

Russ Blagdon, Department of Education
Lenora Fagan, Department of Education

NOVA SCOTIA

Bette Kelly, Department of Education
Turney Manzer, Department of Education

ONTARIO

Michael Kozlow, Ministry of Education
André Vézina, Ministry of Education

QUEBEC

Sylvie Mazur, Ministry of Education
Allan Patenaude, Ministry of Education

SASKATCHEWAN

Rick Jones, Saskatchewan Education
Beverley Mazer, Saskatchewan Education

CHINA

Liu Yuan-tu, Central Institute for Educational Research
Teng Chun, Central Institute for Educational Research

ENGLAND

Clare Burstall, National Foundation for Educational Research
Derek Foxman, National Foundation for Educational Research

FRANCE

Pierre Jouvanceau, Ministry of Education
Martine Le Guen, Ministry of Education

HUNGARY

Peter Vari, National Institute of Education

IRELAND

Michael Martin, Educational Research Center, St. Patrick's College, Dublin

ISRAEL

Naomi Gafni, National Institute for Testing and Evaluation
Zehava Sass, The Van Leer Jerusalem Institute

ITALY

Alberta De Flora, IRRSAE/ER, Ministry of Education

JORDAN

Victor Billeh, National Center for Educational Research and Development
Bahjeh Bitar, Ministry of Education

KOREA

Kil-Ho Jang, National Board of Educational Evaluation
Yong-Ki Kim, National Board of Educational Evaluation

MOZAMBIQUE

Abdulcarimo Ismael, Pedagogical Institute

PORTUGAL

Lourdes Neves, Ministry of Education
Lourdes Serrazina, Higher School of Education

SCOTLAND

Cathy MacGregor, Moray House College of Education
Brian Semple, Scottish Education Department

SLOVENIA

Marjan Šetinc, Educational Research Institute

SOVIET UNION

Galina Kovalyova, Academy of Pedagogical Sciences
Klara Krasnianskia, Academy of Pedagogical Sciences

SPAIN

Mariano Alvaro, Ministry of Education
Reyes Hernandez, Ministry of Education

SWITZERLAND

Urs Moser, Office of Educational Research of Public Instruction for Bern Canton
Erich Ramseier, Office of Educational Research of Public Instruction for Bern Canton

TAIWAN

Jong Hsiang Yang, National Taiwan Normal University

UNITED STATES

Janice Askew, Educational Testing Service
Tillie Kennel, National Computer Systems

INTERNATIONAL COORDINATION

CANADIAN DATA ANALYSIS GROUP

Jean Guy Blais, University of Montreal
Maurice Dalois, GRICS
Michel Frechette, GRICS
Leo Laroche, Quebec Ministry of Education
Solange Paquet, Educan, Inc.

EDUCATIONAL TESTING SERVICE

Archie Lapointe
Nancy Mead

WESTAT

Adam Chu
Leslie Wallace